THE POLITICAL ECONOMY OF HOLLYWOOD

In Hollywood, the goals of art and business are entangled. Directors, writers, actors, and idealistic producers aspire to make the best films possible. These aspirations often interact with the dominant firms that control Hollywood film distribution. This control of distribution is crucial as it enables the firms and other large businesses involved, such as banks that offer financing, to effectively stand between film production and the market. This book analyses the power structure of the Hollywood film business and its general modes of behaviour. More specifically, the work analyses how the largest Hollywood firms attempt to control social creativity such that they can mitigate the financial risks inherent in the art of filmmaking.

Controlling the ways people make or watch films, the book argues, is a key element of Hollywood's capitalist power. Capitalist power—the ability to control, modify, and, sometimes, limit social creation through the rights of ownership—is the foundation of capital accumulation. For the Hollywood film business, capitalist power is about the ability of business concerns to set the terms that will shape the future of cinema. For the major film distributors of Hollywood, these terms include the types of films that will be distributed, the number of films that will be distributed, and the cinematic alternatives that will be made available to the individual moviegoer. Combining theoretical analysis with detailed empirical research on the financial performance of the major Hollywood film companies, the book details how Hollywood's capitalist goals have clashed with the aesthetic potentials of cinema and ultimately stymied creativity in the pursuit of limiting risk.

This sharp critique of the Hollywood machine provides vital reading for students and scholars of political economy, political theory, film studies, and cinema.

James McMahon currently teaches at the University of Toronto, Canada. His main research interests are the Hollywood film business, New Hollywood cinema, social theories of mass culture, political economic theory, and the relationship between institutional power and cultural practices.

THE POLITICAL ECONOMY OF HOLLYWOOD

Capitalist Power and Cultural Production

James McMahon

Routledge
Taylor & Francis Group

LONDON AND NEW YORK

First published 2022
by Routledge
4 Park Square, Milton Park, Abingdon, Oxon OX14 4RN

and by Routledge
605 Third Avenue, New York, NY 10158

Routledge is an imprint of the Taylor & Francis Group, an informa business

© 2022 James McMahon

The right of James McMahon to be identified as author of this work has been asserted in accordance with sections 77 and 78 of the Copyright, Designs and Patents Act 1988.

British Library Cataloguing-in-Publication Data
A catalogue record for this book is available from the British Library

Library of Congress Cataloging-in-Publication Data
Names: McMahon, James, 1981– author.
Title: The political economy of Hollywood : capitalist power and
    cultural production / James McMahon.
Description: New York : Routledge, 2022. | Includes bibliographical references
    and index.
Identifiers: LCCN 2021041086 (print) | LCCN 2021041087 (ebook) |
    ISBN 9780367552640 (hardback) | ISBN 9780367552633 (paperback) |
    ISBN 9781003092629 (ebook)
Subjects: LCSH: Motion picture industry—California—Los Angeles. | Motion
    pictures—Distribution. | Motion picture industry—Political aspects—
    California—Los Angeles. | Motion picture industry—Economic aspects—
    California—Los Angeles.
Classification: LCC PN1993.5.U65 M386 2022 (print) | LCC PN1993.5.U65
    (ebook) | DDC 384/.80979494—dc23/eng/20211124
LC record available at https://lccn.loc.gov/2021041086
LC ebook record available at https://lccn.loc.gov/2021041087

ISBN: 978-0-367-55264-0 (hbk)
ISBN: 978-0-367-55263-3 (pbk)
ISBN: 978-1-003-09262-9 (ebk)

DOI: 10.4324/9781003092629

Typeset in Bembo
by Apex CoVantage, LLC

CONTENTS

FIGURES

TABLES

ACKNOWLEDGEMENTS

I completed this book with the encouragement, advice, and feedback of many. I would like to thank as many of them as I can.

This book was built on my doctoral dissertation. I was very fortunate to have Scott Forsyth and Asher Horowitz on my dissertation advisory committee. Their questions, comments and criticisms were valuable at every stage in my research and writing. I am particularly thankful to them for supporting my pursuit of interdisciplinary research.

Thank you to my PhD supervisor, Jonathan Nitzan. The germ of this book originated in his graduate class, and ever since then, Jonathan has freely given his time to my ideas, arguments, doubts and obstacles. I am also deeply grateful for his expertise and honest critiques. These qualities pushed me to be a better researcher and writer, and they will inspire me to keep holding to the democratic ideals of science and philosophy.

The editors and staff at Routledge have been open and supportive from the very beginning of this project. In particular, Andy Humphries saw potential in a book version of my interdisciplinary research. He gave me a wonderful opportunity and helped get the manuscript over the finish line with guidance and encouragement.

I have the good fortune of having wonderful teachers and friends. My gratitude to all whom, at some stage of my research, gave me energy to stay sitting at my desk and write on the Hollywood film business. I want to thank some by name: Kristen Ali, Emily Anglin, Feyzi Baban, Joseph Baines, Caleb Basnett, Shannon Bell, Myra Bloom, Jordan Brennan, Elliott Buckland, Troy Cochrane, Blair Fix, Andrew Flood, Sandy Hager, Jason Harman, Nadia Hasan, Chris Holman, Arthur Imperial, Andrew Martin, Yasmin Martin, Paul Mazzocchi,

Brian McCreery, David McNally, Stephen Newman, Mladen Ostojic, Devin Penner, Omme Rahemtullah, Sune Sandbeck, Saad Sayeed, Radha Shah, Matt Strohack, Neil Shyminsky, Richard Welch, and Donya Ziaee.

I would like to thank my parents, John and Theresa, and my brother and his partner, Stephen and Nicole. I would also like to thank the Tibor family, especially Romulo and Luz. I could not have gotten this far without all of your love.

This book is dedicated to two special women. My grandmother, Irene Martin, passed away when I was writing this book. She gave nothing but unconditional support to her grandchildren. When my writing slowed or my self-confidence dipped, I leaned on her support, which is now residing in my heart. I have lost count of the number of times my partner, Marian, gifted me with her love and inspired me with her intelligence, humour and honesty. Without her, there would be no acknowledgements because there would be no book in the first place. Thank you, again and again.

1

INTRODUCTION

In Budd Schulberg's novel *What Makes Sammy Run?*, Al Manheim becomes obsessed with trying to understand the behaviour of Sammy Glick, his work colleague and pseudo-friend. Manheim first becomes puzzled when he notices that Sammy never really walks anywhere – he literally runs from spot to spot. Sammy's general mode of behaviour is also much like that of a driver who is willing to run over anything in their way. And when Sammy runs over other people in his pursuit of success, he does not slow down to look behind him.

A flabbergasted Manheim witnesses Sammy Glick successfully lie, sweet-talk, bullshit, backstab and plagiarize his way up the ranks, first as a journalist in New York and then as a screenwriter in Hollywood. While working in Hollywood, Manheim comes to realize that the film business might be better suited for the Sammy Glicks of the world. Although Manheim is older and wiser than Sammy, and although he actually writes his own screenplay assignments, he fails to synchronize himself with the pace of the Hollywood "Dream Factory".

And why not? If Manheim cannot keep pace with a capitalist institution like the Hollywood film business, what makes Hollywood run? What does Hollywood want, and what are its strategies to achieve its goals?

1.1 General overview

This book combines an interest in political economy, political theory and cinema to offer an answer about the pace of the contemporary Hollywood film business and its general modes of behaviour from 1950 to 2019. More specifically, this book seeks to find out how the largest Hollywood firms attempt to control

DOI: 10.4324/9781003092629-1

social creativity such that the art of filmmaking and its related social relations under capitalism do not become financial risks in the pursuit of profit.

Controlling the ways people make or watch films, the book argues, is an institutional facet of capitalist power. Capitalist power – the ability to control, modify and, sometimes, limit social creation through the rights of ownership – is the foundation of capital accumulation. For the Hollywood film business, capitalist power is about the ability of business concerns to set the terms that mould the future of cinema. For the major film distributors, these terms include the types of films that will be distributed, the number of films that will be distributed, and the cinematic alternatives that will be made available to the individual moviegoer.

Parts of the book substantiate this argument with empirical research on the financial performance of *Major Filmed Entertainment*, which is my preferred term for what have been, since 1950, the six largest business interests in Hollywood: Columbia, Disney, Paramount, Twentieth Century-Fox, Universal and Warner Bros. (the use of firm names and "Major Filmed Entertainment" are explained in Section 1.5). Other parts of the book, including all of Part I, develop the theoretical framework that will frame the empirical research that follows in Part II.

A detailed presentation of the theoretical framework is crucial, as this book rejects certain assumptions about the capitalist economy. Most analyses of mass culture and Hollywood cinema are undermined by one of the cardinal assumptions of mainstream political economy – that politics and economics are, ultimately, analytically separate. Economics and politics are usually separated analytically because of a desire to delimit and isolate a specific dimension for study. However, this separation begets mismatches and confusions about the very essence of capitalist society. It generates a dualist methodology that has trouble explaining how a set of concepts for capitalist production (economics) does or does not relate to another set for ideology, power and authority (politics).

In order to offer insights into how various social elements of cinema come under the same heel of control and capital accumulation, this book makes use of the capital-as-power approach, which was first developed by Shimshon Bichler and Jonathan Nitzan.[1] In support of this political economic approach, the reader will find a supporting team of economists and political theorists. In particular, there are key references to the works of Friedrich Pollock, Franz Neumann, Herbert Marcuse, Theodor Adorno, Cornelius Castoriadis and Thorstein Veblen. This collection of thinkers is important to building an alternative framework to analyse the capitalist character of Hollywood cinema. The so-called non-economic elements of mass culture will have new meaning, as we will be able to understand their *direct bearing* on the accumulation of capital. In contrast to both neoclassical and Marxist theories of capital, Bichler and Nitzan (2009) argue that capital does not measure utility or socially necessary abstract labour time. Rather, capital is a quantitative, symbolic expression of organized power over society; it is a measure of the ability of capitalists in general and dominant capitalists in particular to strategically sabotage social relations for the purposes of pecuniary gain.

Much of this project's historical and empirical research seeks to demonstrate that, because of what capital is according to Bichler and Nitzan, Hollywood's dominant firms have a very specific orientation to the aesthetic potential of cinema. Like other firms, the ones that compose Major Filmed Entertainment obey the forward-looking logic of capitalization, which involves discounting of expected future earnings to present prices. Consequently, these firms value film projects as income-generating assets, the price of which depends on what is happening in the world of cinema, mass culture and, indeed, society at large. Thus, Major Filmed Entertainment capitalizes its stakes in the art of film according to how social dimensions of culture might affect earning potential.

The overall logic of capitalization can be broken down further into primary components. One of these components is risk. In the capital-as-power approach, risk concerns the degree of confidence capitalists have in their own expectations. In this study of Hollywood, we will find that risk relates to Hollywood's reluctance to let the world of cinema grow and evolve without limits instituted "from above". Thus, the control of creativity is motivated by a business concern to mitigate the risk of *aesthetic overproduction*. Aesthetic overproduction is not about the cultural or political value of cinema but about the risk such overproduction poses to cinema's earning potential. In fact, the degree of confidence in the expected future earnings of Hollywood cinema tends to increase when the industrial art of filmmaking and the social world of mass culture are ordered by capitalist power. In this cultural environment – which we will describe as an *order of cinema* – limitations are imposed on what cinema can or cannot do, an imposition which in turn allows for the financial trajectory of film projects to become more predictable for those who have a vested interest in future streams of earnings. Indeed, risk perceptions and, more generally, the logic of capitalization demand that assessments of a film's social significance be translated, with a degree of confidence, into quantitative expectations about the film's future income.

1.2   Outline of Part I

The overall objective of Part I is to outline and rectify some of the methodological problems that obscure our understanding of how capital is accumulated from culture. In a world in which businesses, both large and small, explicitly attempt to produce culture for profit, the capitalist facet of modern culture is visible to many. However, political economic theories of value are designed to look beyond the phenomena of prices. In this case, a theory needs to explain what is getting accumulated through the production of culture. Is it utility? Is it the exploited labour time of workers? Is it something else?

Notwithstanding particular differences among schools of thought, it is common practice to build a concept of capital on the assumption that economic and political activity are distinguishable because economic value is, essentially, a *measure of productivity*. Part I analyses how this assumption about economic value produces theoretical problems for a political economic analysis of mass culture. Marxism stands as the theoretical foil for this analysis. Because Marxism defines *capital* such that only economic activity (i.e., labour) can create value, it assumes there is a defined separation between economic and political processes. Some Marxist theorists have no issue with this separation; they trust their abilities to freely mix politics and economics with a dialectical theory of capitalist society. Yet Part I shows why this assumption about the nature of capital is actually a methodological problem that grows from the heart of Marxist economics. For productive labour to be the source of "real" economic value, the Marxist labour theory of value cannot avoid making a series of problematic assumptions about differences between economic and non-economic processes. Marxist theories must also ignore that it is impossible to directly confirm that value is created in the places one states are productive, while, in the rest of society, non-economic processes are purported to only support or assist the circuit of capital.

With this backdrop in mind, Part I introduces the capital-as-power approach and uses it as the foundation to study Hollywood with an alternative political economic theory of capital. The capital-as-power approach views capital not as an economic category, but as a category of power. Consequently, this approach will rearrange and reframe the picture of how capital is accumulated from mass culture. Our particular path to the capital-as-power approach is influenced by the Frankfurt School, whose members began to rethink the role of political power and the economics-politics separation in the age of monopolies, concentrated ownership and automated technology. The capital-as-power approach goes further with respect to the definition of capital: it rejects the economics-politics dualism and argues that the quantities of capital are symbolic expressions of organized power over society.

Chapter 2 demonstrates why the economics-politics separation needs to be reconsidered and why capital accumulation needs to be reframed in light of power. By examining the works of three thinkers of the Frankfurt School – Pollock, Neumann and Marcuse – we can identify various reasons to see the politics-economics separation as a barrier to understanding capitalist power in advanced capitalism (i.e. capitalist societies in the twentieth and twenty-first centuries). Moreover, their writings indicate why Marxism cannot easily overcome problems that stem from an analytical separation between economics and politics. While the Frankfurt School's arguments inspired twentieth-century Marxism to see accumulation, ideology and power holistically, whereby social processes create a totality, holistic Marxist approaches still require an unhelpful split between capital and power. With or without the base-superstructure model of its classical methods, Marxism must split social elements within a totality to privilege, by its own definition of capital, the productivity of labour in the capitalist pursuit of profit.

Chapter 3 looks at Marxist economics more closely. This chapter demonstrates why the Marxist assumption about the nature of economic value has, when applied to mass culture, little explanatory power. In general, we cannot objectively measure the magnitudes of the Marxist concept of capital. And since this short-coming is general, Marxist theories of culture have no solid basis from which to assume that socially necessary abstract labour time is the unit of value that under-pins the heterogeneous appearances of cultural commodities, prices and profit. Moreover, since the labour theory of value lies at the root of the Marxist method, it is difficult to see how this methodological problem could be solved when some cultural theorists include the desires and attitudes of consumers in a broader concept of productive valorization.

Chapter 4 develops a more comprehensive concept of capitalist power by putting power at the heart of capital accumulation. First, the writings of Garnham, Babe, Adorno and Marcuse act as precedents for thinking about the polit-ical economy of mass culture from the viewpoint of institutional power. Second, Veblen and the capital-as-power approach both argue that organized, institutional-ized power is the essence of business enterprise and the financial logic of capitaliza-tion. The capital-as-power approach is particularly useful because it breaks the separation of politics and economics before it builds a theory of institutionalized power in capitalism. Thus, we can use this approach to study the power processes that other studies of mass culture have noticed as well but in a manner that avoids separating power from a "real" magnitude of economic production, whether that magnitude be utility or socially necessary abstract labour time.

For example, by greatly relying on subjectivity, desire and matters of taste and plea-sure, the business of mass culture is filled with many qualitative social aspects. The capital-as-power approach does not pretend otherwise. Rather, it claims that the control of culture is capitalized, which only means that capitalists incorporate the qual-itative aspects of culture into their future expectations regarding *protected claims* on streams of earnings. In other words, culture is produced and consumed, but this pro-duction and consumption have no inherent capital value, whether "measured" as material or immaterial capital (Nitzan & Bichler, 2009, p. 254). As a symbolic expres-sion of organizational power, capital value is *only* attached to the protected claims of ownership that allow capitalists to withhold industrial processes – in this case, the unfettered production and consumption of culture – from society at large. Veblen called this socio-legal process of exclusion and control "strategic sabotage".

1.3 Outline of Part II

Part II focuses on the Hollywood film business. It investigates how and to what extent Major Filmed Entertainment attempts to accumulate capital by lowering its risk. The process of lowering risk – and the central role of capitalist power in this process – has characterized Hollywood's orientation toward the social-historical character of cinema and mass culture. This push to lower risk has been most apparent since the 1980s. In recent decades, Major Filmed Entertainment has used its oligopolistic control of distribution to institute an order of cinema based on several key strategies: saturation booking, blockbuster cinema and high-concept filmmaking. Of course, there is much more to cinema, and even Hollywood cinema, than these three key strategies. Yet the purpose of Major Filmed Entertainment is to create an order of cinema that benefits its business interests. And when Major Filmed Entertainment has the institutional means to shape the movements of the cinematic universe – social relations and all – it possesses a greater ability to affirm, modify or deny film projects and ideas according to their perceived function in capital accumulation.

Chapter 5 examines the capital-as-power approach in greater detail. First to be examined is the concept of differential accumulation. In this book, differential accumulation denotes the process of accumulating capital faster than dominant capital, proxied by the 500 largest firms in the Compustat database. The second issue to be examined is the role of risk in the logic of capitalization. Since lower risk increases capitalization, differential reductions of risk lead to differential accumulation. As with our definition of *differential accumulation*, our analysis of differential risk concerns the ability of Major Filmed Entertainment to lower its risk faster (or have it rise slower) than dominant capital as a whole.

Chapter 6 explains why the Hollywood film business seeks to create and reinforce deterministic social relations in the world of cinema. An order of cinema is a defence against the threat of aesthetic overproduction. This threat, which is financial, can appear when the future social significance and aesthetics of cinema seem uncertain. This uncertainty derives from social-historical shifts in meaning, desire and, more generally, cultural norms and values. Again, shifts in the social meaning of cinema do not undermine filmmaking and film consumption as cultural and political activities; in fact, these shifts in meaning might foretell a cinematic renaissance or democratic potential of art (Holman & McMahon, 2015). But they can undermine the goals of business interests, which value film production, distribution and exhibition as, primarily, capitalist techniques. Therefore, the capitalist control of cinema requires that vested interests shape the relationship between new creativity and already established meaning.

Chapter 7 examines, analytically and quantitatively, how and to what extent Major Filmed Entertainment has been able to reduce risk in the contemporary period of the Hollywood film business, from 1950 to 2019. The chapter outlines some of the business strategies that have been instrumental ever since the US Supreme Court demolished aspects of the classical studio system in 1948. Key post-1948 strategies have been saturation booking and blockbuster cinema, and both were successful in reducing the risk of Major Filmed Entertainment, both absolutely and relative to dominant capital.

These empirical conclusions are antithetical to mainstream theories. By relying on the neoclassical concept of consumer sovereignty, many theories claim that the systemic risk of Hollywood is always somewhere between high and extremely high, whereas in reality this risk has been dropping. In fact, the chapter demonstrates that Major Filmed Entertainment is now able to confidently determine which films will be very successful in the saturation-booking system of theatrical exhibition.

Some of the data analysis in Chapter 7 shows that the highest level of risk occurred in the late 1960s and 1970s. Risk dropped significantly in the early 1980s and then continued to drop steadily to the 2010s. Chapter 8 analyses how this historical trajectory of Major Filmed Entertainment's risk parallels the sector-wide transition from "New Hollywood", a creative period where business interests embraced the visions of American New Wave cinema (~1968–1977), to a glossier, blockbuster-centric Hollywood from 1980 to the present day. This transition was marked by a growing emphasis on the production of high-concept cinema. High-concept filmmaking demands that large-budget films have simple and straightforward stories, character types and imagery. High-concept cinema was never just an aesthetic standard; it was a business solution after American New Wave became a financial burden for Major Filmed Entertainment. The general institution of high-concept filmmaking enabled Major Filmed Entertainment to refrain from distributing film projects that were deemed too complex, too ambiguous or, in light of what American New Wave was seeking to achieve, too political for its twin-engine strategy of saturation booking and blockbuster cinema. Staying within the scope of high concept cinema helped Major Filmed Entertainment achieve significant reduction in differential risk and a concomitant increase in differential earnings.

1.4   On the scope of analysis

This book tries to cover many decades of Hollywood history, which is now over 100 years long. Traversing this scale of time with analysis and research has its challenges, but added difficulties are produced from changes to the geography and technology of Hollywood cinema. The twenty-first-century version of the Hollywood film business looks very different than previous periods of its history. The Hollywood of 2020 is global, has adapted to digital technology and the internet, and creates intellectual property for media conglomerates. Movie consumption has also been re-invented with digital media, cellphones and other portable devices. What can an analysis of the Hollywood film business say about these present-day facts?

This book will not ignore novel characteristics of contemporary Hollywood, but there are empirical limitations to studying them. Table 1.1 summarizes my collection of data by subject type and scale. Two columns indicate if enough data are available to make long time series (~10 years or more) or if data are broken down by national source (e.g. domestic vs international revenues).

TABLE 1.1 Summary of availability and granularity of data on Hollywood

Level	Data	Long time series available?	Breakdown: inside and outside US
Regional	Consumer	★	★
	Financial	★	★
National	Consumer	★	★
	Financial	★	★
Corporate	Revenues	★	
	Income	★	
Platform	Theatrical	★	★
	Video / DVD		
	Digital		
Film	Theatrical Sales	★	★
	Non-Theatrical Sales		
	Profits		
	Budget	★	

When accounting for what is readily available, the reader should not be surprised to see my analysis focus on (a) the US film market (which can include Canada in some data sets) and (b) the revenues of Hollywood films in the theatrical market. When data are available or when a qualitative argument is suitable, this book addresses relevant topics, such as the risks of piracy in online streaming or Hollywood's global reach in the twenty-first century. But data-driven arguments are beholden to what is available in databases. Furthermore, the reader will see how the theatrical market has not diminished in importance, notwithstanding technological changes to film distribution and consumption.

1.5 On the usage of firm names and Major Filmed Entertainment

This book describes and analyses the capital accumulation of what will be called Major Filmed Entertainment. This category comprises the six major studios in Hollywood: Columbia, Disney, Paramount, Twentieth Century-Fox, Universal and Warner Bros. Many of these studios were key players in Hollywood's "studio era", and they have dominated American film distribution since 1950. Some distributors excluded from this list, such as United Artists, MGM or Lionsgate, are occasionally competitive with the previously mentioned six studios; and with its initiation into the Motion Picture Association in 2019, Netflix is currently a legitimate member of Hollywood's oligopoly. However, the six studios in Major Filmed Entertainment have been dominant for decades, and the analyses of risk reduction and differential accumulation operate on this time scale. For present-day readers curious about Netflix, I can say that I am

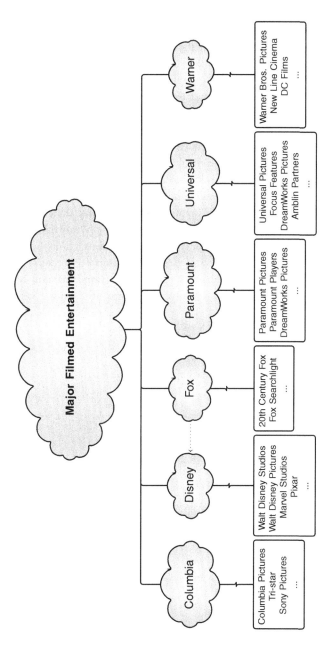

FIGURE 1.1 Conceptualizing Major Filmed Entertainment

Note: Disney acquired 20th Century Fox studios and its related intellectual property near the end of 2018. These filmed entertainment assets were previously owned by Rupert Murdoch's News Corporation. Fox News and related operations are still owned by Murdoch. Prior to the sale to Disney, Fox filmed entertainment operations were spun-off into a separate company, 21st Century Fox.

just as curious. Some of my plans for future research are presented in this book's conclusion.

Some film historians will disapprove of me abstracting up, rather than going down into the finer details of corporate history. However, I patiently ask the reader to consider the difference between the presentation of a concept like Major Filmed Entertainment and the detailed research that prepared the concept for written argument. The construction of Major Filmed Entertainment involved research that included film history and theory, as well as firm-level research of annual reports and US Securities and Exchange Commission (SEC) filings. Small pieces of this research are not always presented individually. Rather, details are often recombined as sector averages and trends, as my interest is in identifying and understanding how the oligopoly that lives at the centre of Hollywood successfully accumulates capital. Moreover, we have to collectively recognize that the Hollywood film business is often presented with *some level of abstraction*. In reality, companies are legal entities, and it is difficult for their names to signify entire networks of employees, subsidiaries, consultants, contracts, investors and beneficiaries. General statements like "Columbia makes and distributes neo-*noir* films" also hide the details of production, the contracts involved and the people therein.

Figure 1.1 is a visualization of how I am conceptualizing Major Filmed Entertainment. The top two levels signify where conceptual abstractions occur. The bottom level excludes the conglomerate parents for a simpler visualization but presents samples of the empirical reality I researched: companies and business divisions that comprise what we commonly imagine to be "major Hollywood studios".

Note

1 All of their writings are freely available at http://bnarchives.yorku.ca.

PART I

2

THE ECONOMICS–POLITICS
SEPARATION AND MARXISM

2.1 Introduction

In both academic theory and public opinion, there is an inclination to think that material production has its own distinct place in capitalism: in the sphere of economics. Our subjective experiences often fuel this inclination. For example, economics often appears to be a circuit of activity defined by space: factories and offices are distinguishable from residences, schools, churches, army bases and government ministries, and goods are exchanged in a place neither familial nor governmental. Hegel (2005a), for instance, described "civil society" as a place where individuals negotiated their needs in relation to the "work and satisfaction of the needs of all the others" (§188). Hegel's description of civil society was influenced by Adam Smith's concept of the market. Smith argued that the extent of the market could solve the problems of individuals trying to meet their own needs through exchange. Each object brought to market had specific, limited utility – like a pair of shoes, or a hunting bow – but the market could mediate an individual's needs and create social relationships based on supply and demand (A. Smith, 1991, pp.15–19).

Beneath such descriptions of the market and the places of material production is a deeper assumption about the composition of capitalist society. Different theories of capitalism, each with its own intentions, assume economics is separate from politics. Caporaso and Levine (1992) explain how one can even unintentionally affirm this separation: "When we speak of the economy, we already assume the existence of a separate entity: . . . a distinct set of relations between persons not in essence political or familial" (p. 28). But can we really speak of the economy? Should theory try to isolate economic relations from other social relations?

DOI: 10.4324/9781003092629-3

Neoclassical and Marxist approaches would disagree on many other aspects of capitalist society, but their respective concepts of capital both produce an analytical distinction between political power and economic production. Political power creates and institutes laws, norms and social values on the basis of institutional authority. This authority can take different forms – the authority of a king or queen can be "sanctioned" by divine right – but it is also theoretically possible for laws and norms to be instituted on the authority of the *demos*. Regardless, the exercise of power is identifiable because, as Hobbes noted, if there is authority, there is an author. Political power, whether it represents the interests of the commonwealth or not, is "done by Authority, done by Commission, or Licence from him whose right it is" (Hobbes, 1985, p. 218).

Economics appears to be analytically different in this regard because "nobody" is the author of market activity. Governments still impose rules and regulations through command, but somehow, when market activity is itself the object of study, it seems that capitalist economics is in the "grip of subterranean forces that have a life of their own" (Heilbroner, 1992, p. 18). From this perspective, power and authority are denoted as non-economic entities that affect competitive market activity from the outside. And in the competitive market proper, commodities are said to be produced and sold at prices that neither buyers nor sellers author. The motions of a capitalist economy are, unlike the motions of politics, said to be governed by laws of equilibrium, material conditions and the measures of input, output and productivity.

Nitzan and Bichler (2009) argue that the economics-politics separation, as it is commonly understood, needs to be thoroughly reconsidered. It is commonly assumed that capital is an economic magnitude that is rooted in material production. Consequently, value is defined as a measure of material productivity (utility or socially necessary abstract labour time), and political power can only ever distort economic activity (neoclassical economics) or assist, support or condition the mode of production (Marxism). According to Bichler and Nitzan, dividing economics and politics with a definition of material productivity is where the problem lies. If a given concept of capital privileges material productivity, the resulting theoretical framework is ill equipped to explain a capitalist historical reality in which *the so-called economic sphere is itself a composite of power processes*. In fact, the explanation becomes burdened with logical fallacies and empirical obstacles.

Aside from a few comparative references to neoclassical economics, this chapter focuses on Marxist political economy. Focusing almost all our attention on Marxism is justifiable. As Bichler and Nitzan (2012) note, Marx was "concerned with *social power writ large*. For Marx the question is how production and exploitation, organized through the process of accumulation, dictate the totality of human relations in capitalism" (p. 8). Unlike neoclassical approaches that try to ignore the effects of power on society, Marxism argues that social power is a necessary condition for the class structure of capitalism to function in spite of its contradictions. Whether expressed through the political power of the state, the ideology of the media or the subject formation of the modern individual, power is a key factor in the social reproduction of capitalist society. Power is also expressed in the struggle over the terms of the labour–capital relationship, which includes the wage rate and the length of the working day.

Yet methodological problems still appear within Marxism because its theory must explain the causes for quantitative magnitudes within capitalist society – why, for example, a labourer is paid $12 per hour, a pair of shoes sells for $100, or why IBM's net income in 2010 was almost $15 billion. Marxism's quantitative mode of analysis is based on a commitment that, fundamentally, economics and politics are separable. If capitalism is, in essence, a mode of production, and if the circuit of capital is, beyond the appearances of price, rooted in labour values, a delineated economic sphere must exist. Otherwise, there is no logical reason why prices and profit should reflect material productivity, ever, or at all. Ignoring for the moment the empirical dilemmas of measuring socially necessary abstract labour time and applying the labour theory of value to business sectors like culture, a Marxist theory of capitalist accumulation needs analytical boundaries between productive economic processes and everything else. Otherwise, it becomes unclear why the difference between production prices and profit is, essentially, the difference between "the value paid by the capitalist for the labour-power" (Marx, 1990, p. 302) and the exchange value of the commodity.

This chapter analyses the problem of the economics–politics separation within the writings of Neumann, Pollock and Marcuse. These three members of the Frankfurt School are important for our purpose because their political economic ideas, which are sometimes fragmentary, reside in the grey areas of Marxism. While the Frankfurt School never intended to overcome Marxism entirely, its members reconsidered the assumptions of Marxist political economy from within. Wanting to answer questions about the essence of capital accumulation in advanced capitalism, the Frankfurt School begin to outline a political economic process of power.

There are numerous reasons to redefine capital in light of the ability to accumulate through power. Social power is everywhere in what Marcuse calls "advanced capitalism": mass culture influences psychology, desire and social behaviour; technological infrastructure and the scientific worldview require their own forms of instrumental rationality; and, perhaps most important for a concept of capital accumulation, giant firms have power over small firms and society at large. Thus, we will see how Pollock, Neumann and Marcuse each erase, ignore or modify the politics–economics relationship when it obscures the role of power in capital accumulation. Gone is the idea that cultural and political processes only ever support or assist what is, in the last instance, an economic system rooted in material productivity. Rather, monopolization and the structure of the modern corporation, for example, indicated to them that institutional power was no longer on the margins of market activity.

The effects of this rethinking can be significant, but these three writers also never made it their goal to fully replace Marxism with an alternative political economic theory. As a consequence, literature tends to situate the Frankfurt School's political economic ideas within the internal evolution of Marxist thought. However, we can take a different perspective on the Frankfurt School's movements within Marxism's theoretical worldview. The Frankfurt School are key examples of Marxist thought rejuvenating dialectical thinking after "classical" Marxism, yet this interest in capital accumulation as a power process would, if followed through, be much more explosive than expected: it would erase the need to create a concept of capital with a primary separation of politics and economics.

This perspective on the Frankfurt School will refer to Marxist the concept of totality, which is a concept that is associated with Western Marxism. Beginning with the writing of Georg Lukacs, the idea of a social totality was key to superseding the base-superstructure models of early twentieth-century Marxism. However, the desire to think of capitalist society holistically has methodological problems when the desire is borne within Marxism. It is the Marxist concept of capital that is creating a fundamental split between its political and economic categories. Historical materialism can reject the base-superstructure model, but its more holistic versions must still retain well-defined ideas of what is and is not economic exploitation. In other words, the conceptual tool that describes the mode of production and the accumulation of surplus value is dialectical *only up to a point*. Dialectical mediation, which remains an important methodological principle for both the Frankfurt School and Marxism, is arrested by the necessity to keep any critical insights about the role of power in advanced capitalism from transforming the Marxist concept of capital into something else. As Lukacs saw in his own writings, the eventual cost of a holistic method is Marxism losing the "centre" of its system (Jay, 1984, p. 85).

2.2 Economics–politics and the definition of capital

The conceptual boundaries of any academic discipline influence the scope and methods of its research. In the case of political economy, the range of analysis is categorized, weighed and interpreted according to the method through which it understands the connection between politics and economics.

Based on the assumption that politics and economics are separate, most theorists tend to explain capitalism with dualist methodologies that have two sets of categories: one set for capital (economics) and another for ideology, power and authority (politics; Nitzan & Bichler, 2000, 2009). A simple but relevant example is found in the measurement of gross domestic product (GDP).

Notwithstanding the more technical debate about whether GDP is even a relevant measure of a country's prosperity (Stiglitz, Sen, & Fitoussi, 2009), GDP only counts some social activity on the fundamental assumption that activity in the economy produces wealth, while political activity cannot. For instance, government transfer payments – for example welfare, social security and subsidies – have great effects on society because they redistribute income (by authority of the state), but they are not counted in measurements of GDP. If economics is about the production of wealth, political exercises like transfer payments can only shape, support, influence, bend or distort the economy from the "outside".

For many thinkers, the separation that delimits economic activity is what distinguishes capitalism from pre-capitalist societies. There is common agreement that to understand material production in pre-capitalist societies, one cannot winnow out politics. Before capitalism, the economy was visibly political; the meaning of material production was defined in relation to the institution of a political order. We can certainly look at a past society and distinguish work and its details from other activities, such as leisurely dialogue or religious prayer. Past social hierarchies also reveal how unproductive rulers separated themselves from the mass of labourers who toiled and got their hands dirty. Nevertheless, many theorists find no point in drawing a circle around economic activity in pre-capitalist societies because the relations of production, exchange, distribution and consumption were not autonomous. Rulers and social institutions actively determined the form, means and ends of economic activity; material production could help actualize the good life or it could fuel war, territorial expansion and crusades against foreign peoples; and who worked, how they worked and what they were working for was affected by myth, tradition and custom, as well as by a ruling authority, be it democratic or autocratic.

The Sumerian debt system, for instance, was largely the prerogative of state rulers. Their decrees about the terms of debt and the interest rate had more to do with religious sanction and mathematical simplicity than profit and productivity rates (Hudson, 2000). Through systems of absolute power, the rulers of ancient Egypt controlled the social division labour in order to build grand public works and monuments like the pyramids, which celebrated "the cult of Divine Kingship" (Mumford, 1970, p. 29). Could we understand the building of pyramids without an idea of how this excessive and wasteful expenditure of human energy was politically sanctioned? It would be silly to shear politics and explain the existence of ancient pyramids from a "purely" economic standpoint. In fact, Bataille (1991) shows us how the reduction of symbolic power to economic laws unveils the absurdity of Keynes's suggestion for economic recovery: "the pyramid is a monumental mistake; one might just as well dig an enormous hole, then refill it and pack the ground" (p. 199).

Some theorists seek to identify instrumental systems of behaviour in pre-capitalist production and exchange. To the modern academic, the means and ends of production and exchange are the territory of the economist, yet the functional logics of pre-capitalist economic systems – for example how much to produce, how much to exchange, what is "fair" trade – are theorized with cultural and political categories. In his study of feudal societies, Moore (1993) argues that a "folk conception of justice" can create a historical equilibrium in the relationship between lord and peasant. This conception of justice is not the same across all feudal systems, but a social belief about what makes a lord "fair" can prevent peasants from revolting at every small change to a lord's exaction (Moore, 1993, p. 471). From a comparison of different societies, Polanyi (2001) arrived at a similar conclusion about the drives of pre-capitalist economic behaviour: "Custom and law, magic and religion cooperated in inducing the individual to comply with rules of behaviour which, eventually, ensured his functioning in the economic system" (p. 57). As Weber argues, pre-capitalist economic behaviour never approximates the cold formal rationality of economic calculation in capitalism. Too much of pre-capitalist behaviour was entangled with and limited by cultural, religious and political traditions (Weber, 2002, p. xxxi).

What then is different or "special" about capitalist societies? Often, in the interest of affirming what is novel about the economics–politics relation in the capitalist universe, theorists tend to treat commodity production and exchange as a distinct domain of market economics. For instance, the capitalist economy is sometimes understood to be its own "thing" because people now behave and act according to a behavioural principle that originates in the market itself. According to Polanyi (2001), the capitalist pursuit of gain for the sake of gain is characterized, first and foremost, as an economic motive that requires no "extra" reference to "social standing . . . social claims . . . or social assets" (p. 48). Seen as a distinct domain, the capitalist economy demands specialized theoretical categories and sets of tools to understand such phenomena as capitalist investment, wage labour and the value of production. Some theorists even treat economic categories as exceptional social categories, as it is assumed that capitalist economics has determinable laws of motion, much like natural phenomena. Marx (1999), for example, stated that not only is the capitalist economic system the key to explaining its class structure but also that this system can, unlike our "legal, political, religious, or philosophic" systems, "be determined with the precision of natural science" (p. 21).

Philosophers, historians, political scientists and economists do not make a cut between economics and politics in the same place. Additionally, what happens after the cut is impacted by one's theoretical worldview. Yet a dualism in political economy is produced by the belief that a cut between economics and politics is *necessary* for the study of capitalism. By variations of degree and style, the sociopolitical concepts of tradition, myth, command and power are marginalized by a fundamental idea of there being something they cannot explain: the mechanisms and processes of the capitalist economy, which has its own *eidos, archē* and *telos.*

The marked shift in perspective regarding capitalist societies produces a new form of dualism, one that assumes that the immanent laws of politics and economics are each understandable in isolation. Nowhere is this dualism more celebrated than in neoclassical economics. As Nitzan and Bichler (2009) explain, the existence of power politics can disturb capitalism's economic system, but, for the neoclassical economist, the presence of power in the world never alters the basic meaning of capital:

> According to the neoclassicists, capital is the utilitarian manifestation of multiple individual wills, expressed freely through the market and incarnated in an objective productive quantum. As a voluntary, material substance, capital itself is orthogonal — and therefore impermeable — to power politics, by definition. (p. 27)

Mancur Olson (1982), for instance, goes to great lengths to list contemporary forms of what he calls "distributional coalitions" – rigid organizations that use power to protect their specific interests against the collective good. Olson finds that, like the Indian caste system or the British class structure, modern institutions like the Organization of the Petroleum Exporting Countries, labour unions, lobbying organizations and professional associations use their size and complexity to control the distribution of material and intellectual resources. However, Olson also assumes that the institutional power of distributional coalitions, no matter how large, complex or ubiquitous, can never change the categories we should use to understand economic activity. Distributional coalitions can accumulate "power and income", *but they can only depress the economy*, which, for Olson, is still analytically separable. According to the neoclassical definition, economic activity is only about growth and productivity.

What about Marxism? By having different social and political interests than neoclassical economics, Marxist political economy takes a different approach to the politics–economics relationship. Marxism's curiosities about the capitalist mode of production and the accumulation of capital are intimately connected to a political theory of liberation, whereby those outside the capitalist class have a real interest in overcoming the contradictions of capitalism. Marxism's theoretical foundations also precede the neoclassical movement, which first began in 1870s. Along with Adam Smith and David Ricardo, Marx was a major figure in the classical tradition in political economy. These intellectual roots prevent Marxist studies from keeping economics "pure".[1]

It is noticeable that Marxism mixes economics and politics with enthusiasm. For instance, the economics–politics relationship is key to understanding how the historical development of the capitalist mode of production has been contemporaneous with liberalism, fascism, imperialism, colonialism, post-colonialism and neo-liberalism. Furthermore, Marx had great insight on social power because he understood that political force balanced the otherwise unstable contradictions of production and accumulation. As Habermas (1991, p. 122) notes, Marx disagreed with liberal claims of a power-free marketplace: hierarchical power must be present lest a class society quickly collapse from its inequalities, injustices and other irrationalities.

But regardless of how complex its analysis becomes, Marxism needs to keep its two main ingredients, economics and politics, separate. Because of the way in which capital is defined in Marxism, political processes must recede into the background when it is time to explain, in technical detail, what is directly responsible for the production of value (Nitzan & Bichler, 2000). Power, law, violence, education, repression, ideology and other such mechanisms are still important to Marxism's theory of class societies, but on questions of economic value, these social phenomenon support another set, those that exploit human labour's singular capacity to create value. Thus, the Marxist concept of capital always necessitates, at key points, exclusive tasks for its economic categories. Only economic categories are used to explain the technological composition of material production, the productivity of labour and the effect of socially necessary abstract labour time on the exchange values of commodities.

Bichler and Nitzan, cited earlier, are not forgetting the dialectical methods of Marx (Nitzan & Bichler, 2000). Capital, for Marx, is a complex, historical-social relationship, and the complexity and historicity of that relationship make it impossible to reduce capital to a simple thing. For example, the Marxist concept of capital references, in its own definition, other concepts like primitive accumulation, expanded accumulation, capitalists, workers, labour, technology, commodity, value, money, price and surplus (Ollman, 2003, p. 14). Yet this dialectical mediation of concepts cannot go so far as to cause the labour theory of value to lose its relevance. In other words, the theory that describes the accumulation of surplus value is dialectical only up to a point. Political concepts such as power and ideology cannot qualitatively transform the Marxist theory of value, lest it be suggested that the exploitation of labour is secondary or inessential to accumulation.

Some of what has been said above is not problematic in the abstract. In fact, as long as the economics–politics split is treated as a reasonable idea for political economic theories of capitalism, one might infer that nothing yet has been said about the consistency or inner workings of Marxism's theoretical model. However, severe problems with the measurement of capital become visible when we start think more about using Marxism's methods to study a capitalist reality. Even if we assume that the labour theory of value is logically consistent and can function as a theoretical model without fallacies, the *historical* development of capitalism can put the attention back on the theory's deepest assumptions about what is primary or essential about capital accumulation.

For example, the Frankfurt School's methods and study of modern society in the twenty-first century led them to rethink the nature of capital accumulation.

Following lines of research on power and repression in capitalism, the Frankfurt School would push their arguments to points where it was no longer clear that socially necessary abstract labour time was the economic substance that "gives commodities their value and makes them commensurate" (Nitzan & Bichler, 2009, p. 88).

2.3   The Frankfurt School and the historical development of capitalism

At the end of the first volume of *Capital*, Marx (1990) reminds the reader of where the class struggle is heading should "the immanent laws of capitalist production" keep their grip on both the capitalists who own the means of production and the wage labourers who have nothing to sell but their labour power:

> Along with the constant decrease in the number of capitalist magnates, who usurp and monopolize all the advantages of this process of transformation, the mass of misery, oppression, slavery, degradation and exploitation grows; but with this there also grows the revolt of the working class, a class constantly increasing in numbers, and trained, united and organized by the very mechanism of the capitalist process of production. (p. 929)

On the same page, Marx also emphasizes how "capitalist production begets, with the inexorability of a natural process, its own negation". These prophetic words acquired a different meaning after Marx's death. They began to function as painful reminders that Marxism needed to explain why the capitalist system kept postponing its own negation.

In spite of significant crises such as the First World War, inflation in the 1920s and the Great Depression in the 1930s, the general actions of the European proletariat in the early twentieth century did not confirm Marx's theory of capitalist crisis. To the surprise of Marxist intellectuals living through the first decades of the twentieth century, workers all over Europe were, in fact, going in the "wrong" direction. Rather than being a great moment of historical self-consciousness in which the proletariat recognized how "the centralization of the means of production and the socialization of labour [had reached] a point at which they become incompatible with their capitalist integument" (Marx, 1990, p. 929), Europe in the 1920s and 1930s was characterized by worker apathy, social democracy and, most disturbingly, fascism.

As a consequence of these historical developments, a new intellectual movement percolated within Marxism. Various European thinkers, while still sympathetic to Marxism's political goals, openly reinterpreted the Marxist method of social theory. Georg Lukacs's *History and Class Consciousness*, for example, was one of the first texts to explicitly present a Marxism-for-the-twentieth-century. According to

Lukacs, ideology and the related issues of subjectivity and class-consciousness were now too important to have marginal places in Marxist theory. He also felt that some of his contemporaries, like Otto Bauer, were missing the point when they argued that Marxist economics simply needed to be "brought up to date". Classical Marxist economics was not only blind to the "ultimate fate of capitalism as a whole" (Lukacs, 1968, p. 31); its methods also betrayed its "inability to understand either the connections of the so-called 'ideological' forms of society and their economic base or the economy itself as a totality and as social reality" (Lukacs, 1968, p. 34).

The Marxism of Lukacs gave credence to the methods of the Frankfurt School. Reductionist versions of Marxism, thanks to Lukacs's interrogations, did not need to be defended when one rethought the relations between theory and practice. Indeed, the obstacles to revolutionary leftism in early twentieth-century Europe suggested that Marxism take a new approach: abandon classical Marxism and reconsider the essence of historical materialism. Events of the twentieth century gave, according to Marcuse (1968e), "a new import to many demands and indices of [historical materialism], whose changed function accords in a more intensive sense the character of 'critical theory'" (p. 142).

The Frankfurt School's development of critical theory sought to explore new ways to understand the totalizing nature of contemporary social domination (Marcuse, 1968e, p. 158). In this theoretical development, we find, among other things, the Frankfurt School's contributions to political economy. Given space limitations, only the contributions of Pollock, Neumann and Marcuse will be presented in this section.[2] These three thinkers developed political economic concepts, such as "state capitalism" and "Totalitarian Monopoly Capitalism", and they attempted to account for the modern corporation and the rise of automation in industrial production. Their analyses were premised on the principle that a historically grounded dialectic was the only way for critical theory to be both negative and emancipatory.

In my view, the writings of the Pollock, Neumann and Marcuse illustrate why the economics–politics separation needs to be thoroughly reconsidered and the concept of capital reconceptualized. The political economic insights of the Frankfurt School are, essentially, observations that the theoretical picture of Marxist economics was not matching contemporary reality. Thus, Pollock, Neumann and Marcuse all began to respectively reframe capital accumulation according to how they understood the roles of command, authority and domination in advanced capitalism. Yet their observations also do not lead to a full reconsideration of Marxism's key economic assumption that value is rooted in labour time. They pushed against economic assumptions but only to a point where their following hypotheses were incompatible with the Marxist concept of capital in at least three ways:

1   economic laws do not force modern firms to compete for profit on terms of productivity,

2   that it is doubtful that there is a link between material production and prices, and

3   that a concept of capital cannot automatically privilege production over power.

As Kellner notes in his intellectual history of the Frankfurt School, the school's complicated relationship with classical Marxism is the consequence of its thinkers attempting to strengthen, rather than weaken, historical materialism (Kellner, 1989, p. 70). Nevertheless, the writings of the Frankfurt School's first generation are now in the hands of its interpreters, who tend to interpret the political economy of writers like Pollock and Neumann with the same "domestic" goal: to support one's understanding of how the politics–economics relationship should function within a Marxist framework. To the best of my knowledge, no one considers an alternative: using the Frankfurt School as a platform to think about a non-Marxist, yet critical, political economy of capital accumulation. Let us consider this alternative.

As we will see in our analysis of Pollock, Neumann and Marcuse, the very historical development of capitalism challenges the theoretical primacy of labour time in the valorization and accumulation of surplus value. In fact, the Frankfurt School pushes us to see how the Marxist labour theory of value obscures our understanding of capital accumulation in contemporary times. We now live in a world where modern firms (a) erase the distinction between economic and political activity and (b) acquire the power to accumulate capital in ways that are not primarily about material productivity: law, ideology, price control, and so on.

Additionally, there is a difference between restating how economic and political categories work within Marxism and reconceptualizing a theory of capital in light of the capitalist ability to accumulate through power. This difference is not one of dialectics *per se* but of the Marxist distinction between economic valorization and political power. Holistic forms of Marxist theory certainly mix the two with enthusiasm – it has to do so in order to explain the social reproduction of the capitalist system. Yet economics must still be isolated in this theoretical mixture, lest a multidimensional picture of capitalist society undermine the key assumption that one specific social activity, labour, is the source of value.

2.3.1   Pollock on political power and state capitalism

Writing just after another member of the Institut für Sozialforschung, Henryk Grossman, had argued that classical Marxist economics was just fine – a claim that seemed to have been vindicated by the Wall Street Crash of 1929 – Pollock's perspective in 1941 was unusual by comparison (Kellner, 1989, p. 57). Since the early 1930s, argued Pollock, capitalism had found ways to solve its own crises. The concentration of ownership and the size of large-scale production transformed capitalist societies into "planned economies". Consequently, in order to theorize how a "new set of rules" had replaced "the methods of the market", a critical theorist needs to make a conceptual shift (Pollock, 2005, p. 75). Pollock suggested that we use the concept of "state capitalism". Market activity still existed, just as production and distribution were still theoretically relevant, but old assumptions about their specifically economic essence had to be jettisoned:

> During the non-monopolistic phase of private capitalism, the capitalist (whether an individual or a group of shareholders represented by its manager) had power over his property within the limits of the market laws. Under state capitalism, this power has been transferred to the government which is still limited by certain "natural" restrictions but free from the tyranny of an uncontrolled market. The replacement of the economic means by political means as the last guarantee for the reproduction of economic life, changes the character of the whole historic period. It signifies the transition from a predominantly economic to an essentially political era. (Pollock, 2005, p. 77)

Economic problems were now "problems of administration", and political concepts, like power, could be used to explain the control of production and distribution.

Members of the Frankfurt School reacted in different ways to Pollock's political economic theory of state capitalism (Horkheimer, 2005a; Neumann, 1942). Neumann, for example, disagreed with Pollock's distinction between economics and politics. A social formation is "no longer capitalistic" if "the new economy is . . . one without economics", "the profit motive is supplanted by the power motive", and "force, not economic law, is the prime mover of this society" is (Neumann, 1942, pp. 182–183). If politics has supplanted economics, a state could be called "a slave state or a managerial dictatorship or a system of bureaucratic collectivism – that is, it must be described in political and not in economic categories" (Neumann, 1942, p. 183).

The disagreement between Pollock and Neumann was rooted in the assumption that economics and politics begin as separate domains. If economics and politics are separate and the latter sphere has conquered the former, a new political ruling class must also have superseded the class of private capitalists, whose habitat was the economy. Thus, in Neumann's eyes, Pollock's shift to the political suggested that we now needed to focus on a new group of elites: "industrial managers, party bureaucrats, high-ranking civil servants, and army officers" (Neumann, 1942, p. 182). This new focus concerned Neumann because it appeared to keep capitalism's primary instinct, the drive to accumulate, out of sight.

But it seems that Neumann misread Pollock's intentions. Pollock argued he was still looking at a capitalist system. The term *state capitalism* simply tells us where Pollock thought power lay in the capitalist societies of the 1920s and 1930s.

Moreover, power was still capitalist in form: "profit interests still play an important role" and the political economic system being described is "not socialism" (Pollock, 2005, p. 72). In fact, Pollock's seemingly unorthodox conflation of profit and power produced two important insights about the character of capitalist societies since the early twentieth century.

First, Pollock wanted us to think about the *control* of production and distribution (much like the writings of Thorstein Veblen, which is given more attention in Chapter 4). The concentration of ownership and the role of the state have changed the political economic environment: output is planned and prices are administered through political power (Pollock, 2005, p. 76). Second, and most important, the exercise of control over production and distribution is still understood and applied in the language of business enterprise. In capitalism, the power to "define the needs of society", allocate resources, "coordinate and control . . . all productive resources", and "distribute the social profit" is now very much a matter of how monopolies secure "monopoly profits at the expense of the non-monopolistic market prices" (Pollock, 2005, pp. 74–76). Thus, in the furnace of "modern giant enterprises", the once separate logics of the entrepreneur, the financier and the government bureaucrat have mixed to become an alloy, whose purpose is to seek profit on the wings of administered prices:

> Specific means of control include modern statistical and accounting methods, regular reporting of all changes in plant and supply, systematic training of workers for future requirements, rationalization of all technical and administrative processes and all the other devices developed in the huge modern enterprises and cartels. In addition to these traditional methods which have superseded the occult entrepreneurial art of guessing correctly what the future market demand will be, the state acquires the additional controlling power implied in complete command over money and credit. (Pollock, 2005, p. 79)

2.3.2   Neumann on totalitarian monopoly capitalism

Interestingly, both Pollock and Neumann tried to overcome the same analytical problem. When no longer grappling with "politics" and "economics" in the abstract, Neumann was much closer to Pollock's position than he would have been willing to admit. Neumann did not like what "state capitalism" implied, and he also thought that Pollock simply supplanted the profit motive with the power motive. But the progressive concentration of ownership compelled Neumann, like Pollock, to reinterpret the relationship between capital accumulation and power.

Neumann's political economic study of Nazi Germany, *Behemoth*, has its own term to describe capitalist power: *Totalitarian Monopoly Capitalism*. This term explains the heart of Nazi Germany's business structure. It also denotes changes in the politics–economics relationship. Nazi Germany was an example of how a modern capitalist society could be both "a monopolistic economy" and "a command economy" (Neumann, 1942, p. 214).

For Neumann, the study of capitalist power enables us to see real differences between different types of property ownership. "In our language", writes Neumann (1942), "domination over means of consumption and over means production is called by the same name: 'property'" (p. 210). However, describing the power of individuals and the power of business enterprises with the same term is a "legal mask". The size of massive industrial infrastructure and joint-stock companies have created qualitative differences between capitalist power and consumer power. Power over industrial capacity has shattered the classical economic assumption that "a large number of entrepreneurs of about equal strength" can do nothing but "compete with each other on the basis of freedom of contract and freedom of trade". Rather, the size and scope of contemporary industry gives its elite group of owners power over others: "power over workers, power over consumers, power over the state" (Neumann, 1942, p. 210).

In contradistinction to Pollock, Neumann still wanted to hold on to "economics" as an independent idea. However, the rich historical details in *Behemoth* demonstrate that he was rethinking the meaning of "economics" in light of historical developments in ownership and the size of modern institutions. There are too many details to cover here, but we can provide three examples that show that Neumann understood that capital accumulation was now rooted in power.

First, prices no longer find market equilibrium because they no longer float in a "power-free" environment.[3] Only in "a purely competitive economy", in which firms are of roughly equal size and the concentration of ownership is low, will "prices crystallize as a result of supply and demand" (Neumann, 1942, p. 255). When this competitive environment does not exist, one must, according to Neumann, develop a theory of price control.

Here, on the topic of price control, Neumann's misinterpretation of Pollock's framework has a beneficial result. Pollock's concept of state capitalism, in Neumann's eyes, suggested that prices are now administered by the state. Thinking that Pollock was unaware of other types of price control, Neumann studied the opportunities for large firms to set prices on the basis of their "strength". Neumann's interest in pricing through strength bears similarities to the theory of Michal Kalecki, who argued that giant corporations fix prices at levels higher than marginal cost. These higher levels are, according to Kalecki (1971), indicative of a firm's "degree of monopoly".

For Neumann (1942), pricing through monopoly power unravels the theoretical relationship between price and production:

> The slightest check on competition – either as a result of a natural shortage in the supply of elements of production or of an artificial regulation of supply or demand in any particular sphere – must disrupt the system of functional

equations that constitutes the "price level", and must prevent the proportions of production from directly following the price equations as well as preventing the price equations from exactly reflecting the proportions of production. This is the case both when monopolies bar competition in particular fields and when centralized controls are established to "stabilize" any set of given correlations of several elements of production or even of all of them. (p. 255)

The distinction between "natural" supply and "artificial" shortages suggests that, beneath it all, Neumann still assumed that power "distorts" true economic value. However, Neumann tried to incorporate historical development into his theory of capitalism, such as the systematic application of price control and the existence of an uncompetitive market. In this state of affairs, finding "pure" economic value from nominal prices was less of a theoretical concern. The much more important task was to learn what giant corporations were able to achieve in society with their degree of monopoly.

This takes us to our second example: the increase in size of a corporation is not exactly about making gains in efficiency, or what is sometimes called "economies of scale". Firms with large amounts of retained earnings – net profits that are not distributed as dividends – have the ability to expand or acquire industrial infrastructure. But, as Neumann notes, a reserve of undistributed profits is "not merely used for plant expansion and for an increase in stock". It can also be "utilized for the extension of power of the monopolies over other enterprises" (Neumann, 1942, p. 264).

For Neumann, this particular phenomenon of giant firms acquiring smaller firms to extend their monopoly power rather than to become more efficient revealed the fallacy of Nazi ideology. The anti-capitalist views of the Nazi Party "always exempted productive capital" according to a distinction between productivity (industrial firms) and predation (banks). This distinction proved to be fallacious when so-called industrial firms acted like banks – they could be just as predatory with their undistributed profits (Neumann, 1942, p. 263). Neumann's descriptions of predation are interesting to us because they are attached to his theory of price control. If a giant corporation can set prices on the basis of its strength, the acquisition of other firms can extend or even increase the ability to price through fiat. Indeed, the institutional power behind the setting of prices forces us to fundamentally reconsider why a firm is of a certain size in advanced capitalism (Nitzan, 2001; Nitzan & Bichler, 2009).

Third, Neumann found that the big firms of modern business do not perceive legislative and judicial acts to be extra-economic factors in the pursuit of profit. Rather, legal and political measures are essential to monopoly profits because they keep market competition depressed. Competition is never fully extinguished, and it is rare for monopolization in a sector to be perfect. Yet Neumann understood that capitalism's biggest players are not simply seeking material and technological advantages through utility or efficiency. Rather, these players use political and legal measures to refrain from competitive games. Market competition and a supply-and-demand environment undermine the ownership of modern technological apparatuses, which are so large that they require "enormous investments". Thus, "rich and powerful corporations" seek protection from "outsiders, new competitors, labour unions" – entities that could undermine the ability to price and purchase through monopoly power (Neumann, 1942, p. 213).

Business enterprise in Nazi Germany provided Neumann with a brutal example of how a legal system was much more than simply a mechanism to regulate economic behaviour and competition. The "Aryanization" of German business was a "powerful stimulant to capital concentration and monopoly" (Neumann, 1942, p. 100). Anti-Jewish legislation gave the biggest firms of Nazi Germany the opportunity to increase their profits through non-productive, anti-competitive means. With significant undistributed profits at their disposal, only the biggest firms had the means to increase their holdings in this manner. For instance, the policies that followed the vom Rath murder and Kristallnacht created monopolistic business opportunities that had nothing to do with labour time, technological efficiency or productive output. A mixture of ideology and authoritarian law redistributed national income, and the gap between the holdings of big and small firms widened as a result of what was essentially an ethnic/racial daylight robbery.

2.3.3 Marcuse on automation and capitalist rationality

Marcuse showed little hesitance to modify the tone and colour of political economic ideas. "A theory which has not caught up with the practice of capitalism", writes Marcuse (1972), "cannot possibly guide the practice aiming at the abolition of capitalism" (p. 34). Marcuse's approach to catching up with the practice of capitalism differs from those of Pollock and Neumann. Marcuse generally assumes that capital is a productive magnitude, but he speaks of productivity in such a way that capital is simultaneously an "element" of power and control over society at large. The "technical apparatus of production and distribution", by virtue of its new size and scope, has obliterated "the opposition between the private and public existence, between individual and social needs" (Marcuse, 1991, p. xlvii). A quotation from *Counterrevolution and Revolt* also demonstrates Marcuse's (1972) unique application of economic terminology:

> [I]n the internal dynamic of advanced capitalism, "the concept of productive labour is necessarily enlarged", and with it the concept of the productive worker, of the working class itself. The change is not merely quantitative: it affects the entire universe of capitalism. . . . This enlarged universe of exploitation is a totality of machines – human, economic, political, military, educational. (p. 13)

Marcuse's political economic ideas are shaped by his views of critical theory. Rigid analytical divisions in theoretical analysis would prevent us from understanding how advanced industrial society "contains no facts which do not communicate the repressive power of the whole" (Marcuse, 1991, p. 11). For instance, political and economic categories must be reconsidered in light of how "the productive apparatus tends to become totalitarian" (Marcuse, 1991, p. xlvii). Moreover, the determinate negation of contemporary society is both material and ideological:

> Validated by the accomplishments of science and technology, justified by its growing productivity, the status quo defies all transcendence. Faced with the possibility of pacification on the grounds of its technical and intellectual achievements, the mature industrial society closes itself against this alternative. Operationalism, in theory and practice, becomes the theory and practice of containment. (Marcuse, 1991, p. 17)

From the edifice of his own critical theory, Marcuse experiments with an abstract idea of capitalist power. This experimentation comes in bursts, and it is sometimes qualified with reminders about his political and philosophical commitment to a critical Marxism. But these experimental moments are still there for us to consider because, as Holman (2013) comments, Marcuse treated "Marxist theory as a living body of ideas constantly in flux, as a lively bundle of forces and tendencies that recombine and reorganize themselves in various ways" (p. 5).

Let us look at two examples of Marcuse thinking about capitalist power. First, Marcuse (1991) argues that the implementation of automation in productive processes makes the Marxist labour theory of value an anachronistic concept:

> The technological change which tends to do away with the machine as individual instrument of production, as "absolute unit", seems to cancel the Marxian notion of the "organic composition of capital" and with it the theory of the creation of surplus value. According to Marx, the machine never creates value but merely transfers its own value to the product, while surplus value remains the result of the exploitation of living labor. The machine is embodiment of human labor power, and through it, past labor (dead labor) preserves itself and determines living labor. Now automation seems to alter qualitatively the relation between dead and living labor; it tends toward where productivity is determined "by the machines, and not by the individual output". . . . [T]he very measurement of individual output becomes impossible. (p. 28)

Quoting at length, a few pages later, Marx's own prescience about the death of his labour theory of value at the hands of automation,[4] Marcuse (1991) then reconsiders the economic meaning of automated technology replacing the "extensive utilization of human labor power in material production" (p. 37). When labour time becomes irrelevant to the output of automated production processes, the transfer of value to a commodity is indeterminate. Moreover, the multiple inputs and multiple outputs of automated technology "transubstantiate" labour power. Individual labour cannot be isolated in this conceptual soup of "joint" production; in fact, it is not exactly clear how new capitalist production processes still depend on the direct exploitation of human labour.

To be sure, Marcuse (1991) connects the implementation of automation to the Marxist thesis that capitalists attempt to raise "the productivity of labour" through advances in technology (p. 37). His conclusions about automation, however, are certainly unorthodox with respect to the economics–politics separation in Marxism. By undermining the economic rationale for capitalism's reliance on labour power, the institution of automation suggests that the class struggle between the wage labourer and the capitalist is now much more about authority and control than productivity, even on the factory floor. When capitalism is understood as a "system of domination", capitalists "value" the working class for what they *refrain* from doing when work is tightly controlled: using their power in numbers and their collective human creativity to disturb technological rationality and the pecuniary interests of the ruling class (Marcuse, 1991, p. 35).

Second, Marcuse reconceptualizes the implicit separation between economics and politics in Weber's distinction between formal and substantive rationality. On the basis of Weber's definition of formal rationality, the capitalist economy is separate from political systems. The quantitative terms of economic rationality are formal, and processes such as profit estimates and the distribution of goods can be calculated in "value-free scientific purity" (Marcuse, 1968c, p. 210). Conversely, there is no purely formal logic of political power. Politics contains irrational elements like charisma, and political decisions always have social values and morals embedded in them. Hence, in Weber's framework, politics operates according to a *substantive* rationality.

Marcuse updates Weber's presentation of how formal and substantive rationalities relate to each other in modern society. For Weber, the borders of these two types of rationality would touch because economic rationality also refers, by virtue of being formalistic and abstract, to the "external source" that defines the ends of its instrumental calculations. For Marcuse, political power is no longer "outside" economic activity; no longer is substantial rationality something reserved for governments, courts and other political authorities. Thus, the seemingly formal rationality of business enterprise is also substantive. Giant firms do not simply calculate profits and losses, nor do they produce according to the "value-free" ends of a market. Rather, they themselves have the institutional means to create a technological apparatus that is the "congealed spirit" of their own vested interests. Thus,

Marcuse (1968c) concludes that capitalism, "no matter how mathematized and 'scientific', remains the mathematized, technological domination of men [and women]" (p. 215).

Marcuse's description of capitalist rationality is similar to his concept of technological rationality, which he developed twenty years earlier. Technological rationality also blurs the line between economics and politics because, again, the techniques of economics do not comprise a subsystem oriented by politics from the outside:

> As the laws and mechanisms of technological rationality spread over the whole society, they develop a set of truth values of their own which hold good for the functioning of the apparatus – and for that alone. Propositions concerning competitive or collusive behavior, business methods, principles of effective organization and control, fair play, the use of science and technics are true and false in terms of this value system, that is to say, in terms of instrumentalities that dictate their own ends. (Marcuse, 2005c, p. 146)

Like his analysis of Weber's concepts of rationality, Marcuse's concept of technological rationality identifies the historical change of business enterprise in the twentieth century – the increasing size and scope of large-scale industry, which supersedes, among other things, the small individual entrepreneur.

2.4   Should we look beyond Marxism?

So far, we have seen how Pollock, Neumann and Marcuse renovated the theoretical separation between economics and politics in order to better understand the role of power in capital accumulation. This type of renovation gives us a platform to rethink capital by looking beyond Marxism. Rethinking capital in such a manner is the preferred alternative to making repeated attempts to rearrange the economics–politics separation within a Marxist framework. Marx built an economic theory on the idea that productive labour was the only true engine of capital accumulation. Lest they become something else entirely, Marxist theories of capital accumulation are stuck rearranging the ways politics "assists", "supports", "amplifies" or "protects" an economic system of production.

There is certainly no shortage of contemporary academics who would disagree that critical political economy needs to look beyond Marxism. Much work has been done to bring the labour theory of value into the twentieth and twenty-first centuries. Updates involve the expansion of the world market (Mandel, 1976), economic and financial crises (Foley, 2012) and the evolution of technology and the need for capitalists to employ immaterial labour (Dyer-Witheford, 1999). Many of these scholars assume that the economic exploitation of productive labour remains the theoretical touchstone of capital accumulation. Either long-standing forms of productive work are now exploited more intensely (Braverman, 1998) or new avenues of exploitation are found in labour that has been subsumed under capitalism, such as intellectual and cultural work (S. Shapiro, 2009). The centrality of productive labour is also seen in the negative: many of the crises of the twentieth century revolved around the structural compulsion for capitalists to realize surplus value (Kliman, 2012).

One might also be hesitant to drift from the political and philosophical aspects of Marxist thought. Marx provided a very rich picture of how, in the history of capitalism, the treatment and conditions of the proletariat are visible expressions of capitalism's repressive and irrational tendencies. Moreover, standing under the umbrella of historical materialism are creative thinkers like Walter Benjamin, whose writings on history, literature, technology, and consciousness have only faint connections to the technical details of Marxist economics (Benjamin, 1968a, 1978). But what is the cost to an anti-capitalist political position that uses Marxist economics to define the essential differences between economics and politics in capitalist society? When Marxist economic theory appears to be objectively true, the fundamental assumptions that produced this theory look definitive and Marxism's view of liberation is emboldened. But what should be done when the truth of the same theory is doubted? How much is capital accumulation in advanced capitalism explained by the productive output of labour? One-hundred per cent? Fifty per cent? Even less? Marxist political economy often gives an unconvincing answer to this line of questioning because its reasons for applying the labour theory of value are becoming more theoretical than empirical – with the "right" understanding of Marx's method, the historical evolution of capitalism does not contradict Marx's labour theory of value.

As mentioned earlier, the Frankfurt School had no explicit intention to break from historical materialist philosophy. However, the school's nascent ideas of capitalist power cannot help but have incompatibilities with Marxism's assumptions about the economic nature of capital; the latter roots economic activity in the productivity of labour, not institutional power. In this respect, the Frankfurt School is in an intellectual position that is similar to Nicolaus Copernicus's position in medieval European astronomy. Copernicus was personally obedient to Aristotelian physics and Ptolemaic astronomy when he developed his heliocentric theory of planetary orbits, yet his ideas about earth's movements had implications that could not be reconciled with a medieval Christian picture of the universe. Arthur Koestler speaks to the force of what Copernicus only ever *implied* in his understanding of the universe:

> The notion of limitlessness or infinity . . . was bound to devour the space reserved for God on the medieval astronomer's charts. They had taken it for granted that the realms of astronomy and theology were contiguous, separated only by the thickness of the ninth crystal sphere. Henceforth, the space-and-spirit continuum would be replaced by the space-time continuum. This

meant, among other things the end of intimacy between man and God. . . .
Hence Pascal's cry of horror [*"Le silence éternel de ce espaces infinis m'effraie!"*].
(Koestler, 2014, p. 194)

Secondary studies commonly attempt to reconcile, in one way or another, the
Frankfurt School's interest in capitalist power with the Marxist concept of capital.
One type of approach, which is represented by Marramao's (1975) and Postone's
(1996) arguments, claims that a "return" to Marx's labour theory of value can
temper the Frankfurt School's enthusiastic reconfiguration of politics and economics. Pollock's interest in state capitalism, Neumann's concern with fascism and
Marcuse's welfare–warfare state are all historically grounded, but this characteristic,
ironically, irritates Marxist approaches that maintain that capital accumulation
during this period was misunderstood: the labour theory of value and its theoretical truths only *appeared* to have been superseded by totalitarianism and state
power. Another approach is more progressive by comparison, as it sees the Frankfurt School and a few others, like Lukacs and Korsch, generating better methods of
dialectical thinking (Jay, 1984; Kellner, 1989). According to this view of the
Frankfurt School's writings, the Marxist concept of totality is a beneficial alternative to the base-superstructure model of capitalist society, which is what led classical Marxism to make unhelpful splits between economics and politics.

Although these two secondary interpretations have different methods of reconciliation, both fail to adequately consider the Frankfurt School's inadvertent effect
on the economic assumptions of Marxism. The Marxist framework requires that,
when needed, the economics of value creation be conceptually isolated from concepts of power, including ideology and state repression; otherwise, the mixture of
politics and economics makes it impossible to claim that only the exploitation of
productive labour is directly responsible for the creation of surplus value.

2.4.1   Reincorporating the labour theory of value

Marxist political economists will sometimes put the Frankfurt School "in context"
by arguing that its writers had political–economic blind spots. These blind spots
existed because writers such as Neumann and Pollock experienced an exceptional
phase of twentieth-century capitalism. The size and reach of state institutions
were easy to see in the 1930s and 1940s, but totalitarian politics also hid the economic contradictions of capitalism from view (Marramao, 1975). Consequently,
the Frankfurt School overstated its case when it suggested that, in advanced capitalism, the growth of political power and the intensification of social domination had
qualitatively transformed the character of capital accumulation. For example, when
Pollock inferred that "economics as social science has lost its object under state capitalism", this was, according to Marramao, a mistake. Pollock was experiencing "the
illusory character of the 'alien power' of the fetishized forms of the economic

process, while accepting as reality the uncontradictory and 'one-dimensional' facade of socialized despotism" (Marramao, 1975, p. 74). In other words, Marramao deems the theoretical reconciliation of Marxism and the Frankfurt School to be straightforward: the Frankfurt School should never have traveled so far from the mode of production and the Marxist labour theory of value in the first place.

Similarly, Postone (1996) argues that the Frankfurt School, like Sweezy and the monopoly capital theory, imagined a qualitative difference where there was none. Advanced capitalism may have jettisoned "the non-conscious, 'automatic', market-mediated mode of distribution", but the holistic truth of Marx's labour theory of value is undamaged as capitalism evolves:

> [Value] is not merely a category of the market, one that grasps a historically particular mode of the social distribution of wealth. Such a market-centered interpretation – which relates to Mill's position that the mode of distribution is changeable historically but the mode of production is not – implies the existence of a transhistorical form of wealth that is distributed differently in different societies. According to Marx, however, value is a historically specific form of social wealth and is intrinsically related to a historically specific mode of production. (Postone, 1996, p. 25)

Thus, according to Postone, Marx's theory of economic value was built to evolve *with* any maelstrom of socio-political transformations: even as some things change, twentieth-century capitalism has "commodity-determined labour" at the core of its mode of production.

These criticisms of critical theory can be very impressive for their nuanced breakdowns of dialectical logic, but they still put the cart before the horse. Marramao and Postone do not empirically confirm that, at their respective times of reading Marx, the Marxist essence of capitalism can be found behind its appearances. Certainly some historical changes are too insignificant to convince anyone to rethink their agreement with the Marxist labour theory of value. Yet Marramao and Postone are not empirically testing their counter-arguments; instead, they operate purely within the realm of theoretical interpretation. Thus, the labour theory of value essentially acts as some sort of transcendental "corrective", telling writers like Postone that it would be logically true that the appearances of state capitalism or totalitarian capitalism are just that: misleading appearances. Capitalist societies can oscillate between market fundamentalism and repressive authoritarianism, the technological infrastructure can multiply in size and complexity and monopoly power can grow with the concentration of ownership and the depression of market competition – but any form of capitalist domination will necessarily obey the same temporal logic of labour time: the "magnitude of value of an individual commodity is … a function of the socially necessary labor time required for its production" (Postone, 1996, p. 193).

As Alfred Schmidt (1981) argues (in his critique of Althusser), arguments about the logical structure of Marxist theory can easily misrepresent Marx's dialectical method. For Marx, a theoretical framework becomes "poorer in definition" as more and more historical moments are deemed "external", "accidental", or "inessential" to the theory (Schmidt, 1981, p. 68). Thus, it is hardly a victory for Marxism if Marramao and Postone show us where the Frankfurt School's historical insights diverge from Marx's labour theory of value. In fact, the burden of proof is reversed; it is on the shoulders of Marxism to demonstrate that its theory of value is still usable when visible changes to the structure of capitalism suggest that productive quantities of labour inputs cannot adequately explain capital accumulation. Unfortunately, on this point, Marramao and Postone are going sideways rather than forward.

How might we verify that writers like Pollock, Neumann and Marcuse were justified in thinking that modern capitalism was breaking old economic laws? There is a vast ocean of phenomena to reconceptualize when productivity is removed from the heart of capital. For the moment, consider the modern phenomenon of inflation. In the era of classical political economy, inflation was not a key factor. Instead, the theoretical frameworks of great theorists like Marx were, according to Bichler and Nitzan, developed in a "deflationary context" in which "consumer prices in Great Britain and wholesale prices in the United States both dropped by more than one third". Thus, it "was only natural [for classical political economy] to concentrate on production and the coercive discipline of 'market forces' and to ignore inflation" (Nitzan & Bichler, 2009, p. 367).

Figure 2.1 uses inflation data to visualize Bichler and Nitzan's argument about significant historical change in the capitalist political economy. Using data from twelve countries, the box plots show 25-year distributions of 10-year inflation rates. Outliers are removed because we want the figure to focus on rates that were "normal" for each period.[5] Figure 2.1 shows two key differences between the distributions before and after the early twentieth century. First, the "normal" rate of twentieth-century inflation was higher than the rate of the nineteenth century, which is when Ricardo, Mill and Marx contributed to classical political economy. Just as importantly, the medians and interquartile ranges (middle 50% of a distribution) of twentieth-century inflation are almost all above zero. As prices in the nineteenth century would have appeared to have stable averages – as a phase of inflation would be followed by one of deflation – rising prices in the twentieth century (and early twenty-first century) would rarely deflate in the next phase.

Pollock, Neumann and Marcuse do not give us all of the details of capital accumulation, but they demonstrate they are receptive to the general transformation in Figure 2.1. As Nitzan and Bichler demonstrate, the ability to accumulate through inflation is much more consistent with writing that emphasizes institutional power, not production. The power of dominant firms to establish higher-

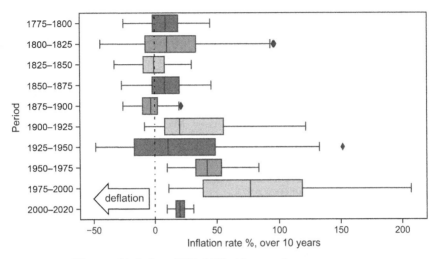

FIGURE 2.1 History of inflation, 1775–2020, 12 countries

Source: Global Financial Data for the annual inflation rates of Belgium, Canada, Germany, Denmark, France, Great Britain, Italy, Japan, Netherlands, Norway, Sweden and United States.

than-average markups is not only a significant means of income redistribution but also "positively related to firm size. . . . [The] larger the firm, the greater and more systematic its differential gains from inflation" (Nitzan & Bichler, 2009, p. 374).

The ideas of Pollock, Neumann and Marcuse might also not be limited to a so-called exceptional phase of capitalism. Using price inflation to serve capitalist interests is a *repeated* event of advanced capitalism. Figure 2.2 indicates that, beginning in the 1930s, waves of inflation have been leading indicators of capitalists increasing their income over the general population. In Figure 2.2A we have three series. Two series are measures of 10-year inflation rates, which have both been shifted 10 years. The third series is Bichler and Nitzan's (2016) "power index" for the United States. The power index is a ratio of stock index price (such as the S&P 500) to the average wage rate. This power index is a representation of how capitalists (who have significant stakes in the stock market) succeed or fail relative to the underlying population (who primarily rely on wage income). Figure 2.2B uses a 25-year correlation to show the relationship between the US power index and long-term inflation, 10 years earlier. A strong positive correlation is frequent after 1930. By looking backward from 1930, we can see an entirely different relationship between inflation and the gains of the stock market over wage income. And if we speculate about Marx's viewpoint with the earliest 25-year correlation in the data set (1875–1899), it is unlikely that this relationship was positive and strong at the time of his writing.

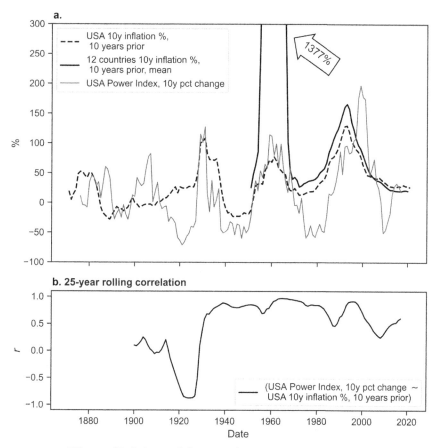

FIGURE 2.2   Waves of inflation and the United States power index

Source: Global Financial Data for the annual inflation rates of Belgium, Canada, Germany, Denmark, France, Great Britain, Italy, Japan, Netherlands, Norway, Sweden and United States. Bichler and Nitzan (2016) for United States power index, 1865 – 2016. Data available at http://bnarchives. yorku.ca/494/

2.4.2   The Marxist concept of totality

As much as Postone critiques the Frankfurt School for its political economic ideas, he also recognizes that the writings of the Frankfurt School helped twentieth-century Marxists rejuvenate the dialectical method of historical materialism. Moreover, Postone acknowledges that he follows in the footsteps of the Frankfurt School and uses dialectical logic to construct a concept of the capitalist totality. The capitalist totality, in the words of Postone, "refers to the domination of people by abstract, quasi-independent structures of social relations, mediated by commodity-determined labor, which Marx tries to grasp with his categories of value and capital". Consequently, the study of the entire capitalist universe will relate to what we can see in its grain of sand, the capitalist mode of production:

> [T]he Marxian critique is a critique of labor in capitalism, rather than merely a critique of labor's exploitation and mode of social distribution, and ... the fundamental contradiction of the capitalist totality should be seen as intrinsic to the realm of production itself, and not simply a contradiction between the spheres of production and distribution. (Postone, 1996, p. 124)

Other Marxist theorists commend the Frankfurt School for resuscitating the philosophical rigour of Hegel and Marx, and for replacing the base-superstructure model with a concept of totality (Jay, 1984, 1996; Kellner, 1989; Ollman, 1976). From this perspective, the base-superstructure model is the perceived reason for Marxism developing a bad dualism between economics and politics. Consequently, Marxist theory can overcome the "vulgar" versions of itself, which have forgotten that "that the economy, which can never be isolated, is made by human individuals, as is politics, which can never be isolated" (Bloch, 1988, p. 27).

The Frankfurt School's concept of totality helps keep politics and economics in a good dialectical relationship, which enables us to understand how production and power are mutually constitutive. However, is a *Marxist* concept of totality, and all that it implies methodologically, sufficient to answer our critique of the economics–politics separation in political economic theory? In order to clarify that the issue is not dialectics *as such*, let us briefly address the dialectical method and the foundations of critical theory. The specific problem for Marxism is that *its* privileging of material production creates the requirement that, within its own logic, there is a defined separation that analytically isolates economics from politics. This requirement for separation is sometimes overlooked in contemporary Marxism, as some of its theorists enthusiastically mix economics, politics, and other social dimensions. But the impulse to creatively think about a capitalist totality – with its mutually constitutive relations and its multiple social dimensions – must stop at defined points if the goal is to be holistic *within* a Marxist framework. In other words, the cost to Marxism for breaking too many walls between economics and politics is being able to explain capital accumulation with a theory of value that is rooted in the material productivity of labour. This cost appeared when writers like Pollock, Neumann and Marcuse wandered "too far" in their analysis of power.

When looking beyond Marxism, the concept of totality should not be discarded. It is methodologically crucial because capitalism is not just a mode of production; it is a mode of being, a society and a way of life. The idea of totality helps us ground seemingly disparate facts in the same social condition. Marxist philosophy was the first to integrate the concept of totality into political economic theory.

Its theorists recognized that a concept of totality is dialectical thinking unleashed: "the dialectical conception of totality can enable us to understand *reality as a social process*" (Lukacs, 1968, p. 13). Marx's method is also holistic largely because it is dialectical. "The concrete is concrete", writes Marx (1993), "because it is the concentration of many determinations, hence unity of the diverse" (p. 101). This "concentration of many determinations" is conceptualized when theory searches for the social reality that each thing or idea presupposes. Exchange value, for example, "presupposes population, moreover a population producing in specific relations; as well as a certain kind of family, or commune, or state, etc. It can never exist as an abstract, one-sided relation within an already given, concrete, living whole" (Marx, 1993, p. 101).

Overall, the concept of a capitalist totality overcomes the bad habit of dividing society into strict analytical categories. Fallacies accumulate when we think that spheres of society have clearly demarcated boundaries – almost as if institutional structures and networks of social relations self-align according to the rigid division of academic disciplines. To develop their concepts of the capitalist totality, members of the Frankfurt School took their research in all sorts of directions, including science, aesthetics, psychoanalysis and philosophy. The school also considered the epistemology of holistic social analysis. These studies of epistemology have a distinct flavour. As described by Martin Jay (1996), the general tenets of critical theory were, from its inception, "expressed through a series of critiques of other thinkers and philosophical traditions" (p. 41). For example, Horkheimer's critique of "traditional theory" was the first major project of the Frankfurt School. This critique enabled Horkheimer to propose that an alternative "critical theory" could build a much more holistic analysis of social and political domination.

Traditional theory is defined by its ignorant relationship with the larger social processes that condition each branch of knowledge. This ignorance is not the same as conceptual isolation, which is often required for scientific activity to focus its experiments on measurable variables. Instead, the ignorance of traditional theory concerns the social values, structures, institutions and relations that condition the application of theoretical knowledge. Consequently, traditional theory not only prides itself for its intellectual self-sufficiency or value-free neutrality, but it also lacks a "concrete awareness" of its role in the greater social division of labour (Horkheimer, 2002b, p. 216). For Horkheimer, it is telling that the value-free neutrality of traditional theory and its place and function in society contradict. The "real social function of science is not made manifest; it speaks not of what theory means in human life, but only of what it means in the isolated sphere in which for historical reasons it comes into existence" (Horkheimer, 2002b, p. 197).

With respect to its formal structures, critical theory is similar to traditional theory. "The critical theory of society", writes Horkheimer (2002b), "also begins with abstract determinations. . . . In critical theory, as in traditional theory, specific elements must be introduced in order to move from fundamental structure to concrete reality" (p. 225).[6] However, critical theory consciously seeks to overcome traditional theory's ignorance. Capitalist society runs on an engine of particular social values – class, wealth, profit, power, modern technology, and so on – and traditional theory is unable to recognize "its positive role in a functioning society, [its] indirect and obscure relation to the satisfaction of general needs, and [its] participation in the self-renewing life process" (Horkheimer, 2002b, p. 216). Thus, critical theory reminds itself that a theory becomes one-sided when the complex totality of modern society is lost from view:

> [S]eparated from a particular theory of society as a whole, every theory of cognition remains formalistic and abstract. Not only expressions like life and promotion, but also terms seemingly specific to cognitive theory such as verification, confirmation, proof, etc., remain vague and indefinite ... if they do not stand in relation to real history and receive their definition by being part of a comprehensive theoretical unity. (Horkheimer, 2005b, p. 426)

To my knowledge, Horkheimer did not use the term *traditional theory* in any published writing other than "Traditional and critical theory". However, the term clearly inspired Horkheimer to continue critiquing theoretical systems for not overcoming "the one-sidedness that necessarily arises when limited intellectual processes are detached from their matrix in the total activity of society" (Horkheimer, 2002b, p. 199). For example, he detected one-sidedness in the metaphysical systems of Western philosophy. From the heights of metaphysics, the details of history are almost invisible. And similarly to traditional theory, metaphysics then reifies what its methods cannot adequately describe: it "takes the most general characteristics, the elements as it were, which are common to all men in all times and calls them 'concrete'" (Horkheimer, 2002a, p. 18).

Horkheimer and other members of the Frankfurt School also argued that the base-superstructure model was producing a one-sidedness within Marxist theory (Kellner, 1989, p. 11). In *Counterrevolution and Revolt*, Marcuse (1972) argues that the base-superstructure model is an impediment to dialectical thought because it freezes historical analysis in a manner similar to traditional theory: "To isolate the identical capitalist base from the other sectors of society leaves Marxian theory at its very foundation with an unhistorical, undialectical abstraction" (p. 33). In the section of *Minima Moralia* titled "Baby with the Bath Water", Adorno takes a similar stance. Addressing the problematic way in which culture is stripped of any autonomy in the base-superstructure model, Adorno criticizes those who put all of their theoretical and practical energy into the so-called objective tendencies of the capitalist economy (Adorno, 2005a, p. 44).

To the present-day reader, there is likely no visible controversy to accepting the Frankfurt School's position on the base-superstructure model. In fact, contemporary defenders and critics of Marxism can come together and agree that the base-superstructure model is far too rigid for any theory that calls itself "dialectical". For instance, Castoriadis's (1998) *criticism* of Marxism mirrors Terry Eagleton's *defence*:

> [T]here is not, nor has there ever been, an inertia of the rest of social life, nor a privileged passivity of the "superstructures". These superstructures are no more than a fabric of social relations, neither more nor less "real", neither more nor less "inert" than the others, and just as "conditioned" by the [base] as the [base is] by them, if the word "conditioned" can be used to designate the mode of coexistence of the various moments or aspects of social activities. (p. 20)

as opposed to

> Politics, culture, science, ideas and social existence are not just economics in disguise. . . . They have their own reality, evolve their own histories and operate by their own logic. . . . The traffic between economic "base" and social "superstructure". . . is not just one way. (Eagleton, 2011, p. 113)

Like Eagleton, Bertell Ollman defends Marxist methods by dissuading us from associating Marxism with economic determinism. While determinism appears to surface in places like the preface to *A Contribution to the Critique of Political Economy*, many of Marx's writings, according to Ollman, are not fundamentalist about the linearity of the base-superstructure model. In fact, when Marx's method is understood in the proper light, "'Economic Determinism'. . . appears to be a caricature foisted upon Marxism by readers who misread [Marx's] general claims" (Ollman, 1976, p. 9).

When standing from a distance, these claims appear to demonstrate that Marxist methodology is not a barrier to the Frankfurt School's ideas about advanced capitalism. Thus, if writers like Neumann find evidence of capital accumulation through political power, a holistic Marxism will refrain from bending or cutting this evidence for the sake of a deterministic model of base and superstructure. As Eagleton suggests, we appear free to study the reality, history and logic of accumulation-through-power. However, the barriers are there; they are found when we look closer at the places where the Frankfurt School made modifications to a critical political economy of capitalism. By rethinking the essence of capital accumulation in the twentieth century, the Frankfurt School played with ideas that are at the root of Marxist economics. Pollock, Neumann and Marcuse did not simply add more concepts to the "traffic" between economics and everything else; they showed flashes of a radical rethinking, which can undermine labour's privileged position in capital accumulation.

The writings of Pollock, Neumann and Marcuse do not supply robust alternatives to Marxist political economy, but they portend Marxism's problem with the facts of historical transformation. In Marxism, the necessity to isolate production in general and labour in particular demarcates the limit of dialectical mediation, even without the base-superstructure model. Interestingly, this point is sensed by one of Marxism's most esteemed writers on the place of culture in historical materialism: Raymond Williams. While Williams believes theorists should study much more than the economic structure of capitalism, he also thinks Marxist theorists of all types should recognize that the idea of totality can undermine the core purpose of Marxist theory:

> The totality of social practices was opposed to this layered notion of base and a consequent superstructure. . . . Now the language of totality has become common, and it is indeed in many ways more acceptable than the notion of base and superstructure. But with one very important reservation. It is very easy for the notion of totality to empty of its essential content the original Marxist proposition. For if we come to say that society is composed of a large number of social practices which form a concrete social whole, and if we give to each practice a certain specific recognition, adding only that they interact, relate and combine in very complicated ways, we are at one level much more obviously talking about reality, but we are at another level withdrawing from the claim that there is any process of determination. . . . If totality is simply concrete, if it is simply the recognition of a large variety of miscellaneous and contemporaneous practices, then it is essentially empty of any content that could be called Marxist. (Williams, 2005, pp. 35–36)

The general thrust of Williams's concern is warranted; weak or missing theoretical principles will produce amorphous theories. Yet Williams is also affirming the need for Marxist economics to organize non-economic theory. He is telling the reader that as long as *one starts from the assumption that economic exploitation is a definable process*, theorists can then branch out and explain the existence of the state, the military, the church and the educational system; they can research the ideological character of affirmative culture, positive philosophy and common sense; and they can study developments of technology, science, art and language.

2.4.3 Staying within Marxism's orbit

Postone, Jay, Kellner, Williams – this is not a band of fiercely dogmatic thinkers, and it is my hope that I have given no suggestion that the Frankfurt School is up against an orthodoxy that cannot see faults within Marxism. Rather, the image in my mind is one of a planet having gravitational pull. In the space of political economy, Marxism is undoubtedly the size of a Jupiter or Saturn. Thus, if an orbiter of Marxism witnesses someone generate enough escape velocity to free themselves from its gravitational force, they might not initially see why this would be anyone's desire. Moreover, the opportunity to leave planet-Marxism comes with a fear that something too big is being left behind or that there is no other home for a critique of capital accumulation. Williams, for example, is not telling the reader to blindly accept Marxist economics; he is fearful of sentencing himself to floating in space.

The problem of remaining within Marxism's orbit, however, is about the composition of what is being orbited. Even if the Marxist concept of capital is assumed to be correct, the mixture of politics and economics produces an impossible methodological step: we need to demonstrate that, from within this mixture, Marxism's categorical distinction between power and productive processes is observable in the capital accumulation of surplus value. Unfortunately, Marxism's assumption that value is a productive magnitude makes it difficult to know how much or how little social-political activity is influencing magnitudes of labour time.

In "Ideology and Ideological State Apparatuses", for instance, Althusser (2001) relies on the Marxist definitions of economic value and the reproduction of labour power to mix his presentation of ideology and institutional power with material production. The basis for this particular politics–economics mixture is Marx's claim that the market value of labour power is always tied to what social reproduction means in each culture. In agreement with Marx and Engels, Althusser (2001) states that the "quantity of value (wages) necessary for the reproduction of labour power is determined not by the needs of a 'biological' Guaranteed Minimum Wage . . . alone, but by the needs of a historical minimum" (p. 88). Althusser then paints a picture in which almost every social institution, except for the police and the military, is a factor in the ideological reproduction of the worker.

To be sure, Althusser's presentation initially appears to be an impressive showcase of how ideological social reproduction and material labour are not separate but, rather, mutually constitutive elements in a dialectical whole. But Althusser's enthusiastic mixture of ideology and labour time actually does Marxist economics no favours. The economic aspect of the argument must somehow decipher how this multitude of ideological state apparatuses affects the quantitative level of the wage rate, the value of which is expressed as "a definite quantity of the means of subsistence" (Marx, 1990, p. 276). Forgetting for the moment the more important problem that the wage rate is expressed in prices, and not in measurable units of abstract labour time, the exchange value of labour power, both simple and complex, now somehow refers to an ideological complex of media, religion, law, education and family. But which political and cultural aspects of social reproduction are simultaneously economic factors, and how do we calculate the value of ideology as a means of subsistence? We have wage data in prices, but to know the value of labour power, we must first know what constitutes the "means of subsistence" in advanced capitalism. What aspects of advanced capitalism allow the "owner of labour-power" to maintain what Marx (1990) called the "normal state as a working individual" (p. 275)?

For example, what is the relationship between television and the reproduction of labour power? Is the culture of watching television popular enough to be considered a necessary factor in the ideological diet of a contemporary worker? If so, the cost of reproducing contemporary labour power must include the economic value of television sets and cable subscriptions. But can this type of inclusion be anything other than an arbitrary decision? And if we assume we can make a decision on television's inclusion in social reproduction, we must also have definitive views on the role of a great multitude of commodities. Social reproduction might also include cinema, religion, family, coffee, alcohol, cars, sports, the internet and so on.

Figure 2.3 reveals there are even bunches of small assumptions hidden behind the mixture of ideology and the market value of labour power. This figure plots American Time Survey data (from the Bureau Labor of Statistics). In each row we have different activities. By column, the data are split into the average time of the "in group" – those who engage in the activity – and the per capita average. Figure 2.3 is an empirical picture of leisure activity, but the difficulty involves translating the pieces of the picture into magnitudes of economic value. First, there is the issue of quantitative comparison. Is 1 hour of television equal to 1 hour of reading? Second, no leisure activity is universal across an entire society. This forces one to decide if a measure of leisure time should be the average across all society (per capita) or the average time of those who engage in the activity. This is not a simple decision to make because some activities could be "essential" for those who are engaged in them. Measured per capita, the consumption of arts and entertainment (excluding sports) is a minuscule part of the average American's leisure time, yet for those do engage in this activity, they are spending significant portions of their leisure time. Can I say that, for those who do engage in the arts, their consumption is necessary for social reproduction? Third, there are *qualitative* changes to the content of leisure time. This fact might not first appear to be problematic, but the problem appears when we need to know how each annual change relates to social reproduction's "historical minumum". For instance, the bottom-right panel in Figure 2.3 tells us that the average American was watching 2.58 hours of television a day in 2003 and 2.81 hours in 2019. If the task was simply to count the hours of two *identical* activities, the answer is simple: in 2019 the average American is watching 1.089 times more television than they were in 2003. However, as an input for the *value* of labour power, this change could mean many things. It could signify that a worker in 2019 demands a greater level of ideological reproduction (assuming that 1 hour of television in 2003 is equal to 1 hour in 2019), but it also could signify that a worker needs higher doses of "lower-quality" television to reproduce the same amount of labour power (assuming that television is 8.9% less effective in 2019).

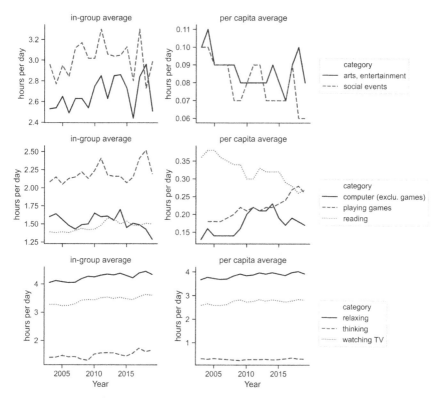

FIGURE 2.3   How free time is spent in the United States, 2003–2019

Source: https://www.bls.gov/tus/ for "Table A-1. Time spent in detailed primary activities and per cent of the civilian population engaging in each detailed primary activity category, averages per day by sex, annual averages, total".

Note: Category names have been abbreviated from original titles. "In-group" defined as "hours per day for persons who engaged in the activity"; "per capita" is the total American population.

Because of the economics–politics separation in Marxism, the role of ideology in capital accumulation must pass through a confusing two-step method, whereby politics and culture are unproductive themselves, but they are also the "social conditions" of productive processes. The confusions about this two-step method multiply as institutional power and ideology increase in importance and complexity. Note, for instance, that Althusser is not directly saying that capitalists can accumulate through ideology. Rather, ideology is unproductive political and cultural power that is a social input in the formation of productivity; ideology is somehow a large, multisided factor in the value of labour power, which then determines how long it will take a rate of exploitation to create a surplus of value.

Conversely, a holistic Marxist theory will also pay a heavy price if it is unwilling or uninterested in applying, in more historically specific terms, the assumptions about what is and is not included in magnitudes of value. When boldly journeying into the realms of politics and culture without a clear distinction between political power and economic exploitation, the Marxist framework is limited to producing *abstract* descriptions of capital accumulation. Marcuse (1972) is sometimes guilty of drawing, for example, an imprecise picture of the accumulation of surplus value in advanced capitalism:

> The directing and organizing power of *Gesamtkapital* [(capital as a whole)] confronts the productive power of the *Gesamtarbeiter* (collective labour force): each individual becomes a mere fragment or atom in the coordinated mass of the population which, separated from control of means of production, creates the global surplus value. (p. 11)

Similarly, Postone seems content to speak about economic exploitation at a high level of abstraction. With little interest in being more specific about how we measure capital accumulation in a social totality that is comprised of economics, politics and other dimensions, Postone can only use Marx's concepts of use value, exchange value, commodification and labour time as general social-philosophical terms. Consider part of Postone's answer to an interviewer who wants to know how we can avoid "slipping into a kind of metaphorics" when describing the dual character of the commodity:

> Marx grounds the form of production in capitalism as well as its trajectory of growth with reference to his analysis of the dynamic nature of capital. I tried to work out the general character of the dynamic as a treadmill dialectic. It's this treadmill dialectic that generates the historical possibility for the abolition of proletariat labor. It renders such labor anachronistic while, at the same time, reaffirming its necessity. This historical dialectic entails processes of ongoing transformation, as well as the ongoing reproduction of the underlying conditions of the whole. As capital develops, however, the necessity imposed by the forms that underlie this dialectic increasingly remains a necessity for capital alone; it becomes less and less a necessity for human life. In other words, capital and human life become historically separated. (Postone & Brennan, 2009, p. 314)

Much like the abstractness of metaphysics (Horkheimer, 2002a), here we have truth claims stacked on top of truth claims about a historical process that should have concrete, observable details.

When the methodological implications of the economics–politics separation are overlooked, secondary interpretations of the Frankfurt School can also remain content with explaining capital accumulation with abstract ideas. Jameson (2007), for example, states that Adorno's presentation of the social division of labour and the mechanization of human beings in capitalist production is "itself dialectical and includes Marx's analysis of the organic composition of capital as such" (p. 71). To a Marxist political economist, this coupling of Adorno and the organic composition of capital is at best misleading. The organic composition of capital is fundamentally a quantitative relationship $(\frac{c}{v})$ that is related to the rate of surplus value $(\frac{s}{v})$ and the rate of profit $(\frac{s}{c+v})$. Furthermore, the organic composition of capital is a weak concept when presented in the abstract; Marx argued that historical circumstances, such as foreign trade and the depression of wages below the value of labour power, could act as "counteracting tendencies" to the falling rate of profit (Fine & Saad-Filho, 2004, p. 113).[7] Adorno's writings are monumentally important to a critical theory of society, but nowhere in them do we find such a commitment to understanding the technical details of value theory. His uses of the category "exchange-value" are meant to explain the capitalist form of domination; his writings do not contain solutions to the methodological problems with measuring the quantification of exchange value.

2.5   Conclusion

Although the Frankfurt School is not free from some of the methodological problems that are being critiqued in this chapter, Pollock, Neumann and Marcuse are influential for recognizing that theories of capitalism, prevailing at their time, might not have been keeping pace with the types of historical development that began in the early decades of the twentieth century. In fact, their curiosity about the nature of capital accumulation in advanced capitalism is a testament to how critical theory understands itself to be dialectical. "The name of dialectics", writes Adorno (1973),

> says no more . . . than that objects do not go into their concepts without leaving a remainder, that they come to contradict the traditional norm of adequacy. . . . Dialectics is the consistent sense of nonidentity. It does not begin by taking a standpoint. My thought is driven to it by its own inevitable insufficiency, by my guilt of what I am thinking. (p. 5)

No longer can an abstraction stand as a "timeless eternal" form; a concept is only valid if it is relevant to a social reality and "the practice of the associated individuals" (Marcuse, 1968b, p. 87).

The Frankfurt School disrupts our impulse to assume that, in capitalism, economic categories should specifically or mostly focus on the productivity behind the creation and distribution of value. When power processes intervene in the theoretical link between capital accumulation and material production, it cannot be true that production and power are distinguished by virtue of what the former explains and the latter does not: the so-called real productive engine of profit.

Such a separation lingers within Marxism, despite its intention to provide a critique of capitalist processes and their effects on individuals inside and outside of work. The Marxist framework, even when holistic, still forces an unhelpful split between economics and politics.

Alternatively, the political economic adventures of the Frankfurt School give us a greater opportunity to rethink the economics–politics relationship. If capitalists can accumulate through power, then we can redefine the concept of capital according to the modern uses of monopoly, command, automation, ideology and so on. Such a redefinition might leave some of Marxism's key economic assumptions behind, but this would be the cost of building a better understanding of social domination under advanced capitalism. Because, as Marcuse's (2005b) reflections on his disillusionment with Heidegger's philosophy show, we have to be careful about the conceptual barriers that can hide in plain sight:

> To me and my friends, Heidegger's work appeared as a new beginning: we experienced his book . . . as, at long last, a concrete philosophy: here there was talk of existence, of our existence, of fear and care and boredom, and so forth. . . . Only gradually did we begin to observe that the concreteness of Heidegger's philosophy was to a large extent deceptive – that we were once again confronted with a variant of transcendental philosophy (on a higher plane), in which existential categories had lost their sharpness, been neutralized, and in the end were dissipated amid greater abstractions. That remained the case later on when the "question of Being" was replaced by the "question of technology": merely another instance in which apparent concreteness was subsumed by abstraction – bad abstraction, in which the concrete was not genuinely superseded but instead merely squandered. (p. 176)

Notes

1 This fact is celebrated in the introduction to the edited volume *Cultural Political Economy*. Jacqueline Best and Mathew Paterson argue that Marxism is a good example of how political economy can have a rich life when it avoids the neoclassical path. Marxism is not "deadened by the insistence that 'the economy' can be analyzed without reference to the specific sorts of people which inhabit and produce it (its cultures), the forms of power embedded in it (its politics) and the normative questions which animate both it 'in itself' and reactions to it" (Best & Paterson, 2009, p. 24).
2 A larger analysis would certainly include Horkheimer (2005a). D. Cook (2015) identifies the influence of Pollock's thesis of state capitalism on Adorno's thinking.
3 This is a point of Neumann's that Pollock would agree with. Pollock writes: "Nothing may seem on the surface to have changed, prices are quoted and goods and services paid for in money; the rise and fall in prices may be quite common. But the relations between prices and cost of production on the one side and demand and supply on the other . . . become disconnected in those cases where they tend to interfere with the general plan [of administered prices]. . . . In the last decades administered prices have contributed

much toward destroying the market automatism without creating new devices for taking over its 'necessary' functions" (Pollock, 2005, p. 75).

4 The quotation is from the *Grundrisse*, and Marcuse (1991, pp. 35–36) provides his own English translation in *One-Dimensional Man*.

5 Above the 80th percentile there is evidence that hyperinflation has occurred in different periods of capitalism. For instance, French society between the French Revolution and the War of 1812 experienced an almost 2,500% 10-year inflation rate.

6 In similar fashion, Marcuse (1991) thinks that the abstractness of critical theory is not automatically a concern: "critical philosophic thought is necessarily transcendent and abstract. Philosophy shares this abstractness with all genuine thought, for nobody really thinks who does not abstract from that which is given, who does not relate the facts to the factors which have made them, who does not – in [her] mind – undo the facts. Abstractness is the very life of thought, the token of its authenticity" (p. 134).

7 Fine and Saad-Filho explain how "counteracting tendencies" also have a quantitative relationship to the organic composition of capital: "If we write $r = \frac{s}{c+v}$, it follows that anything that reduces c or v, and anything that increases s, tends to increase r. The production of relative surplus value does all these, because the increase in productivity implies a reduction in the value of c and v (whether directly in the wage goods sector or indirectly through its use of lower valued raw materials) and an increase in s, through the reduction of v (given the real wage)" (Fine & Saad-Filho, 2004, p. 133).

3

CAPITAL AND THE STUDY
OF MASS CULTURE

3.1 Introduction

I suspect that if I asked readers to outline the characteristics of culture in capitalism, few would hesitate to connect the production and consumption of culture to the broader context of living in a capitalist society. This connection makes sense: almost every cultural object, event or activity of the past 100 years has had some price attached to it; advertisers, marketers and firms work tirelessly to sell culture to consumers; and the "free time" we have for art and entertainment is visibly impacted by structures of work and the social demand to have enough income to survive.

Yet, paradoxically, the *capitalist character* of culture might be something that is easy to recognize as a lived experience but hard to explain more comprehensively as a theory of capital accumulation. Mass media is now big business, and profit can be made from the buying and selling of artworks and cultural practices. Yet the difficulty involves using a theory of economics to explain why culture is or is not a source of value for the accumulation of capital. This type of explanation can prove to be difficult because theorists must use the methods of their chosen economic theory to address such issues as deciding what is a source of value, or explaining how aesthetics and meaning can be priced for exchange.

Marxist political economy offers a theoretical framework to explain the accumulation of capital from culture. In addition, some of its theorists work to demonstrate that, in some form, the Marxist labour theory of value is still relevant, despite mass culture having many immaterial and ideological aspects to its production and consumption. Unfortunately, significant theoretical problems are visible in the application of Marxist economics to culture. Confusions and contradictions

DOI: 10.4324/9781003092629-4

appear when we take a step forward and apply Marxist frameworks to understand how magnitudes of socially necessary abstract labour time are behind the production, sale and profit of cultural commodities. And for every confusion we resolve with a stated assumption, we risk ballooning theoretical assumptions about labour productivity to sizes that are unmanageable for empirical analysis.

Certainly we cannot forget that Marxist theory is bigger than its labour theory of value; the historical materialist approach has been responsible for producing many insightful critiques of mass culture, consumerism and ideology (Adorno, 2004b; Horkheimer & Adorno, 2002; Lukacs, 1968; Marcuse, 1991). Nevertheless, the idea that capital is valorized through the exploitation of labour remains foundational to Marxism's explanation of how capital accumulation works. Moreover, social, political and cultural theorists readily cite Marx as a source for explaining the economics of commodification and exchange value. Thus, it seems more than fair to think about how Marxism explains

1   the nature of value, the source of equivalency between commodities;
2   what produces economic value, in distinction from what only uses or transfers already existing value; and
3   how much value each productive entity contributes.

This chapter comments on two tasks that Marx's labour theory of value needs to accomplish before we can use the labour theory to explain the valuation and accumulation of capital from culture:

1   reduce concrete labour to a universal unit of measure, socially necessary abstract labour and
2   determine what types of labour are productive.

In practice it is difficult, if not impossible, to objectively satisfy both of these tasks. Moreover, these methodological dilemmas exist at the *root* of the Marxist method; they precede any modification that reshapes the labour theory of value for a particular business sector, such as mass culture.

3.2   Theoretical assumptions about capitalist production

To proceed with our evaluation, it is first necessary to establish that socially necessary abstract labour time is treated as an *objective measure of value*. Essentially, the objectivity of value, revealed in magnitudes of socially necessary abstract labour, is what gives Marx the platform to speak about capital accumulation as an ongoing system with structures, tendencies and rules. Many modern readers are resistant to emphasizing this side of Marx's theory, as it evokes images of "vulgar" economic Marxism and risks overshadowing the masterful nuances of his philosophical and social analysis. Yet blind devotion to Marxist economics is not necessary for one to surmise why Marx's theory of capital needs an objective core. It is there for us to look beyond superficial differences in business activity, to instead understand how the exploitation of productive labour is neither accidental nor incidental to the accumulation of capital. Marx wanted to know what was *essential* to capital accumulation, and he certainly was not satisfied to simply offer a moral critique of the capitalist class. He sought to use his value theory, in the words of Joan Robinson (1964), in order to "escape from sentiment and win for [his approach] the status of a science" (p. 25). His theory used classical economic categories to explain the contradictory laws of capitalism and the logic of capital (i.e., $a \rightarrow b$).

For Marx, value is not objective because it refers to some "thing" that transcends the historical movements of capitalist societies (D. Harvey, 2006, p. 124). Instead, value is objective because every commodity is measured by a systemwide expression of average productivity: the socially necessary labour time of production. By always referring to a social average, every exchange value is, under competitive conditions, independent of the buyer's and seller's wills (Marx, 1990, p. 477). Moreover, individual capitalists are generally forced to play this competitive game in a certain way: increase productivity in the production processes they control. Thus, as Paul Baran (1954) explains in a letter to Herbert Marcuse, the averaging of socially necessary labour time is unlike the averaging that individuals can do in their minds:

> The fact that all profits are subject to averaging in the arithmetical sense is not the issue. *Ex post* for purposes of some calculations you can average out the profits of your corner grocer and of GM – this is of no consequence. Marx assumed – and rightly so for a competitive economy – that the averaging out process takes place in reality (not merely in statistics), i.e. that equal capitals earn equal returns in different employments in reality. (Baran, 1954, p. 1)

Theoretical assumptions follow from a belief in the reality of socially necessary abstract labour time. The most fundamental assumption is that value is counted in units of labour time (e.g., 5 hours of labour, 2 days of labour etc.). This assumption is the backbone of so many of Marxism's economic arguments, even when they are more philosophical than empirical. For instance, formal analyses of logical consistency and discussions of different models – from simple commodity production to expanded reproduction – must presuppose that labour time is a measurable quantity (e.g., D. J. Harris, 1972; Wolff, 1981). More qualitative theorizations of labour and capital accumulation must also rely on the quantitative dimension of Marx's value theory. Frequently will Marxist thought reference *equivalent* commodity exchange and exploited labour *time*. Its qualitative claims still assume that capital is about the *growth* and appropriation of *more and more* surplus value, which is the *remainder of a greater sum* of produced value. And although many Marxist thinkers will have no numbers in their writing, they might stress that there is a structural imperative to *increase* the exploitation of labour (Braverman, 1998, p. 69). Things fall apart if the implied quantities of this language can never be measured explicitly.

Therefore, we are justified to analyse the labour theory of value according to Marx's own ambition to use *quanta* of value in his study of capitalist society. To set the stage for this analysis, let us review a few other assumptions about the labour theory of value and its measure of productivity.

First, value is always counted in units of abstract labour time. Whether we are considering constant capital, the means of subsistence or any other expression of value, labour time is the unit of value:

> How, then, is the magnitude of [abstract human labour] to be measured? By means of the quantity of the "value-forming substance", the labour, contained in the article. This quantity is measured by its duration, and the labour-time is itself measured on the particular scale of hours, days etc. (Marx, 1990, p. 129)

As Castoriadis (1984b) argues, this "value-forming substance" must then be an invariant unit of measurement, just as the kilometer, as a unit to measure distance, cannot vary with time and space. If Marxist economics lacked an invariant unit of measurement, it would be impossible to include different capitalist processes under the same "economic laws" of productivity. For example, the organic composition of capital can rise or fall with time, but this change can only exist, let alone be understood, when any two points in the history of capitalism are comparable with exactly the same set of formulas and units of measure. Similarly, if Canadian and Japanese labours are each examples of "variable capital", they must be identical with respect to the unit of measurement, which is labour time.[1]

Aristotle (1999, bk. 1, 3, 1094b) helps us see that when Marx speaks about value in a certain way, he is actually creating a standard for using value theory "accurately": "the educated person seeks exactness in each area to the extent that the nature of the subject allows. . . . [I]t is just as mistaken to demand demonstrations from a rhetorician as to accept [merely] persuasive arguments from a mathematician".[2] Thus, it is warranted to treat the following quotation as an example of Marx (1990) relying on the mathematics of proportionality:

> Let the value of the linen remain constant, while the value of the coat changes. If, under these circumstances, the labour-time necessary for the production of the coat is doubled, as a result, for instance, of a poor crop of wool, we should have, instead of 20 yards of linen = 1 coat, 20 yards of linen = ½ coat. If, on the other hand, the value of the coat sinks by one half, then 20 yards of linen = 2 coats. (p. 145)

As labour time can be divided, so it can be added, subtracted and multiplied. Commodities can be added together to find the "total labour-power of society, which is manifested in the values of the world of commodities" (Marx, 1990, p. 129). We can go in the other direction and decompose an aggregate bundle of commodities, such as the means of subsistence, into composite parts (Marx, 1990, p. 276). Likewise, since labour time is a measure of (productive) duration, an hour of abstract labour can be broken down into minutes of labour, just as hours can be aggregated into days, days into weeks and so on.

Finally, Marxism differentiates the social substance of value from the symbolic expressions of a price system. This differentiation of value and price need not take us all the way to the infamous "transformation problem". Rather, the philosophical foundation of Marx's framework is just as significant. As Castoriadis (1984b) reminds us, Hegel's influence on Marx was such that the latter did not use the terms "appearance", "substance" and "essence" naively (p. 265). For Marx, value is the essence behind the appearance of equivalence – in contrast to other economists who mistakenly confused the value-form of commodities with the value of commodities (D. Harvey, 2006, pp. 9 - 13).

In line with this distinction between value and its appearance, many of Marx's claims about the productivity of labour could never be corroborated with just wage and commodity prices. For example, jobs of all types remunerate work, but only some forms of labour will produce value; some commodities have prices but no value; or some commodities, like diamonds, have value but their prices might never be "proportional" to their values (Marx, 1990, p. 130). In fact, price and value are likely to diverge because the ratio between money wages and profits and the rate of exploitation, measured in labour time, can fluctuate independently of each other (J. Robinson, 1976, pp. 38–42). Therefore, Marxist political economy needs a unit of value that can be measured independently from price. Otherwise, it remains a mystery whether values remain constant when nominal prices remain constant, or if, beneath a stable level of prices, values are growing or shrinking.

Having established that the objectivity of value is key to Marx's theory of value, we can begin to subject Marxism's productivist approach to a stress test. In particular, we can assess the usefulness and clarity of the labour theory of value when it is applied to the production, circulation and consumption of culture under capitalism.

3.3 Reducing concrete labour

From the perspective of Marxist economics, any productive process in the capitalist mode of production – whether it takes place on a movie set, a car factory or a chemical plant – valorizes its commodities with the same "value-forming substance". Consequently, the concept of abstract labour is a keystone of the Marxist framework. It is the basis for the exchange of two commodities that are otherwise incommensurable with respect to their use values and the "formative" elements of their concrete labour. For example, the concrete qualitative differences between tailoring and weaving can be abstracted away, which uncovers the same human labour in an abstract, "physiological sense": they are each "a productive expenditure of human brains, muscles, nerves, hands, etc." (Marx, 1990, p. 134).

The concept of abstract labour is Marxism's common denominator for comparisons of productive duration. However, using the concept of abstract labour is not as straightforward as it first appears. There are methodological questions concerning how one reduces concrete labour to abstract labour. With respect to mass culture, a key methodological problem involves the nature of artistry and the use of creativity in cultural production. These aspects confound the meaning of abstract labour and, consequently, Marxist approaches to the economics of mass culture.

3.3.1   The creativity and artistry of cultural production

The creativity of the human imagination is not exclusive to cultural or artistic labour.[3] Yet, in the realm of art and culture, the problem of reducing concrete creativity to abstract labour is acute. It is unclear what becomes of the creative, artistic and immaterial elements of cultural production when artistic labour is subsumed under capital and abstracted according to the forces of socially necessary abstract labour time.

By formulating a *general* theory of capital, Marx excluded works of art for being exceptional commodities. Artistic labour was not yet, in the eyes of Marx, formally subsumed under capital. Instead, artistic labour was in a "transitional" stage (Marx, 1994), as it still included artists such as Milton and Balzac, who were neither alienated nor exploited like the proletariat. The proletarian worker loses his individuality by being subsumed under an abstract social definition of productivity. Conversely, the "classical" individual artist is still defined by their individual skill; they are their own measure of output and the duration of their labour is not benchmarked against a society-wide mass of "homogeneous labour" (Marx, 1990, p. 136). Moreover, any broad standard of artistic productivity is potentially meaningless because artistic labour is not necessarily competing to produce the same artwork in less time. For instance, when Picasso finished painting *Guernica* in 1937, it mattered little if *Guernica* took ten days or ten weeks to be completed; with no other *Guernicas* for comparison, it can never be determined whether the time it took Picasso to paint this unique artwork was socially necessary. And without a determinable quantity of value on the basis of abstract labour time, the exchange value of *Guernica* cannot be expressed as x coats, y yards of linen, z pounds of coffee and so on.[4]

The "transitional stage" of Marx's time has carried over into the contemporary era of artistic work, at least in a very important aspect: some artists, by virtue of fame or talent, receive large sums of money for the concrete labour they perform *as individuals*. Thus, the nature of their concrete artistic labour actually affects our understanding of the role of "joint-work" in mass culture. Rather than making it easier to claim that artistry and creativity are beholden to socially necessary abstract labour time, joint-work in mass culture retains aspects of classical bourgeois art. For each branch of mass culture – music, film, theatre and so on – some artists draw (high) wages because their proper names are famous – just like the names of Milton, Balzac or Picasso. John Cleese, for instance, is an exemplary comedian who cannot be substituted with even Michael Palin or Terry Jones, two other members of Monty Python. Thus, can we even abstract the so-called homogeneous element of Cleese's labour if we remove his concrete individuality from his performances? He was on the BBC and in plenty of movies because his brain, his nerves and his muscles produced comedy.

Some theorists not only recognize that artistic labour is a tricky exception to labour under capitalism but also do not think that the concreteness of artistic labour is a methodological problem. Instead, the irreducible concreteness of artistic labour is said to demarcate where the accumulation of capital from culture reaches its real social limits. For instance, Ryan (1992) argues that art's incompatibility with the Marxist definition of abstract labour creates a contradictory labour-capital relationship:

> Unlike many other types of workers, capital is unable to make the artist completely subservient to its drive for accumulation. The reason is simple. Since art is centred upon the expressive, individual artist, artistic objects must appear as the product of recognizable persons; the concrete and named labour of the artist is always paramount and must be preserved. As socially constituted, artists appear to capital as the antithesis of labour-power, antagonistic to incorporation in the capitalist labour process as abstract labour. . . . [The] artist represents the special case of concrete labour which is ultimately irreducible to abstract value. (pp. 41–44)

However, methodological questions still linger. Even if Ryan is justified to claim that the concrete particulars of artistic production cannot, by definition, be flattened into simple abstract labour, how do we avoid applying this definition arbitrarily or tautologically (e.g., an artist is someone who makes art)? Who is an artist and who is not?

Much like a drop of ink in a glass of clear water, the very idea that some creative labour is irreducible to abstract labour dirties the whole picture of contemporary cultural production. For instance, I personally agree with the praise Agee (2005) gives to the four most recognizable comedians in the era of silent cinema – Charlie Chaplin, Buster Keaton, Harold Lloyd and Harry Langdon – but where is the objective platform for me to state firmly that none of their concrete labour translates into socially necessary abstract labour time? What if someone thinks that, of the four, only Chaplin and Keaton are artists? This second discrimination implies that the labour times of Lloyd and Langdon were formally subsumed under capital as abstract labour time. Or what of artists who, while exceptional in their craft, will never have the same publicity as movie stars, or prize-winning writers, pop singers and fashion designers? The whole idea of "irreducibility" plays on our imagination that recognizable artists stamp "signatures" onto their works. And how will value theory account for cultural commodities that can sometimes involve the labour of hundreds? What about the "background" work of exceptionally talented film composers, make-up artists, set designers and others? How do we decide which background artists are famous enough for their labour to fall outside of abstract labour? Does the theoretical place of someone like Hans Dreier depend on whether moviegoers recognize his name?

To some, these questions might appear as being pedantic. However, a solid definition of abstract labour is key to Marxism's argument that, when subsumed under capital, the expenditure of labour is valued not by its own duration, but according to socially necessary labour time. The latter is a competitive benchmark; it forces capitalists to keep designing and redesigning their manufacturing processes on the basis of what, at each moment in time, is deemed socially necessary. Moreover, these redesigns can only be said to follow the laws of value if it is possible to find where productive processes, denominated in abstract labour time, deviate from competitive averages. For instance, Marx (1990) argued that if a "capitalist has a foible for using golden spindles instead of steel ones, the only labour that counts for anything in the value of yarn remains that which would be required to produce a steel spindle, because no more is necessary under the given conditions" (p. 265). Therefore, if it is unclear how artists of various types are even treated as abstract labour, it is also unclear how one could establish that a type of production in mass culture is in "excess" of socially necessary abstract labour time. This issue resurfaces when we come to the concept of productive labour.

3.3.2 Complex labour

Even if we assume that artistic creativity poses no problems for the accumulation of capital from mass culture, methodological issues still plague the concept of abstract labour. Key among these issues is the requirement that complex labour be reducible to simple labour.

Anticipating that abstract labour time would be the common denominator of differently skilled jobs, Marx (1990, p. 137) argued that skilled labour time is only ever a multiple of simple labour. Simple labour is "the labour-power possessed in his bodily organism by every ordinary man [*sic*], on the average, without being developed in any special way". Simple labour may vary "in different countries and at different cultural epochs, but in a particular society it is given". It is crucial that the simple labour of a particular society can be measured. Every type of complex labour is only, according to Marx (1990, p. 137), "intensified, or rather multiplied simple labour, so that a smaller quantity of complex labour is considered equal to a larger quantity of simple labour" (p. 137).

Finding the simple–complex ratio is undermined in at least two ways. First, it is far from straightforward how we can establish which type of labour is simple labour. Does society possess an existing labour process that lacks even the smallest degree of skill? Moreover, is simple labour even isolatable?[5] If simple labour is mixed with any amount of complex labour, we cannot count hours of work and treat them as a benchmark for simple labour (Nitzan & Bichler, 2009, p. 141). Instead, we must first know the quantitative relationship between complex labour and simple labour – that is, by how many multiples complex labour is already a quantity of simple labour: "Socially necessary labour-time is the labour-time required to produce any use-value under the conditions of production normal for a given society and with the average degree of skill and intensity of labour prevalent in that society" (Marx, 1990, p. 129).

Second, it is problematic to reduce complex labour to simple labour from both the input and output sides of production. Reduction from the input side must identify the value of the education and training processes that turn simple labour power into complex labour. For example, Hilferding (1966) argued that the ratio of complex to simple labour is equivalent to the costs required for labour power to develop its skills. However, Hilferding presumes not only that education and training can already be counted in units of simple labour but also that the only countable "hours" of education are the ones that capitalists eventually pay for. In other words, formal education has a price and it theoretically enables a skilled worker to command a higher wage; simple labour can then be found by dividing the value of complex labour by the total labour time of schooling and professional certification. Unfortunately, skill development in a person cannot be isolated this way. To say nothing about how one would account for the qualitative differences between schools that educate people for the same types of work, there is a great sea of "informal" education: one's family, community and culture. These layers of socialization are instrumental to the performance of complex labour, but, in terms of value, they are all obscure because they are *free* (P. Harvey, 1985; Nitzan & Bichler, 2009).

The presence of free, indirect and non-commodified education undermines the logic of equating the complexity of skill with its costs of development. Just as problematically, Hilferding (1966) presents the transfer of value from skilled labour as a linear process:

> Regarded from its standpoint of society, unskilled labour is latent as long as it is utilized for the formation of skilled labour power. Its working for society does not begin until the skilled labour power it has helped to produce becomes active. Thus in this single of the expenditure of skilled labour a sum of unskilled labours is expended, and in this way there is

created a sum of value and surplus value corresponding to the total value which were requisite to produce the skilled labour power and its function, the skilled labour. (p. 145)

With respect to the labour pool behind cultural production, there are too many alternatives to developing skills linearly, especially because this "path to skilled labour" is said to terminate at the point when a capitalist remunerates past education and training. What of internships, apprenticeships or any other training that is not exactly or only partly paid for by a future employer? Or what if, from year to year, the borders between work and education are increasingly blurred? Film directors, for instance, could have gone to film school, but they can also receive a lifelong education from repeated collegial support or from an endless love of old and new cinema. In such an atmosphere, skills development is not always paid for, and a cycle of ongoing education is missing from the initial purchase of complex labour.

Reducing skilled labour from the output side is also problematic. As Nitzan and Bichler (2009) point out, wage income is the only quantitative measure available to compare qualitatively different skills. Consequently, price differentials would be explaining the distribution of complex labour power, rather than the other way around. If we extend this logic to labour in cultural production, the great inequality of wage income suggests that a celebrity earning $20 million per year is producing 250 times the value of someone earning $80,000 per year, who herself is producing four times the value of someone earning $20,000 per year. The theoretical implication that celebrities create 1,000 times more value than someone who earns $20,000 is not problematic simply because the multiple is large. Without a means to measure abstract labour directly, we actually cannot determine whether this multiple is too big or too small. And depending on the celebrity, our estimated ratio is undermined even more: their possession of "skill" might be a debatable point. There is no school to become a certified famous person and we are now in an age where people complain about high-income celebrities having no discernible skills whatsoever. Meanwhile, the majority of working artists, who have actually paid to have formal training in art, are likely to be paid far less for the same output of entertainment.

According to D. Harvey (2006), these criticisms of the complex-to-simple-labour reduction miss the mark because they take the wrong perspective. Too much focus on skilled labour, according to Harvey (2006), risks overlooking how the "reduction from skilled to simple labour is more than a mental construct; it is a real observable process, which operates with devastating effects upon the labourers" (p. 59). In other words, capitalism's real push to mechanize and de-skill labour will eventually short-circuit the complex-simple problem:

The essential measure of the reduction of skilled to simple labour lies in the degree to which capitalism has created skills that are easily reproducible and easily substitutable. All of the evidence suggests that this has been the direction in which capitalism has been moving, with substantial islands of resistance here and innumerable pockets of resistance there. To the extent that the reduction of skilled to simple labour is still in the course of being accomplished, we have to conclude that capitalism is in the course of *becoming more true to the law of value* implied in its dominant mode of production. (D. Harvey, 2006, p. 119 emphasis added)

While it is politically important to critique any systemic process that is repressive, our methodological problem about simple labour is not erased. At least with respect to cultural production for mass culture, the need for *some degree of artistic skill* dirties the cleanliness of Harvey's argument.

For Harvey, Marx's method of only using measures of "simple labour" is "reasonable" because we can observe capitalists breaking and repressing any skill that workers could monopolize. For the case of mass culture, however, it does not appear that the goal is to flatten artistry to the point that every artist is replaceable and creative inputs are all substitutable. The capital–labour relationship of cultural production is still antagonistic (Gill & Pratt, 2008), but the point against Harvey is that the business of mass culture seeks to embrace and exploit rather than repress and destroy the complex skills of artists who have a virtual monopoly on their fame, image and singular qualities (Hozic, 2001; Ryan, 1992).

In fact, our scepticism of Harvey's claim should go beyond the scope of cultural production in the twenty-first century. Harvey's interpretation of simple labour builds from Marx's main object of study: nineteenth-century industrial manufacturing. Because labour processes in the "dark satanic mills" of the nineteenth century were often simple and monotonous, it was reasonable for Marx to assume that an industrial process can substitute the labour power of one worker for another. Since Marx's time, however, it has become difficult to assume that simple labour will become a universal characteristic of every modern labour process. Jobs in the culture industry, like many of the jobs in engineering, law, medicine, science and research, are now complex, even in their most "simplified" or controlled forms. Moreover, the mechanization of work does not *ipso facto* leave workers to act as machinery's simple appendages (Giedion, 1948). Some workers must suffer through brutally monotonous jobs, but others need the qualities of "alertness, responsiveness, an intelligent grasp of the operative parts: in short . . . [to be] an all-round mechanic rather than a specialized hand" (Mumford, 2010, p. 227).

3.4 Productive versus unproductive labour

The Marxist labour theory of value requires that theorists can discriminate between productive and unproductive labour. In this case, "productive" refers specifically to the creation of surplus value and never simply to the physical or mental production of use-values (Mandel, 1976, p. 33). Thus, by definition, the distinction between productive and unproductive labour is fundamental to the overall coherence of Marxist economics (Mohun, 1996, p. 31). If we cannot identify where productive labour occurs, we do not know whether all, some, or no labour processes are valorizing capital, which is said to occur when production is carried beyond "the point where the value paid by the capitalist for the labour-power is replaced by an exact equivalent" (Marx, 1990, p. 302).

Just as it did for abstract labour, cultural production complicates the distinction between productive and unproductive labour. Theoretically, the Marxist definition of productive labour should be consistent across business sectors, including cultural production. In fact, Marx (1994) sought to be consistent by explaining why a "literary proletarian" is productive, while John Milton, the great epic poet, was unproductive:

> Milton, for example, who did *Paradise Lost*, was an unproductive worker. In contrast . . . the writer who delivers hackwork for his publisher is a productive worker. Milton produced *Paradise Lost* in the way that a silkworm produces silk, as the expression of his own nature. Later on he sold the product for £5 and to that extent became a dealer in a commodity. But the Leipzig literary proletarian who produces books, e.g. compendia on political economy, at the instructions of his publisher is roughly speaking a productive worker, in so far as his production is subsumed under capital and only takes place for the purpose of the latter's valorization (p. 484).

Unfortunately, Marx's example does not help explain productive work in mass culture. Even if all productive cultural work were "hackwork" created for profit, the lines between production, circulation and, for some, consumption have been blurring since the early decades of the twentieth century. Therefore, it is difficult to assess when and how different types of cultural activity are even subsumed under capital. Advertising and marketing firms, for example, act as intermediaries for productive processes that "create" value directly. But are these firms themselves productive or unproductive? Moreover, consumers have a significant role in creating, reproducing and circulating the meaning, symbols and images of culture – are these aspects economically productive?

3.4.1   Three definitions of productive labour

By reviewing some of the existing literature, we find three general methods to define productive labour in cultural production. Unfortunately, each of these definitions has a set of methodological problems. The definitions also cannot be combined to produce a synthesized model. As we will see, it would be contradictory to combine arguments that have different assumptions about where valorization can occur in capitalist society.

In order to retain the universality of value theory, the first definition of *cultural production* tinkers with classical Marxism as minimally as possible (Mohun, 1996; Starosta, 2012). This definition assumes that we can apply the concept of "immediate producer" to culture and art just as we do to the production of physical commodities like corn and grain. Terms like "immaterial labour" or "cognitive labour" are considered small-but-reasonable modifications for the particularities of cultural work. Overall, this definition draws sharp lines between productive and unproductive labour: productive cultural work is distinguishable from cultural activity during "free time", and immaterial, cognitive or artistic labour can valorize capital when it is exploited directly. Moreover, this definition does not modify Marx's important distinction between the production of value and the mere circulation of value. For example, intellectual property rights are unproductive because they do not create surplus value.

The second definition of *cultural production* considers how quantitative increases in advertising and marketing have transformed the mode of circulation since Marx's time. The newfound depth and breadth of corporate sales efforts have, according to some, made labour within the mode of circulation productive. Ryan (1992), for instance, argues that processes of circulation, like advertising and aesthetic design, have become indispensable to "the conservation of use-value of commodities" (p. 64). "Immediate producers" still exist, but the circuit between immediate producers and consumers is only completed by the work of sales promotion, which can include "advertising, variation of the products' appearance and packaging, 'planned obsolescence', model changes, credit schemes, and the like" (Baran & Sweezy, 1966, p. 115).

In contrast to the first definition, this conceptualization of productive labour seeks to incorporate the broader social world into the economic value of mass culture. As Bohm and Land (2009) argue, the "classical" definition of productive labour excluded far too much:

> Teaching and education in general are clearly part of the reproduction of capitalist value, and should therefore not simply be regarded as "unproductive labour". In a similar way, feminist writers have pointed to the usually unwaged reproductive labor of women doing housework and care work. Equally, we would suggest that artists and cultural workers contribute to the production of capitalist value while falling outside traditional Marxist categories of "labour". (p. 87)

If the second definition expands beyond traditional Marxist categories by one or two degrees, the third definition's expansion is much more significant. In the second definition of *productive labour*, the valorization of cultural commodities still takes place in the "hidden abode" of privately owned firms, even if this abode now includes advertising, marketing and other aspects of the corporate sales effort (Buzgalin & Kolganov, 2013). By comparison, the third definition of cultural production demolishes the analytical walls between production, circulation *and* consumption. Here, consumption and consumer participation in mass culture produce value (Arvidsson, 2005b; Bohm & Land, 2012).

In order to have a broader view of cultural activity than the other two, the third definition accounts for the behaviour of cultural meaning and imagery in contemporary societies. During both work and "free time", consumers are participants in a broader "social factory" of cultural production (Gill & Pratt, 2008), and the ideological and social dimensions of mass culture – the attitudes, emotions and desires of consumers – now valorize capital (Gill & Pratt, 2008; Haiven, 2012; Lazzarato, 1996). According to Arvidsson (2005b), cultural activity can be subsumed under capital by brand management; the latter turns the "context of consumption" into a productive factor. Bohm and Land (2012) share a similar perspective to Arvidsson. For example, they argue that Apple has successfully captured consumer desire as value. By integrating its products and brand identity into the social practices of

> friendship, play, sex and even love . . . the reproduction of the cultural values and meanings invested in the [Apple] brand, and its related communities, is secured by the active labour of those consuming the brand and thereby valorizing the brand and contributing to its value. (Bohm & Land, 2012, p. 230)

The third definition deviates the most from the bounds of productive labour in classical Marxism, but its motivation to extend into the realm of consumption is justified by the historical development of brand culture. From this standpoint, brands and the symbols and images of mass culture are never "so much things – material artifacts and commodities – as social relations, signifying complexes, frames of action and subjectivity" (Bohm & Land, 2012, p. 231). For example, Haiven (2012) claims the value of Pokémon cards is a good example of why the value of popular cultural objects cannot be found in their costs of material production: "The value of Pokémon cards is clearly imagined. Even in their initial, commodified form, a slip of mass produced, coloured cardboard is by no stretch of the imagination 'worth' the money children pay for them" (p. 15).

3.4.2 Problems with the three definitions

The first definition of productive labour is constructed with categorical distinctions, as its authors are trying to prevent notions of cultural value from dissolving Marx's "classical" picture of where and when labour valorizes capital. Mohun (1996), for example, writes at the twilight of the twentieth century, but invokes Marx's definition to cut between the capitalist spheres of production and circulation: any form of labour that "brings buyers and sellers together" is unproductive because this form of labour "produces nothing in addition to what is already in existence" (p. 44). Starosta (2012) uses Marx to argue that contemporary political economy is mistaken in its belief that capitalism no longer needs the valorization of immediate labour processes, even in the age of digital culture, "cognitve" labour, research and development (R&D) and intellectual property. A close reading of Marx, according to Starosta (2012), will demonstrate these contemporary processes are pseudo-forms of circulation, as they can only mediate the value of what was first created in the production of prototypes or the "first" copies of artworks:

> The value of the aggregate product [i.e., all the reproductions of a commodity] no longer represents the simple addition of its constituent elements. Instead, the total value is determined "first" and then shared out equally by each individual commodity, which now contains a proportional fraction of the former. (p. 374)

Granting, for the sake of argument, that production is productive and circulation is unproductive, how do we confidently apply this distinction when an empirical reality is not clear-cut? For instance, how should we apply this aspect of value theory to the Star Wars franchise? On the one hand, George Lucas originally created characters, environments, objects and images for the production of the first three Star Wars films (*A New Hope, The Empire Strikes Back* and *The Return of the Jedi*). On the other hand, the breadth and complexity of the Star Wars universe have grown with every creative addition since the first three films. Is the first Star Wars trilogy the "original" commodity that determines how every subsequent commodity of the franchise is, in the words of Starosta (2012), an "aliquot part of total value"? How do we account for the reuse of established characters, such as Luke Skywalker or Darth Vader? Is value being created when reproduction takes place in another medium, such as when the image of Han Solo (Harrison Ford) is printed on T-shirts or movie posters? Or is this just unproductive circulation? When more characters, places and things are added to the Star Wars universe, which aspects of the next Star Wars commodity are new (productive) and which ones are "already there" (unproductive)? For instance, Darth Maul was a new villain for *Episode I: The Phantom Menace*, but he is also a particular version of past universal concepts (e.g., Jedi, the "Darth" prefix, lightsabers, the Force). What is the proportion between the creation of new value and the transfer of past value?

It would be impossible to answer these questions about the Star Wars universe because, as Nitzan and Bichler (2009) point out, the line between productive and unproductive moves every time something manifests advertising-like qualities:

> [T]ake advertising. Undoubtedly, this activity is designed to promote sales. But what about the incessant remodeling of automobiles, clothing, detergents, cosmetics, architecture, news media and what not — remodeling that according to some estimates accounts for over 25 per cent of the cost of production? Given that the main purpose here, much like in advertising, is to enhance

circulation, shouldn't we consider the labour put into such remodeling to be unproductive as well? Paradoxically, even a positive answer would not solve the problem here. After all, any new product characteristic can persuade people to buy, so how do we distinguish between the advertising-like aspect of remodeling that merely circulates existing values and its productive aspect that by definition creates new values? (p. 113)

The second definition of *cultural production* appears to circumvent this issue by stating that the mode of circulation is, in fact, productive. However, we now face another difficult question: how would we know when and to what extent labour in the capitalist mode of circulation is productive?

As we saw earlier, some Marxist theorists argue that the mode of circulation is productive because marketing, branding, artistic creativity and design are currently necessary parts in the creation of value. The so-called necessity of it all, however, is difficult to determine. Take, for example, the decision to pay someone like Jennifer Lawrence $10 million to star in the next big action-adventure blockbuster. On top of this high wage cost, there are the added costs of promoting Lawrence's involvement. Does all labour surrounding Lawrence add value to the commodity, the movie? Step one is to determine whether the capitalist purchase of Jennifer Lawrence's labour power was necessary. Unfortunately, this determination requires that we first know the subjective attitudes of consumers. If the commodity in the mind of the average customer was "a Jennifer Lawrence movie", then the cost of hiring her was necessary for accumulation. And if the promotion and advertising had changed people's minds about seeing "a Jennifer Lawrence movie", then this labour of circulation might be considered productive as well. But if it is also possible that moviegoers will watch the movie for entirely different reasons – for example "I just wanted to watch a good popcorn movie and I don't care who the lead actor is" – then it is less clear whether all the labour necessary to circulate the aura of this Hollywood star was necessary and, thus, a productive input.[6]

This methodological confusion about "productive" circulation is exacerbated by the existence of coercive force within capitalist societies. Structural and institutional-based repression unravels any simple one-to-one relationship between consumer behaviour and the labour costs of corporate sales efforts. People are certainly bombarded with advertisements every day, but it is nevertheless difficult to determine whether exercises in glossy advertising or branding are necessary, partially necessary, or superfluous to capital accumulation.[7] Blind spots persist because it is also possible that the length of the working day, stagnant wages, the social division of labour, and the political and environmental conditions of society cause consumers to buy into mass culture. For instance, the largest media firms benefit from what Marx discovered in 1844, namely, that the persistence of alienated labour causes us to dislike labour and treat time away from work as a sanctuary from both physical and mental effort (Marx, 1988, p. 76). Additionally, the sales of mass culture rely on the institutions and social relations that can act as indirect conduits for business interests. Through the family unit, social taboos, a hierarchical distribution of scarcity and the control of technological innovation by vested interests, the instinctual energies of a population are, to varying degrees, already deflected into "socially acceptable" forms of sexuality and pleasure (Horowitz, 1977, 1987; Marcuse, 1966).

The third definition assumes that consumer activity is also a productive input in the valorization of cultural commodities. Consequently, a measure of productivity must extend far beyond the walls of factories and workplaces. In the age of what Arvidsson (2005b) calls "informational" capitalism, much "of the value of brands derives from the free (in the sense of both the unpaid and autonomous) productivity of consumers" (p. 130). Capitalists are said to appropriate this broad influx of value "by positing the brand as a kind of virtual factory, by giving labour a place where its autonomous productivity more or less directly translates into feedback and information."

As with the second definition, the third definition is shaped by a thematic interest in ideology, cultural meaning and social desire. In itself, this interest is reasonable. What is concerning is the moment when this theoretical interest causes theorists to jump feet-first into economic assumptions about productivity. The third definition needs to develop a reliable economic measure of consumer valorization, but, problematically, this broader conceptualization of immaterial and cultural value resorts to a modified version of revealed preferences. Coined by Paul Samuelson, *revealed preferences* is a neoclassical term that uses the act of choosing one good from alternatives to define the utility of one's preferences. Utility cannot be measured directly but, by assuming that utility drives behaviour, an individual's choice to purchase a good will "reveal" the utility of this behaviour, relative to available alternatives.[8] Thus, like the detective of Edgar Allan Poe's "The Purloined Letter", the neoclassicist must deduce the whereabouts of its lost item (utility) from things she can observe (people buying goods at certain prices). Yet, unlike a stolen letter that exists separately from its owner, the "shape" and "size" of utility does not exist independently of the utility–price relationship. Thus, the proof of revealed preferences runs into problems because the economist has to assume the autonomy of individual choice will allow us to see utility through the lens of prices. For instance, the neoclassicist must determine that the market is in a state of perfectly competitive equilibrium; prices would not, without this condition, cleanly reveal utility. Moreover, this logic uses "observed" consumer behaviour to determine where utility lies, when utility is meant to be the subjective cause of consumers having demand for goods. By going in reverse, the proof presupposes that each act of consumer choice is *always* a rational comparison of utility.

The third definition relies on the idea of revealed preferences because so much of its so-called consumer valorization is obscure – as even proponents of the third definition admit (Bohm & Land, 2012, p. 130). Moreover, the quantitative categories of productivity, such as labour time, are inapplicable to the desires and emotions of consumer behaviour. Two people own Adidas shoes, for example. Do they valorize the Adidas brand equally? Do obsessed fans of the Harry Potter novels produce more value than those who read and enjoy the stories with much less intensity? Does so-called value-producing consumption need to be reduced to simple labour? Is consumption a skill that can be possessed to varying degrees?

As a consequence of these potential confusions, the makeshift solution is to work backwards by first looking at prices. One solution is to treat immaterial value as a residual, in which brand value is a firm's market price minus its tangible assets. Problematically, however, this arithmetic still requires that brand value is the proven effect of consumer desires and attitudes. In other words, brand value is the pricing of the future earning potential and risk of *brand equity*, which, under these assumptions, is comprised of all of the productive processes, both inside and outside the firm, that go into establishing brand loyalty and consumer preferences (Moor & Lury, 2011; Willmott, 2010). For example, the problem with finding "real" consumer valorization by working backwards is present in Willmott's (2010) theorization of YouTube's worth:

> YouTube was acquired by Google for $1.65bn in 2006 when it had just 65 employees. That is a potent illustration of how the labour of user-consumers built the brand equity of YouTube that was turned into brand value. The proceeds of the sale of YouTube were shared amongst those legally credited with owning the site . . . to the exclusion of those who provided its content and built its reputation. The capitalist state ensured that, legally, the co-producers of YouTube's brand equity had no entitlement to the dollar value generated by their labour. (p. 527)

Willmott is updating a Marxist theory of appropriation: the shareholders of YouTube were making it rich on the appropriation of labour time, which in this case came from the users that made and uploaded content for free. The suggestion that Google paid $1.65 billion for the sum of all contributing productivity, however, must also imply that consumer labour *could* have been paid for its inputs if it had not been appropriated as surplus value. Yet, the insights of another economist, Thorstein Veblen, help us recognize that, once again, this perspective on labour inputs presumes that price will cleanly reflect each individual input's value contribution. As with other processes in modern industry, the labour of cultural goods cannot simply be deconstructed into atomistic, definable factors of a production function. The complexity of modern industry and the mixture of different commodities in the same production processes blur the lines that would allow us to say that each input contributed a definite quantity of value (Veblen, 2006a, 2006b).

Moreover, the productivity-based approach is undermined by the large free "common stock" of knowledge and ideas, which are repeatedly used to produce objects and ideas (Veblen, 2006b). For instance, the making and uploading of a basketball video on YouTube would never simply be about the labour time of the filmed basketball players or the user who makes, edits and uploads the content. Rather, this productive process of sharing a video on the internet is dependent on an enormous complex of factors in computer, electrical and mechanical engineering. Moreover, a video on basketball depends on the existence of this sport, which was invented (for free) by James Naismith and developed from knowledge in material science, organizational behaviour and the biological capacities of human beings. Additionally, any commentary in the video would rely on a shared human language, such as English or Japanese. The simple idea that the maker of the YouTube basketball video is tacitly relying on the history of a sport and the productivity of semiconductors, binary logic, the invention of synthetic rubber, language, mathematics and so much other modern technology to create and upload a single digital product is Veblen's point about the immeasurable productivity of our *common stock*. The social and technological foundations of modern production render isolated definitions of productivity meaningless. Conversely, many of the precursors of industrial creation are, by virtue of being shared social knowledge, *free to all*, including businesses. Capital value, in contrast, stands on the aspects of industrial capacity that have been made exclusive through the social-legal institution of private ownership. These aspects – the exclusive right to advertise and sell data to others – are what make YouTube an asset to Google. The future earnings of YouTube still depend on all of the social relations that are relevant to making this website a virtual community, but the capital value is attached to the copyrights, patents and ownership titles that allow Google to sell access to what is now withheld from society at large (Veblen, 2004).

The makeshift use of "revealed preferences" is also found at the level of individual consumption, whereby the "premium" price reveals the desires and emotions of consumers who are willing to pay. This "premium" is the new use-value of branded cultural commodities:

> On a first and most basic level, consumers pay for access to a brand. Within marketing and accounting literature this is usually conceived as the "premium price" that consumers pay for a branded item, with respect to a "comparable" non-branded item (a Nike shoe versus an anonymous shoe, for example). What consumers pay for is access to the communicative potential of the brand, the possibility of inserting the brand in their own assemblage of compatible qualities. The use-value of the brand for the consumer is its value as a means of communicative production. (Arvidsson, 2005a, p. 250)

To look at price and work backwards, however, is to employ a faulty logic whereby the value of ideology and other immaterial qualities must be revealed through the prices people pay for consumer goods. The explanation is supposed to go the other way: How do ideology, desire and other immaterial aspects of consumer behaviour *cause* prices? Can the so-called productive value of consumer behaviour be verified independently of market prices? Moreover, defining the premium price of Nike shoes with a comparison to an "anonymous shoe", is problematic if it is not so easy to find a "pure" brand-less item that can act as an objective benchmark for differences in value, which we have still not found. For instance, many countries associate luxury and pleasure with the ownership of expensive cars, but where is the generic, anonymous car to reveal to me the value differential of a BMW, Mercedes or Lexus? Even the "average" car, whatever that may be, is branded property.

3.5 Conclusion

This chapter focused its critique on the application of the Marxist labour theory of value in the realm of culture but not in order to reject the social philosophy of historical materialism *in toto*. Instead, the goal has been to explain where and how studies of capital accumulation and the business of mass culture can entangle themselves with questionable assumptions about the measurement of socially necessary abstract labour time. Mass culture is a good example of how entangled an economic theory can get. When trying to see the value of culture as magnitudes of productive inputs, one must answer a long series of questions about how to know which element of culture can even be accumulated as value.

In the survey of Marxist political economy, we came across many thinkers who were not naive about the significance of value theory. We also witnessed instances of nuanced theoretical analysis; few Marxist political economists would be unaware of critiques about the reduction of concrete labour to abstract labour or the differentiation between productive and unproductive labour. Nevertheless, I believe this chapter demonstrates the need to develop and use entirely different assumptions about the nature of capital. Why go to this extreme? Using the labour theory of value to explain the accumulation of capital from cultural production forces one to dissect labour, creativity and the social environment of culture according to a definition of productivity. This dissection is ultimately subjective, as theorists are not measuring value in culture (independently of prices) but instead making categorical claims about where valorization occurs (behind the appearances of prices).

This subjective approach to explaining productive valorization might not always be visible, but we can see it when we remember that socially necessary abstract labour time is defined as an objective substance. Thus, every time a theorist claims that, by definition, a type of production is either inside or outside the labour theory of value, it is assumed that, *in reality*, the mechanics of the entire value system are arranged in the same way. Make the claim, for example, that culture cannot be properly subsumed under capital, and you imply that, *objectively*, vast swaths of capitalist society are not producing value. If one claims instead that consumers valorize capital with immaterial labour, one must commit to the objective existence of a "social factory", whereby capitalists can capture desires and pleasure *as units of socially necessary abstract labour time*. Otherwise, how would capitalists, in a world where Marxist economics is correct, accumulate capital from consumer desires?

Unfortunately, without a method to test interpretations of value *independently* from prices and without adding more assumptions with ontological definitions of what is and is not productive, we are stuck looking for reassurance like Irimias in Krasznahorkai's (2012) *Sátántangó*, who observes aloud in a police station that, "The two clocks say different times, but it could be that neither of them is right" (p. 23). The way forward, in my opinion, involves putting power at the centre of a theory of capital. From this perspective, we gain the freedom to rethink how aspects of society – ideology, desire, signification, intellectual property rights, nationalism and many other political processes – are just as important for accumulation as labour and machines are. Investment will still involve some type of production, and the treatment of labour under capitalism still matters socially and politically. But our methodology does not tangle itself in the idea that capital is a magnitude of productivity. Instead, a theory of capitalist power can continue to account for the ways in which firms use the repressive elements of their institutional power to profit on the basis on their strength.

Notes

1　The magnitudes of Canadian and Japanese labour power can certainly differ from each other because the reproduction of labour power, for Marx, depends "on the level of civilization attained by a country". Yet it is also Marx's (1990) point that we are comparing value with value, like with like: "The value of labour-power can be resolved into the value of a definite quantity of the means of subsistence. It therefore varies with the value of the means of subsistence, i.e., with the quantity of labour-time required to produce them" (p. 276). In other words, when we compare the value of labour powers in different countries, we apply the same formal method: "in a given country at a given period", we break the means of subsistence down into smaller quantities of labour time.

2　The use of this quotation is inspired by Castoriadis's (1984b) interpretation of Aristotle.

3　Therefore, this section's focus can be widened to ask even more questions. For example, how is a biological yardstick – brains, nerves, muscles – helpful when the concrete labour of a doctor or a shoemaker is always a complex composite of mental and physical coordination?

4　For a critique of theoretical assumptions that try to pin the price of art to the value of its production, see Suhail & Phillips (2012).

5　For a critical examination of the Marxist skilled labour–unskilled labour relationship, see (Nitzan & Bichler, 2009, pp. 141–144).

6　Although I am using my own hypothetical example, this point comes from Nitzan and Bichler (2009), who use "Mexican flowers" as their example (p. 116).

7　It is noteworthy that Adorno (2004c), one of the fiercest critics of mass culture, came to a similar conclusion about the ideological strength of consumerism: "the culture industry has . . . become total", but it is "doubtful whether the culture industry and consumer-consciousness can be simply equated with each other" (p. 195).

8 For a clear introduction to the neoclassical theories of consumer behaviour, including the idea of revealed preferences, see Asimakopulos (1978). For critiques of utilitarian consumer behaviour, see Keen (2001) and J. Robinson (1964).

4

A POWER THEORY OF MASS CULTURE

4.1 Introduction

Chapters 2 and 3 focused on the limitations of the Marxist framework. These limitations stem from Marxism's method of defining the economics–politics relationship in capitalism. The Marxist concept of capital privileges labour on the assumption that magnitudes of capital are essentially measures of economic productivity – in this case, labour time. Thus, for all of its dialectical insights, and despite the strong desire for Marxism to account for many social dimensions of capitalist society, economics and politics must ultimately be analytically separable according to this assumption. In the final analysis, surplus value, the object of capitalist appropriation, is defined as the product of exploited labour time, nothing else.

Marxism has, by its own definition of capital, committed itself to the argument that, within the dense composition of capitalism, nothing other than the abode of production, however defined, is the so-called real source of value. Other aspects of modern business, like finance, are deemed to operate with quantities of fictitious capital, and the state and other institutions of civil society are understood to only ever promote or assist capital accumulation as external forces. As with neoclassical economics, this method of delineating economic activity makes it difficult for Marxism to explain the relation between nominal prices and real economic values – a difficulty that is connected to the empirical problem of isolating a pure measure of productivity in reality. Unlike the conservative presentation of "distortions" in neoclassical economics, Marxism inadvertently hides this problem within a dialectical framework that aimed at studying the capitalist totality.

Labour is certainly an important factor to any comprehensive study of capitalist mass culture, but it is our assumptions about economic productivity and not the

DOI: 10.4324/9781003092629-5

ubiquity of wage labour that tells us we have to look at the latter in terms of productive output. Therefore, if we use entirely different assumptions about capital accumulation, we might be able to create stronger links between profit, creativity and the social composition of mass culture. Stronger links reside, I believe, in a political economic approach that uses an alternative to the Marxist concept of capital. The capital-as-power approach, first developed by Bichler and Nitzan, is the basis of this book's power theory of mass culture.

Bichler and Nitzan conceptualize capital accumulation as a *mode of power*. Various elements to this mode of power, such as the strategic sabotage of industry and the capitalization of expected earnings, are presented to the reader in the second half of the chapter. The first half is preparatory. It will survey theoretical precedents and provide examples that relate to a power theory of mass culture. This preparation is not occurring because the content of the second half is difficult to understand. Rather, it is my experience that the captial-as-power approach is easy to misinterpret, intentionally or accidentally. A longer route to Bichler and Nitzan's writings will give us the material to see how, by comparison, the capital-as-power approach is taking steps to create a political economic *project*, which can grow in both its theoretical and empirical dimensions. Others might conceptualize the existence of power in capital accumulation, but few are, like Bichler and Nitzan, carefully considering how concepts would transform into research questions, how research questions would require empirical methods, and how empirical methods would measure capitalist power.

4.2   Theoretical precedents

While the path to breaking the dualism between economics and politics lies in a concept of capital that is different from what is found in Marxist frameworks, the latter does contain ideas that we can use to begin our journey. Within a broader methodological debate about how to theorize culture, Marxist political economy often presents itself as the best method for studying the effect of power on the cultural aspects of capitalism. This interest in power, despite our deeper issue with the labour theory of value, can help explain the role of control and authority in the creation of culture and the circulation of meaning. Thus, by reviewing some of these Marxist approaches to power and culture in capitalism, we travel towards a political economic framework that uses a concept of capitalist power to rethink the nature of capital accumulation.

4.2.1   Cultural studies versus Marxist political economy

In the March 1995 issue of *Critical Studies in Mass Communication*, a "colloquy" between academics addressed theoretical issues that tended to divide leftist theories of culture into two groups. For the sake of simplicity, the groups had generic titles.

One group was called "political economy", and the other was called "cultural studies".

One of the participants, Nicholas Garnham, made the case for using Marxist political economy in the fields of culture, communication and media. For Garnham (1995), the discipline of political economy is effective in criticizing the capitalist character of culture and communication. Marxist political economy performs this function by connecting the ideological qualities of culture to its historical mode of production. This theoretical link between ideology and material structure is the means to investigating how "a delimited social group, pursuing economic or political ends, determines which meanings circulate and which do not, which stories are told and about what, which arguments are given prominence and what cultural resources are made available and to whom" (Garnham, 1995, p. 65).

Garnham uses his understanding of Marxist political economy to correct what he thinks cultural studies misunderstands in this debate over methodology. Cultural studies is similarly interested in power, but its analyses of culture have, in the eyes of Garnham (1995), hastily rejected the methods of Marxist political economy. Scholars on the side of "cultural studies" show a lot of dislike toward the "economistic" or "reductionist" aspect of Marxist political economy (p. 62). This dislike biases the ways cultural studies interprets the Marxist concept of the capitalist superstructure, the "place" that houses cultural activity. Cultural studies scholars like Stuart Hall and Angela McRobbie, as cited by Garnham (1995, p. 62), believe that there is a correlation between Marxism's economic determinism and its problematic arguments about the so-called false consciousness of ordinary people.

Robert Babe, who refers to this colloquy in his book *Cultural Studies and Political Economy*, returns to this war over method because, as of 2009, "the fields remain riven" (p. 6). According to Babe (2009), cultural studies is a "multidisciplinary study of culture" that "refers to arts, knowledge, beliefs, customs, practices and norms of social interaction". This approach differs from political economic theories of culture, which focus on "the economic, financial and political causes and consequences of culture" (Babe, 2009, p. 4). Similar to Garnham's argument in 1995, Babe claims that the post-structuralist turn within cultural studies was the unfortunate effect of other scholars believing that political economists had mishandled the immaterial aspects of culture. Like Garnham, Babe (2009) argues that political economy is unfairly indicted for engaging in economic reductionism and for not "inquiring into the ideological and interpretive practices of audiences" (p. 4).[1]

The arguments of Garnham and Babe certainly aim to defend their interpretations of Marxist political economy.[2] Beyond their more particular interests in Marxism, however, they make a particular argument that interests us here – that cultural studies and political economy should reconcile and integrate their methods to study power. A political economic analysis of the "structure of domination" is the solution to problematic instances when "the source of power remains, in general, opaque" (Garnham, 1995, pp. 67–69). The "cultural industries" are examples of these "structures and organization of power" and their mysteries are clarified with a method that draws links between the "power relations embedded in the production, distribution and consumption of cultural forms as commodities" and "the use-value of that commodity to the consumer" (Garnham, 1995, p. 65). With links of this kind, a critical analysis of culture is able to juggle both the symbolic and material aspects of capitalism in a single unified theory. Similarly, Babe (2009) argues that a holistic method is effective at analysing modern culture as a political economy of power and control: "the median and dialectical position . . . acknowledges mutual interaction and mutual dependency in the systems theory sense among culture, economy, and polity/policy" (p. 8).

4.2.2 Adorno

According to Babe, a prototype of a political economy of power can be found in the cultural writings of Adorno. The interdisciplinary qualities of Adorno's writings on culture demonstrate that it is

> insufficient merely to depict general relations between various cultural products (say, musical genres) and social life. Rather one needs to explore how cultural products help organize society (allocate leisure time and promote passivity and conformity in audiences, for example), and address in detail the production, reproduction, distribution, exchange and consumption of cultural commodities. (Babe, 2009, p. 24)

And while Adorno's theory of culture is still Marxist, it is moving outwards. By abandoning both the "basic tenets as class warfare between capital and labour" and the idea that the materialist dialectic in capitalism is the inevitable "working out" of contradictions on the way to socialism, Adorno is, according to Babe, able to outline the new "fundamentals" for a "critical political economy of media and culture". This critical political economy is much more holistic, as it includes

> the claim of marked asymmetries in the distribution of communicatory power; an emphasis on the oppression, manipulation, and control through media by an elite; the notion of domination of media as a prerequisite to attaining and maintaining political-economic power; media as devices for influencing if not controlling consciousness and limiting resistance; economic power as affecting cultural production. . .; transformations wrought by commodification (exchange value suppressing use value); . . . creative arts as a possible but waning key to critical understanding; emphasis on

the social totality; and the importance of contradiction, reflexivity and dialectics. (Babe, 2009, p. 31)

Babe, like other readers who identify Adorno's political economic overtones (D. Cook, 1996, pp. 103–105), is not trying to credit Adorno for doing more than he does. Adorno's writing on mass culture can be abstract, and this would have consequences on how another political economic study of mass culture could use his arguments for historical and empirical research. Yet Adorno's writing is foundational in the sense that, from his explorations of more philosophical spaces, he developed concepts and themes that can be the buttresses of a more detailed political economic project.

For example, there is Adorno's presentation of the dialectic between culture and administration. This conceptual presentation illustrates why the autonomy of cultural creation is simultaneously a struggle against external control. Just as enlightenment is never ultimately separate from myth in the dialectic of enlightenment, culture is never separate from administration. Equally important, the latter two concepts, while intertwined, still cannot be reduced to the same common denominator. Between culture and administration, there is a tension of non-identical purposes:

> Whoever speaks of culture speaks of administration as well, whether this is his intention or not. The combination of so many things lacking a common denominator – such as philosophy and religion, science and art, forms of conduct and mores – and finally the inclusion of the objective spirit of an age in the word "culture" betrays from the outset the administrative view, the task which, looking down from on high, is to assemble, distribute, evaluate and organize. (Adorno, 2004a, p. 105)

The lack of a common denominator is the effect of culture being irreducible to the means–ends logic of instrumental reason. The objectification of culture in art, symbols, imagery and meaning can certainly be treated as means to the ends of dominant social interests – for example cultural production for the purposes of glory, prestige or profit. But culture can also be created without any regard to "functional relationships within society". Conversely, administration can never disregard these functional relationships, as its very purpose is to control social relationships according to some mandate, whether official or tacit (Adorno, 2004a, p. 108). Thus, writes Adorno (2004a),

> The demand made by administration upon culture is essentially heteronomous: culture — no matter what form it takes — is to be measured by norms not inherent to it and which have nothing to do with the quality of the object, but rather with some type of abstract standards imposed

from without, while at the same time the administrative instance – according to its own prescriptions and nature – must for the most part refuse to become involved in questions of immanent quality which regard the truth of the thing itself or its objective bases in general. (p. 113)

No solution to the cultural effects of administration can be found in wishing that cultural creation could reject administration "*en bloc*" (Adorno, 2004a, p. 121). Instead, highlighting the traces and effects of administration on the scope of cultural creativity allows for matters of art and culture to be opened for political deliberation. We can use political categories like freedom and happiness to debate the legitimacy of an administrative power controlling the historical possibilities of aesthetics and meaning. Indeed, politics can make what is often invisible in culture visible: the institution of a culture through authority. In other words, self-reflexive criticism of the culture–administration dialectic derives from an awareness that artistic and institutional interests will diverge at points: "Culture is the perennial claim of the particular over the general, as long as the latter remains unreconciled to the former. . . . [Administration] necessarily represents — without subjective guilt and without individual will — the general against the particular" (Adorno, 2004a, p. 113).

In this respect, Adorno's apparent "pessimism" about mass culture is related to the amount of theoretical work that is required to put power back into the mix – so that we can then analyse and talk about the power structure of culture in capitalism. As with one-sided notions of enlightenment, where the very possibility for enlightenment to revert to myth is buried within impulsive affirmations of technological progress and scientific knowledge, a one-sided concept of mass culture is resistant to the language of power when nothing about leisure time and modern entertainment appears to be worthy of a serious critical eye. For example, part of Adorno's criticism of mass culture relates to myths surrounding the historical transformation of artistic production from patronage to bourgeois liberalism.[3] The bourgeois ideals of purposeless art, "pure works of art . . . simply following their own inherent laws", *l'art pour l'art*, and other such notions where art is postulated as its own autonomous sphere, are all formally different from patronage, where artists are, by virtue of the patronage relationship, "subject to the patrons and their purposes" (Horkheimer & Adorno, 2002, p. 127). However, a simplistic narrative positing mass culture as the child of artistic freedom born during the decline of European patronage in the eighteenth century will likely hide the key structural development of institutional power in advanced capitalism: "The triumph of the giant corporation over entrepreneurial initiative is celebrated by the culture industry as the perpetuity of entrepreneurial initiative" (Horkheimer & Adorno, 2002, p. 120).

As is shown in two supplementary commentaries to the 2002 English translation of *Dialectic of Enlightenment*, Adorno's descriptions of monopoly capital and institutional power were entangled in various problems of terminology, some of which concerned how Marxist terminology would be interpreted in juxtaposition with the realities of Soviet Marxism and authoritarian forms of socialism (Noerr, 2002; Reijen & Bransen, 2002). Nevertheless, we can offer two reasons why this emphasis on institutional power is a useful precedent for a concept of capital that stresses power, not productivity.

First, the "culture industry" (*Kulturindustrie*), perhaps the Frankfurt School's most well-known concept, denotes the control of cultural production and distribution, rather than the productivity of these processes. In "Culture Industry Reconsidered", for example, Adorno (2004b) clarifies what he means by the term *industrial*: "It is industrial more in the sociological sense, in the incorporation of industrial forms of organization even when nothing is manufactured – as in the rationalization of office work – rather than in the sense of anything really and actually produced by technological rationality" (p. 101).

Second, Adorno describes the *Kulturindustrie* in such a way that the most emphasized facet of modern corporate activity in mass culture is the ability to control the shape and style of culture through exclusion and repression:

> The explicit and the implicit, exoteric and esoteric catalog of what is forbidden and what is tolerated is so extensive that it not only defines the area but wholly controls it. Even the most minor details are modeled according to this lexicon. Like its adversary, avant-garde art, the [*Kulturindustrie*] defines its own language positively, by means of prohibitions applied to its syntax and vocabulary. (Horkheimer & Adorno, 2002, p. 101)

The motives for this control are "economic", but the efficient cause has more to do with the *negation* of other competitors. For example, corporate advertising is transformed into a negative principle when "the free market is coming to an end". What was once about "orienting the buyer" in a competitive market is now a "blocking device" for firms that can outspend much smaller firms. In an environment in which a lot of money is used to advertise and promote the most dominant firms, "anything which does not bear its [money's] seal of approval is economically suspect" (Horkheimer & Adorno, 2002, p. 131). Furthermore, the so-called economics of advertising changes qualitatively when consumers are already informed about the most popular commodities on the market: "Advertising becomes simply the art with which Goebbels presciently equated it, *l'art pour l'art*, advertising for advertising's sake, the pure representation of social power" (Horkheimer & Adorno, 2002, p. 132).

4.2.3 Marcuse

Compared to Adorno's study of the culture industry, the writings of Marcuse appear to be even further removed from a historically detailed political economy of mass culture. If Adorno (2005b), with Horkheimer, shapes his concept of the culture industry by referring to monopolization, and critiques, in his collaborations and conversations with Horkheimer and Benjamin, the ownership and control of modern aesthetic techniques, Marcuse's (1965, 1968a, 1968d) interests in culture seem to be much more about its general ideological character. However, Marcuse's conceptualization of ideology is an important complement to Adorno's project. Marcuse's critical theory, with its mixture of aesthetic and political theory, produces a picture in which ideology is the *emergent property* of institutional power and its grip on society. Such a presentation of ideology offers an opportunity to include ideological aspects of culture in a theory where capital accumulation is defined as a power process. We also avoid having to take the problematic step of thinking of ideological "value" in terms of productivity, where the desires of consumers are sovereign, or even productive as such. Marcuse inspires us to investigate how popular cultural meanings in a repressive society are connected to the social institution of limitations, constraints and taboos.

As much as ideas, beliefs and values are, so to speak, a matter of the human mind, Marcuse's concept of ideology is primarily interested in the ways in which an established social universe of discourse and action can serve as an objective limit on the dynamics of thought. This objective limit is predominately social. It is mainly the product of vested interests and institutional power repressing historical possibilities through the control of society's intellectual and technological development. Limiting technological and intellectual development according to the established goals and values of dominant powers in society is also the other side of any affirmative rationalization of these goals and values. By circumscribing the scope of technology, work and creativity according to the goals of society's vested interests, the "ideas, aspirations and objectives" of thought, even when expressed through cultural creation, become what Marcuse describes as "one-dimensional". One-dimensional thought can subsist even in light of capitalism's many irrationalities because thought is barred from finding rational solutions in the realm of meaningful social alternatives. The material and intellectual capacities to usher in a qualitatively different, more humane society are either limited by the demands of capitalist society or made ineffectual through attenuation.

Marcuse's (1991) interest in culture is an outgrowth of his more universal concept of one-dimensional thought. Included under the category of one-dimensional thought are modes of thinking that certainly differ in their formal attributes. Yet different systems of thought in philosophy, science, politics and culture can all be manifestations of one-dimensional thought because the term describes the social function of thinking. Logical positivism is not the same as idealist philosophy, and these two are not the same as operational behaviourism in business management. However, all can be one-dimensional on the basis of what they achieve:

they reconcile thought with existing modes of behaviour in an established social order. It is this reconciled relationship that is ideological, rather than specific thinking *per se*. For Marcuse (1968e), the

> concept of ideology has meaning only when oriented to the interest of theory in the transformation of the social structure. Neither a sociological nor a philosophical but rather a political concept, it considers a doctrine in relation not to the social conditions of its truth or to an absolute truth but rather to the interest of transformation. (p. 140)

For example, we might watch a film and conclude that it is ideological for what we see to be problematic or apologetic content. Yet, according to Marcuse's critical theory, the ideological quality of the film is never simply about the film itself. The ideological quality is the mediated quality of what its content refers to at a higher degree of analysis: a greater historical project that may or may not have a vested interest in *rationalizing* injustice, alienation and unhappiness in society. For instance, misogynist imagery is less of an ideological issue if it is actually an unfortunate exception to a greater anti-misogynist culture (which is not to say that individual content is beyond all political critique). Conversely, this very same content is ideological when it stands, like other misogynist films, as a particular representation of an established culture of cinema that has *no interest* in transforming the art of cinema into something better (in other words, the particular and the universal are identical here). One of Marcuse's own examples is also illustrative. An empirical analysis of political polling is not ideological simply by virtue of the fact that it is concerned with the data and facts of an established society. Such a study is ideological when the theoretical scope of its quantitative analysis is limited by an idea of democracy that merely assembles aspects of democratic societies in their already existing forms (Marcuse, 1991, p. 118). In this case, there is no tension between the idea of democracy, which has a long intellectual history, and the facts of the polling research. Without any tension between concept and object, these facts appear to be "adequate", and there is also no intellectual room to judge whether or not actual democratic processes fulfill the "historical intent of democracy" (Marcuse, 1991, p. 117). Therefore, this version of political polling is one-dimensional because it has become "circular and self-validating. If 'democratic' is defined in the limiting but realistic terms of the actual process of election, then this process is democratic prior to the results of the investigation" (Marcuse, 1991, p. 116).

According to this conceptualization of ideology, a critique of ideology examines how the reconciliation between thought and society is *false*. With respect to culture, what is of concern is its spiritual dimension, broadly conceived. While the broad spiritual dimension of culture acts as the "background" of a society, cultural values are susceptible to becoming one-dimensional when their "oppositional, alien and transcendent elements" no longer have an antagonistic relationship with the established social reality. For Marcuse, this is a worrisome situation because many cultural values are, in fact, oppositional by virtue of being ideals and beliefs about how a social order *should* function. As a "background" that frames the meaning of actual social behaviour, culture, says Marcuse (1965), "thus appears as the complex of moral, intellectual, aesthetic goals (values) which a society considers the purpose of the organization, division, and direction of its labor – 'the good' that is supposed to be achieved by the way of life it has established" (p. 190).

Like the examples of cinema and democracy earlier, the ideological character of culture is defined by the ways society handles the non-coincidence between cultural representations of historical possibilities and actual social behaviour. Culture is one-dimensional, for example, when its spiritual character is perceived as a matter unto itself, when the imagined possibility for a "better material existence" has no effect on how we collectively value the creation of cultural meaning. Culture is also one-dimensional when unrealized cultural ideals do not create a living tension between the ideas of the "Good Life" and the established social reality (Marcuse, 1968d, p. 121).

Marcuse's definition of culture is specific, as it seeks to highlight the political quality of cultural values. Such a definition of culture, however, allows Marcuse to point to the elements of culture on which vested interests and institutional power can have great impact. Institutional power's impact on culture is clearer in some of Marcuse's more focused analyses, when he is interested in how needs and wants are satisfied, how values and ideas coordinate the behaviour of a community and how the aesthetic dimension is objectified as art. For the remainder of this section, we will analyse how the ideological transformation of transitive meaning into intransitive meaning contributes to the pacification of the tension between cultural values and the facts of social existence.

The problem of transitive meaning becoming intransitive can be seen in the obverse, through the lens of Marcuse's arguments in favour of conceptual thinking. According to Marcuse, concepts *mediate* the transitive properties between apparently disparate aspects of a social universe. This type of mediation is especially important when, in a social universe that is "broken in itself", there are "modes of being in which men and things are 'by themselves' and 'as themselves', and modes in which they are not — that is, in which they exist in distortion, limitation, or denial of their nature (essence)" (Marcuse, 1991, p. 125). For Marcuse (1991), a concept

> is taken to designate the mental representation of something that is understood, comprehended, known as a process of reflection. This something

may be the object of daily practice, or a situation, a society, a novel. In any case, if they are comprehended, they have become objects of thought, and as such, their content and meaning are identical with and yet different from the real objects of immediate experience. "Identical" in as much as the concept denotes the same thing; "different" in as much as the concept is the result of a reflection which has understood the thing in the context (and in the light) of other things which did not appear in the immediate experience and which "explain" the thing (mediation). (p. 105)

Here we can see the influence of Hegel's philosophy on Marcuse's critical theory. For Hegel (1977), a concept is a "movement of knowing" (§166) and it sublates two limited moments of a thought process. The first moment is a limitation that manifests itself through naïve or stubborn attempts to over-determine and inflate a partial truth. The second limitation is expressed in the partial overcoming of the first, when consciousness, on one hand, grasps the partial-truth as partial-truth, but, on the other hand, still "does not know how to free it of one-sidedness, or to maintain it as free". As Yirmiyahu Yovel explains, these two limitations are arresting to a consciousness that is "driven by the law of non-contradiction . . . to exclude one moment because of the other" (Hegel, 2005b, p. 68). Conceptual thinking, for Hegel (1977), is the movement of self-consciousness, which is no longer stymied by the law of non-contradiction. Self-consciousness works through a "double object" (§167). It sees a partial-truth as both a moment (e.g., rationalism) and as a moment "in conflict and in opposition with itself" (e.g., rationalism in conflict with and opposition to empiricism; Hegel, 2005b, p. 68).

Conceptual thought, as proposed by Marcuse, is a tool to uncover problematic intransitive logics in everyday thinking – for example thinking that my gas consumption in North America has nothing to do with wars in the Middle East. Indeed, this habit of bracketing and separating social spheres of activity into mutually exclusive spheres exacerbates, in the words of Marcuse (1991), "a new ideology which undertakes to describe what is happening (and meant) by eliminating the concepts capable of understanding what is happening (and meant)" (p. 178). Our experiences of individual pleasure are good examples of how mass culture is ideological in this sense. Discourse around our experience of mass culture tends to be the effect of accepting that, in capitalism, pleasure is separate from reason or that play is structurally different from labour. Indeed, our language about mass culture need not refer to the more "serious" issues of society because pleasure is affirmed as something "exclusively subjective" (Marcuse, 1968d, p. 167), while the terms and values of the greater social reality are deemed to be of another loftier type. Consequently, the properties of mass culture become resistant to criticism and the meaning of individual pleasure is satisfied through the closed language of modern consumerism:

"Describing to each other our loves and hatreds, sentiments and resentments, we must use the terms of our advertisements, movies, politicians and best sellers. We must use the same terms for describing our automobiles, foods and furniture, colleagues and competitors – and we understand each other perfectly" (Marcuse, 1991, p. 194).

Again, the issue is not that individuals can find pleasure in the world of mass culture. Rather, mass culture, along with all its pleasures, is structured as a social sphere of "non-interference". The meaning of individual pleasure does not touch, nor is it touched by, real differences between consumptive affluence and the general unhappiness of historical circumstances. To allow pleasure to be framed in the context of greater political problems would open the realm of pleasure to "the historical demand for the general liberation of the individual" (Marcuse, 1968a, p. 101).

Moreover, this non-interference of mass culture is institutionalized as the difference between play and work. Small degrees of individual pleasure can be found in types of work in which the social division of labour is less dehumanizing, precarious, monotonous or alienating than in other jobs. Yet work is generally "a whole dimension of human activity and passivity [that] has been de-eroticized. The environment from which the individual could obtain pleasure – which [he or she] could cathect as gratifying almost as an extended zone of the body – has been rigidly reduced" (Marcuse, 1991, p. 73). The play of immediate gratification, in contrast, is marked by its allocation to a delimited space-time of social life. The great range of pleasures available to the modern consumer is repressive to the extent that sublimated activity (e.g. work) is not a place to create a less repressive structure for future work. As the "scope of sublimation" is both restricted and prevented from being transformed, the immediacy of gratification – that is desublimation – is intensified to the point that it appears that individual pleasure equals desublimated activity (Marcuse, 1991, p. 73).[4]

4.3 Conceptualizing capitalist power

As intellectual precedents to a power theory of mass culture, the ideas of Garnham, Babe, Adorno and Marcuse are limited to the extent that they are still connected to Marxist economics and the problems inherent to it. Thus, a gap remains between where we are now (institutional power in historical materialism) and where we hope to go (accumulation-through-power, seen through the capital-as-power approach). We can traverse this gap by thinking more about what would make power in mass culture capitalist in character. As we will see, a capitalist's investment in mass culture is rooted in having institutional power over the creation of culture. This institutional power operates through the symbols, norms and institutions of business enterprise.

As Marx first recognized, a capitalist is driven to accumulate more and more capital. When power is placed at the centre of a political-economic theory of capital accumulation, the capitalist's drive is to use power to accumulate more power. This drive to accumulate power is hardly new in human history, and, in a broad sense, the capitalist has the same fundamental goal as any individual, retinue, class or elite that sought to increase exclusive privileges, benefits or rights at the cost of other people's welfare. However, the *means* by which a capitalist accumulates power is defined by historically specific institutions (the corporation), social logics (accounting and finance), and methods (property, contract law, and state-sanctioned rights).

In the day-to-day workings of business enterprise, owners, bankers, managers, entrepreneurs and accountants all think in terms of prices and the goal is to profit from investment. As we saw in Chapter 2, prices and profit are the phenomena that many economic theories will claim are the observable effects of productivity. Rather, prices in capitalism rest on the ability for owners to generate income through the threat to *withhold* goods and services from society at large. In the case of profiting from culture, the power to threaten the withholding of cultural goods and services depends on the state of *social creativity*, which will be our general term for the ways a society is producing, distributing and accessing the creation of new ideas, meanings, symbols and objects. In the interests of profit, capitalists attempt to control the scope and capacity of social creativity through the rights of ownership, which is a type of authority that rests on the greater social system of private property. Capitalist power and its control over social creativity are never total; this would be impossible when the possibility for change is a quality of *historical* time. Instead, this power over social creation is the desire to impose limits "from above" and repress the potential for a radically democratic form of social creation.

Reference to a political term like *radical democracy* is inspired by Cornelius Castoriadis, who helps us look at social creativity through the lens of institutional power, whether it is capitalist or of another mode. The presence of power in society makes the human capacity to create forms and meanings (*vis formandi*) a political matter. To be sure, humans possess a bare ontological capacity to be creative, which is what makes time *historical*:

> The perpetual self-alteration of society is its very being, which is manifested by the positing of relatively fixed and stable forms-figures and through the shattering of these forms-figures which can never be anything other than the positing-creating of other forms-figures. (Castoriadis, 1998, p. 372)

The social dimension of human creativity is inherently political, as this bare ontological capacity to create other forms and figures has to be applied in a specific social context and with or against the interests of others. Thus, the political character of human creation circles around questions of how and why. How and why, for example, is the "otherness-alteration" of creativity being affirmed or denied by society and its major institutions?[5]

The potential of creativity is radically democratic at its root, according to Castoriadis (1984a), because only a radically democratic politics can affirm "the fact that brute reality is not fixed, but bears within it immense interstices which allow of movement, assembling, alteration, division; and the fact, too, that man [*sic*] is able to insert himself as a real cause in the flux of reality" (p. 240). With respect to the creation of culture, a democratic cultural project would see the novelty and indeterminacy of social-historical creation as a vitamin rather than an allergen: "When an artist begins a work, and even when an author begins a theoretical book, he both does and does not know what he is going to say — even less does he know what that which he will say will actually mean" (Castoriadis, 1998, p. 74). Under different political circumstances, however, the potentials of autonomous creation are perceived as a threat to what Castoriadis calls "an explicit power".

Whether it be legislative, executive, judicial or even what we are calling capitalist power, an explicit power has an instrumental orientation to the ends of social creativity: its particular conservatism against the "perpetual self-alteration of society" is "rooted in the necessity [for the explicit power] to decide what is and is not to be done with respect to the more or less explicit ends which are the objects of the push and drive of the society considered" (Castoriadis, 1991, p. 155). As an instrumental logic oriented to the goal of profit, capital accumulation is antithetical to the open potentials of radically democratic creation. This certainly does not mean that there is no ingenuity behind many of the great technological and artistic achievements of the modern capitalist era. Instead, it means that the popular conception of capitalism relying on creativity or even a "creative class" to achieve economic growth is missing a very important aspect of social creativity. By virtue of what capitalists hope to accomplish, capitalist power is an act of reducing social creativity to a "coherent set of already produced means (instruments) in which this power is embodied" (Castoriadis, 1998, p. 195). And the apparent compatibility of *applied* creativity and the fundamental values of capitalists is a product of people creating this compatibility in society, through the institution of a social order.

The language of power and control might still seem far removed from the financial language of business enterprise, which would be hard-pressed to speak about the employment of labour in stark political terms. Yet is it a surprise we have trouble imagining that the relationship between capital and labour's creative potential is based on power? Standard educations in economics, business and finance are derived from an assumed separation of politics from economics. When perceived as an economic factor – on the assumption that economics and politics are analytically separable – the *vis formandi* of human beings is not a quality that *inherently* needs to be limited, controlled, coerced, repressed or denied by business interests. Rather, the economic picture is deceivingly harmonious in the sense that capital needs creative people to add value and creative people need capital as a factor of production. Indeed, if a free, competitive market existed for both the supply and demand of creativity, great financial successes could go to *any* type of creative innovation that successfully met market demand, especially when the supply of that type of creativity was still below what it "should" be. On matters of taboo, where some products of human creativity need to be limited by a political power – by laws, codes and standards – the economic picture of creativity and innovation does not change in kind. Instead, if one assumes that the boundaries to human creativity come not from actors inside an economy, but from an external political force, the value of human creativity can still be subjected to "the [economic] mechanics of indifference curves, budget lines, production functions and possibilities frontiers" (Nitzan & Bichler, 2009, p. 75).

For those who try to keep politics separated from economic theories of creativity, a thorny methodological issue will appear. Take the theory of creative destruction in the business of mass culture. The history of creativity in mass culture, for example, appears to be ripe for a perspective that uses Schumpeter (2008) to theorize how creative destruction is a metaphor for beneficial economic dynamism. This sector's hyperactivity in artistic and technological progress is seemingly rational because creative destruction will replace old with new and kick-start another cycle of income. For example, writes Doyle (2010),

> creative destruction [appears to relate] to the music sector where the progress of time has been marked by a succession of advances in audio formats, from gramophone to vinyl records to the arrival of CDs which are now being usurped by MP3 digital files. Each successive innovation has brought opportunity, success and growth for some players. (p. 250)

The thorn in the side of this theory comes in follow-up questions: Why did the new replace the old in that way and at that time? We can clearly see the signs of dynamism in mass culture, but how do we know that creative destruction is beneficial to society? In Doyle's terms, what is the social value that tells us that creative destruction is "good" rather than "destructive destruction" – "i.e. a phase in which businesses are eradicated but without any positive benefits being created"? (Doyle, 2010, p. 251).

These questions demand an answer that goes beyond a tautological reference to prices – for example any technological progress that is profitable is creative destruction, while the evolution of technology is merely destructive and wasteful when it is not. Neither is the answer satisfied by counting creativity in the amount of stuff that is made or how many times an artistic or technological method is renovated by innovation; counting creative destruction would suggest that any large increase or big change is *ipso facto* useful. Instead, the answer is found in the very place that, according to Doyle, makes the economics of culture a problematic theory. What is or is not beneficial, pleasurable or useful about cultural objects depends on what *cultural and political ideas* hold court at a certain moment in time. Similarly, the meaning of creativity is defined by a system of social significations that frame, in the words of Castoriadis (1998), what "is and is not, what is relevant and what is not, [and] the weight, the value . . . of what is relevant" (p. 234).

The social meaning of culture, especially its symbolic meaning (Doyle, 2010, p. 246), opens the floodgates to methodological problems in attempts to keep an economic definition of creativity separate from politics and power. In a historical circumstance in which a creative endeavour has the choice to affirm what already exists as much as it has the capacity to, in the more philosophical language of Castoriadis, become the radical creation of other forms, the business of culture is never simply about what gets produced but about the scope of creativity: Why are some ideas approved, and why are others rejected or severely modified for the purposes of business? Are some ideas naturally unprofitable? Even in the hypothetical situation in which firms are so small that they are necessarily passive with respect to the needs and wants of consumers, the business of mass culture still needs to make decisions that will refer to an established world of social signification. Thus, even a weak decision about what gets produced is already marked by the existence of social power. Unless the world of social significations is the product of the *demos* autonomously limiting itself around a set of values, the business of mass culture is faced with the fact that the meaning of its creativity is less about consumer sovereignty and more about what cultural and political values are reinforced by the presence of society's major institutions – for example education, religion, science, government and the military. What sort of cultural commodity should a firm produce when dominant groups in society have clear preferences for only some ideas, values and norms?

When some capitalist firms are themselves large enough to actively participate in the very construction of social meaning, the presumed societal benefits of creative destruction become even more opaque. Note that for Schumpeter, the practice of creative destruction by big business was meant to be a substitute for what was traditionally accomplished by small entrepreneurs in a less concentrated market. Lest he accept that big business can become a "perfectly bureaucratized giant industrial unit" that "ousts the small and medium-sized firm", Schumpeter (2008, p. 134) believed that even big businesses cannot relax their attention to technological innovation. The giant firm, *even when in a monopoly position*, "will always adopt a new method of production which it believes will yield a larger stream of future income per unit of the corresponding stream of future outlay, both discounted to the present, than does the method actually in use" (Schumpeter, 2008, p. 97).

The partial truth of Schumpeter's writing lies in the fact that these calculations are a matter of prices and profit, not much else. Yet even the largest firms are compelled, according to Schumpeter (2008), to make beneficial contributions to technological progress because "the capitalist engine in motion comes from the new consumer's goods, the new methods of production or transportation, the new markets, the new forms of industrial organization that capitalist enterprise creates" (p. 83). What Schumpeter neglected, however, were the opportunities for dominant firms to transform the principle of creative destruction itself by significantly influencing the very social-historical meaning of "new" technological improvements.

We overlook the ability of dominant firms to shape the social meaning of creativity when, as Nitzan and Bichler (2009) argue, we continue to assume that the market is like a Newtonian container:

> Its particles – the utility maximizing investors-consumers – act and react on one another according to the rules of the market, but they have no bearing on the rules as such. These rules are eternally fixed, making market space independent and absolute. (p. 279)

Things look different when a social space like the market is not independent of the bodies that move and interact within it but rather is the "order of the things" (Nitzan & Bichler, 2009, p. 278). In other words, when some firms are exponentially larger than others (measured by employees, revenues, income or market capitalization), their gravitational force can bend the curvature of the social space they and other firms occupy together. The work of Fix (2019) can help us visualize this difference in the perspectives on capitalist space. To understand the relationship between energy use, hierarchy and income inequality, Fix models the differences between a typical subsistence society and an industrial society (as shown in Figure 4.1). His spatial model of industrial society – modeled from case studies, employment data and firm-size distributions – shows us the sizes of the institutional "pyramids" that exist in contemporary society. From the perspective of Bichler and Nitzan, this is an unlikely environment where a firm, *regardless of size and relative power*, is unable to affect the *terms* of market activity. In fact, the classic assumptions of free market activity have a better "home" in Fix's model of a subsistence society – despite the high likelihood that an actual subsistence society would organize production and consumption through tradition and command (Heilbroner, 1992; Polanyi, 2001).

In the case of mass culture in the twentieth and twenty-first centuries, sets of large firms significantly bend the social space in which they also produce culture for pleasure and profit. Thus, while the largest firms rely on the creative powers of their labour force, the means and ends of controlling social creativity change when capitalists can take a leading role in shaping the world they hope

Subsistence Society

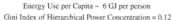

Energy Use per Capita ~ 6 GJ per person
Gini Index of Hierarchical Power Concentration = 0.12

Industrial Society

Energy Use per Capita ~ 350 GJ per person
Gini Index of Hierarchical Power Concentration = 0.76

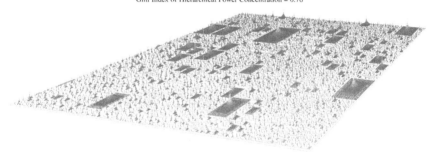

FIGURE 4.1   Differences in space: subsistence versus industrial societies

Source: Fix (2019).

Note: Used with author's permission.

to profit from. Oligopolies in mass culture allow for each repetition, stagnation or repression of social creativity to be called by other names, for example inventive, imaginative, exciting and, most important, new. This effect of redefining the boundaries of mass culture is not just about what is massively popular – for example pop music, blockbuster film, primetime television and so on. It is also about dominant firms having a strong ability to reject, deny or modify the desire of creative labour to experiment, pursue alternatives, and even dislocate meaning through "otherness-alteration". It is the contemporary version of what Castoriadis (1995) described regarding the beginnings of the bourgeois era:

> The result was the appearance, for the first time in history, of the phenome-
> non of the avant-garde and of an artist who is "misunderstood," not "by

accident" but of necessity. For, the artist was reduced at that time to the following dilemma: to be bought by the bourgeois of the Third Republic — to become an official pompier-style artist — or to follow his/her own genius and to sell, if lucky, a few canvases for five or six francs. (p. 109)

When a firm's ability to negate the potential of creativity is this influential, the separation between economics and politics is wholly untenable. Investment will still involve some type of production, but it can now also depend on the ability of alternative forms of human ingenuity to be neglected, marginalized or repressed by the authority of others. Labour and the costs of production still matter, but the strategies of business enterprise have an authoritative element when large firms can also set the terms of social creativity. Furthermore, this power can be specifically characterized as capitalist power the more we pull away from the assumption that institutional power is secondary or external to the "real" story of economic productivity, however measured. Indeed, as Garnham (1995) argued, we should use political economy to understand power in modern culture because giant conglomerates in the business of culture are able to profit from their active influence over the manner in which meaning is created, stories are told and social creativity finds its means to objectify itself in art.

4.4 The capital-as-power approach

The capital-as-power approach, first developed by Shimshon Bichler and Jonathan Nitzan, is a political economic theory that argues that we need to conceptualize captial *as* power rather than seeing power as something that interacts *with* capital. Ideally, the presentation of the capital-as-power approach would work through all its theoretical lineages – some philosophical but mostly in the history of political economic theory. For the sake of space, let us introduce the capital-as-power approach through its major connection with Veblen. The Veblen–Bichler–Nitzan connection: this is where we can start to see how our research interest in mass culture and capital accumulation can go beyond thinking of capitalist power in the abstract. The capital-as-power approach builds a critical research project on top of three aspects of Veblen's political economic theory:

1   the distinction between business and industry,
2   the concept of strategic sabotage and
3   the function of capitalization.

4.4.1 Veblen's concept of capital

In the interest of breaking the theoretical dualism of economics and politics – a dualism that is often exclusively reserved for capitalist societies – we must be willing to rethink our concept of capital. If capital is forever an economic magnitude anchored in production, research questions about political-economic power will always start from the margins. Thorstein Veblen's approach gives a better starting point: from the word "Go!" he rejects the productivist-economic approach to defining value. To be sure, the nature of productive activity is important to Veblen, particularly with the rise of the "Industrial Age". However, he also believes people misunderstand capitalism when they deem productivity to be the substance of profit:

> It has commonly been assumed by economists, without much scrutiny, that the gains which accrue from invested wealth are derived from and (roughly) measured by the productivity of the industrial process in which the items of wealth so invested are employed, productivity being counted in some terms of material serviceability to the community, conduciveness to the livelihood, comfort, or consumptive needs of the community. . . . The aggregate gains of the aggregate material capital accrue from the community's industrial activity, and bear some relation to the productive capacity of the industrial traffic so engrossed. But it will be noted that there is no warrant in the analysis of these phenomena as here set forth for alleging that the gains of investment bear a relation of equality or proportion to the material serviceability of the capital goods, as rated in terms of effectual usefulness to the community. (Veblen, 2006a, pp. 353–354)

While Marxists laugh to themselves that neoclassical economics assumes that price is a reflection of the utility generated by a good, they also assume a material substance of their own: socially necessary abstract labour time. Capitalism in Marxism is understood through the interaction of two layers: nominal price (appearance) and real value (essence). While rejecting one "real" measure (utility), the Marxist economist accepts another (labour time).

As Figure 4.2 shows, too much emphasis on the productivity of labour will likely produce severe empirical blind spots in a political economy of mass culture. This figure looks at the income of major studios in Hollywood and the compensation of employees in US film production. In Figure 4.2A, we have a benchmarked comparison of two series: the average operating profits of the major Hollywood studios (which we are calling Major Filmed Entertainment) and the average employee compensation for US motion pictures. Figure 4.2B is a ratio of the two. Figure 4.2C plots the rate of change of Major Filmed Entertainment's operating income per firm and the rate of change of employee compensation. The ratio of profit to labour compensation and the relationship between their annual changes both *undermine* an imagined relationship between capital and labour productivity in Hollywood, a major sector of mass culture. Hollywood's profitability is moving up and down for some *reason* or

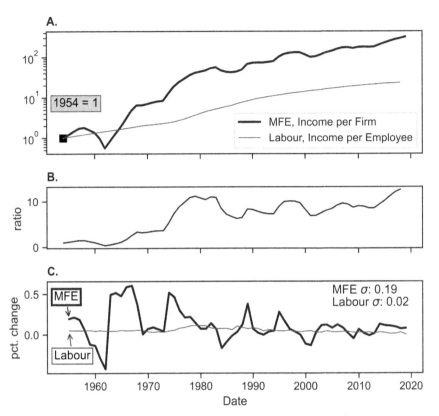

FIGURE 4.2 Major Filmed Entertainment (MFE) income versus labour income in Hollywood, 1950–2019

Source: COMPUSTAT through WRDS for operating income and revenues of Major Filmed Entertainment, 1950–1992. Annual reports of Disney, News Corp, Viacom, Sony, Time Warner (Management's Discussion of Business Operations for information on their filmed entertainment interests) for operating income of Major Filmed Entertainment, 1993–2019. Global Insight for US CPI, Compensation of Employees and Employed, Full & Part Time.

Note: Series in A are smoothed as 5-year moving averages.

reasons, but its profitability does not correlate with changes to the cost of its labour (Pearson's *r* for Figure 4.2C = +0.096).

Veblen's approach to capital accumulation does have a duality of sorts – industry and business – but his dualism avoids the problem of basing "real" value on a conception of productivity, whether defined by neoclassical economics or Marxism. Veblen does not regard capital, which belongs entirely to business, as a two-sided affair of nominal and so-called real economic value. Rather, an asset "is a pecuniary concept, not a technological one; a concept of business, not of industry". The same can be said of so-called tangible capital goods:

> Capital goods, which typically make up the category of tangible assets, are capital goods by virtue of their technological serviceability, but they are capital in the measure, not of their technological serviceability, but in the measure of the income which they may yield to their owner. (Veblen, 2006a, p. 359)

Veblen does not deny the influences of technological efficiency and the sweat of labour on the success of business; production is a necessary condition for business. But capitalization, the discounting of future expected earnings to present prices, does not measure the level of technology or the efficiency of the production process; it simply measures the ability to make a profit. Note the absence of material productivity in this definition of capital:

> The capital value of a business concern at any given time, its purchase value as a going concern, is measured by the capitalized value of its presumptive earnings; which is a question of its presumptive earning-capacity and of the rate or co-efficient of capitalization currently accepted at the time; and the second of these two factors is intimately related to the rate of discount ruling at the time. (Veblen, 2004, p. 219)

What do these observations mean for the measurement of capital? Bichler and Nitzan point to Veblen's essential insight: prices and earnings do not reflect "productivity *per se*" but "the control of productivity for capitalist ends" (Nitzan & Bichler, 2009, p. 223). Without an institutional ability to carve out a piece of society-wide productivity (industry) through the socio-legal power of private ownership, business is a *valueless* institution (Nitzan & Bichler, 2000, p. 78). We know this when we try to measure the social benefits of industry *independently of ownership*. Society-wide productivity can be "valued" without prices, but only in political and cultural definitions of wealth and purpose. Economists wish to translate these political and cultural definitions into economic units of utility, but Veblen sees faults in their approach. First, Veblen argues that industry cannot be broken down into discrete pieces of productivity because each "thing" in industry is a product of "the whole fabric of human knowledge, including the sciences, technology and . . . underlying cultrual traits" (Nitzan & Bichler, 2000, p. 78). Second, economists believe they can explain the distribution of income with discrete pieces of productivity, but, in this belief, business has already divided and distributed industry *from the outside*, through an ability to exclude others from accessing what has become private property.

4.4.2 Business as strategic sabotage

Ownership is always, at root, a form of control over what is owned. In the terminology of Veblen (2004), the owner derives an income from their legal rights to *sabotage* industry, which is an act of business keeping "the work out of the hands of the workmen and the product out of the market" (p. 66). Nitzan and Bichler (2009) emphasize that sabotage through the right of private ownership need not be exercised: "What matters is the right to exclude and the ability to exact terms for not exercising that right" (p. 228). Moreover, the sabotage of industry is strategic. The best strategy for business is to charge what the "traffic will bear" – to use one of Veblen's favourite phrases. Charging what the traffic will bear, for Veblen (2004),

> consists, on the one hand, in stopping down production to such a volume as will bring the largest net returns in terms of price, and in allowing so much of a livelihood to the working force of technicians and workmen, on the other hand, as will induce them to turn out this limited output. It evidently calls for a shrewd balancing of production against price, such as is best served by a hard head and a cool heart. (p. 67)

Elsewhere in *Absentee Ownership*, Veblen (2004) emphasizes this point by calling sabotage "A Conscientious Withdrawal of Efficiency" (p. 218). Conscientiousness in this case is not insignificant, as too little sabotage can be just as disastrous for capitalization as too much. While the community at large may benefit from a free run of industrial production, business would not.

With respect to a political economy of mass culture, Veblen shows us how we can sidestep, rather than wrestle, the types of problems we saw in Chapter 3. The dollars and cents of mass culture do not reflect technological efficiency or the "real" economic value of artists, writers, actors, playwrights, designers, copy editors and so on. As a community of patrons we might find some products of mass culture to be beneficial, pleasurable or useful, but, according to Veblen, these are judgements about the state of industry, which does not directly translate into the pecuniary value of business. The gains of business are differential gains related to the socio-legal institutions that determine the distribution of industrial production (Veblen, 2006b).

By focusing on the Hollywood film business, we can add particulars to our conceptualization of strategic sabotage in mass culture. Figure 4.3 is an attempt to paint a broad picture of strategic sabotage in the history of Hollywood cinema. On the x-axis we have the theatrical releases of the Motion Picture Association of America (MPAA), which is a near-perfect overlap with Major Filmed Entertainment. The releases are plotted as 10-year per cent changes – for example 1950 equals the per cent change from 1941 to 1950. The y-axis presents a 10-year per cent change of US ticket prices, divided by the US consumer price index (CPI). We divide by the CPI because we want to see how Hollywood's major studios and theatrical exhibitors can, relative to rising prices across all sectors, charge what the traffic may bear. As a kernel density estimate of the balancing of production against price, Figure 4.3 demonstrates that the major trend in the business of Hollywood is to reduce or stagnate production and raise prices faster than general inflation. The

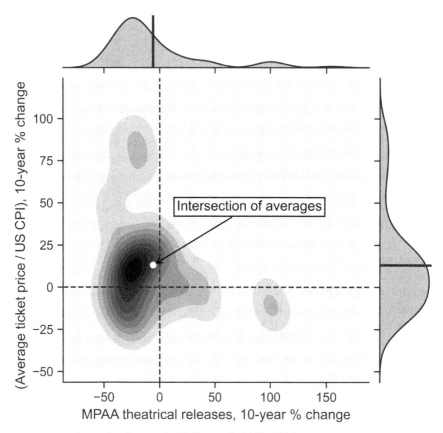

FIGURE 4.3 Strategic sabotage in Hollywood, 1933–2019

Source: Finler (2003, pp. 376–377) for MPAA releases from 1933–2002; MPAA Theatrical Market Statistics for MPAA releases from 2003–2019. http://natoonline.org/data/admissions/ and boxofficemojo.com/about/adjuster for average US theatrical ticket prices from 1933–2019; missing values are interpolated with a linear trend. Global financial data for US consumer price index (CPI).

Note: Per cent changes are from 10 years prior.

minor trend is to allow for an increase in theatrical releases, but at the cost of being able to increase prices in the same period. Noticeably absent is any positive trend between production and increases in ticket price.[6]

For the film business to be able to throttle the pace of the film industry, institutional conditions are required. In order to exist, business enterprise must be able to threaten to withhold the products of industry it controls, because, as Nitzan and Bichler (2009) remind us, free, limitless production is not a sound business strategy:

> The only way... spending [on productive capacity] can become profit-yielding investment is if others are prohibited from freely utilizing its

outcome. In this sense, capitalist investment – regardless of how "productive" it may appear or how much growth it seems to "generate" – remains what it always was: an act of limitation. (p. 233)

To have any price attached to a film, whether profitable or not, there must be an effective claim of ownership on that film. The claim of ownership must mean something to the particular person or group that holds it, and it must be embedded in a general system of private property, where the exclusion of one's property from others is effective. Abstracted from the social structures that support them, claims of ownership are useless pieces of paper or empty entitlements. The real ability to keep everyone else's hands off of your claim is nothing but social power that is expressed through the state, laws, the courts, the police and an established culture of private property and exclusive rights (Nitzan & Bichler, 2009, p. 228).

Seen through the prism of the film business, the products of the film industry should be private property and sold to the consumer at a price. While the absentee owner-investor may know next to nothing about how a film is made (as that is a matter of industrial technique), they may nonetheless be interested in how the material properties of the produced film will serve the goals of strategic sabotage. For instance, relevant to the film business is the "indivisibility" of the film image. Indivisibility refers to how one person's consumption of a film does not exhaust the physical capacity for someone else to watch in tandem (Sedgwick & Pokorny, 2005, p. 13). Certainly, the indivisibility of a film is not infinite. There are technological and physical limits to how many people can watch the same image from the same screen (even though the internet is breaking all sorts of spatial barriers to how people can access motion pictures). However, unlike the physical properties of a car, which excludes potential passengers with a rigid steel frame, there is (currently) no way for the light of the film image to selectively transmit to the eyes of only some people in an audience. Whether Hollywood likes it or not, the number of people who can watch a rented DVD in a friend's living room depends on the size of the living room and not the DVD.

From the earliest days of film, the business side has needed means of exclusion to manage this "problem" of indivisibility. For instance, from the 1900s to the late 1910s, the major power to repress the possibility of indiscriminate exhibition – indiscriminate according to business principles – was the Motion Picture Patent Company, the "Edison Trust". Spearheaded by Thomas Edison himself, the Edison Trust leveraged its pool of patents over film technology to set prices. The Trust also attempted to control how many movies were made, what types of movies were made, and where movies were shown (Litman, 1998, p. 10; Wu, 2010, p. 64). Tim Wu (2010) explains the consequence of such power:

In the name of avoiding "ruinous" competition, [the Motion Picture Patent Company] pooled sixteen key patents, blocked most film exports, and fixed prices at every step of filmmaking and exhibition. There was, for instance, a set price per foot of film that distributors would pay producers, another price (originally $2 per week) that exhibitors paid for use of patented Trust-owned projectors, and so on. (p. 64)

To benefit from the blessings of the trust, producers and exhibitors (owners of nickelodeons) were required to align themselves exclusively with the Trust and not acquire independent or foreign technology for the production and exhibition of films (Litman, 1998, p. 10).

Another example of indivisibility, this time from the sphere of law, concerns the privileges of exhibiting a film for others. The technological evolution of film exhibition, through the inventions of VHS, DVD and Blu-ray Disc, is a *problem* for business if, in the absence of copyrights, open-ended viewing is left unchecked (Decherney, 2012; Wasser, 2002). Copyright law protects the rights of business by setting the terms of what an individual can do with their possession of a film copy. If one exhibits a film for private home viewing, it is unnecessary to acquire a license in addition to what is granted through the purchase for personal consumption. If one begins to imagine they can share their copy of a film outside of a private setting, laws such as the US Federal Copyright Act define all the social environments where one would need to acquire a license for "public performance". Swank Motion Pictures Inc. (2016), a company that is an intermediary distributor for public performances of films, makes it clear that a public performance license would need to be purchased for almost any social setting outside of the home:

> This legal copyright compliance requirement applies to everyone, regardless of whether admission is charged, whether the institution is commercial or non-profit or whether a federal, state or local agency is involved. This means colleges, universities, public schools, public libraries, daycare facilities, parks, recreation departments, summer camps, churches, private clubs, prisons, lodges, businesses and more all must properly license movies to show them publically [*sic*]. (p. 2)

The technologically skilled reader might now be thinking of how easy it is to find a pirated copy of a Hollywood film. This same reader might also be thinking of open-source software, or how copyright law is not governing our everyday interactions with cultural objects, which can be copied, transformed or altered (Coombe, 1998). But Veblen's theory of business enterprise is not incompatible with our contemporary, mostly digital, reality. Business enterprise might tolerate a degree of piracy or embrace some open-source projects, but Veblen's key point about strategic sabotage is that business *cannot* look at the creative value of industry the same way a community of people would. According to Veblen, we can see incompatible perspectives when we think about what "overproduction" means for business enterprise. Based on his split between business and industry, Veblen (2006c) notes that overproduction applies "not to the material, mechanical bearing of the situation, but to its pecuniary bearing" (p. 215). The output of industry may not exceed the "consumptive capacity of the underlying population," but the same level of output may threaten prices that concern the vested interests of business. Thus, the Hollywood film business might not be able to prevent all piracy, or it could sometimes be good for business to allow for the free dissemination of cinematic images through social media or on the internet. But Veblen (2006c) sees very clearly that business interests need to be holding the reins of industry, as these interests "do not see their way to derive a satisfactory gain from letting the industrial process go forward on the lines and in the volume for which the material equipment of industry is designed" (p. 213).

With this in mind, we can start to think of situations that would be beneficial to the art of film but nightmarish for the business of film. From the standards of aesthetics and democratic principles, free public performances and an open culture of sharing could energize the world of cinema. Free public access to motion pictures, for instance, could be the catalyst for an engaged assembly of moviegoers, and engaged assembly could in turn enliven those in the film industry who know that the principle of producing "cheaply and interestingly made distractions" (Bloch, 1988, p. 27) has nothing to do with aesthetics and everything to do with profit. Could absentee owners of film property ever embrace these alternative, democratic principles?

In the words of Adorno (2004c), owners are all too happy for freedom during leisure time to be "functionalized, extended and reproduced by business" (p. 190). Prices and income depend on how the art of film serves the order of business. This "harmony" is never without power. We saw how power is used to manage the material indivisibility of the film image. In addition, film businesses must manage and control the material quality of reproducibility. As Walter Benjamin (1968b) notes, in principle all art is reproducible: "Man-made artifacts could always be imitated by men [*sic*]" (p. 218). However, the techniques of mechanical reproduction represent something new for artistry. While the methods of founding and stamping go back to the time of ancient Greece, the more contemporary methods of reproduction are revolutionary in at least one important respect: reproduction is now inherent in the very technology of artistic creation. This feature is especially true for films and photography. The uniqueness and permanence of an authentic artwork have been superseded by mass production, where there is no concern that an original artwork precedes the reproduction of facsimiles. Benjamin (1968b) explains: "From a photographic negative, for example, one can make any number of prints; to ask for the 'authentic' print makes no sense" (p. 224). If Benjamin sees in film production an opportunity for the *demos* to reject ritual and any heteronomous reverence for the aura of tradition, the film business that he fails to adequately consider sees something else. For the film business at large, the reproducibility of the film image is a potentiality that needs to be tamed and kept at "reasonable" levels. Power from above is needed to repress the promise that Benjamin sees in the film image and contemporary art: the indeterminate, radical potential of mechanical reproduction.

In more recent times, this conflict over the effects of mechanical reproduction connects to business's struggle against piracy in digital culture. The modern notion of piracy has deep origins. Adrian Johns notes the connection to the much older idea of seafaring pirates. Thucydides understood that the stability of the Greek city-states depended on their ability to repress *peiratos*, "seagoing coastal warlords" (Johns, 2009, p. 35). And since the seventeenth century, there has been a new breed of pirates, those who violate someone else's privilege to reproduce or withhold a work. At stake in this violation is the power relationship between "creativity, communication, and commerce" (Johns, 2009, p. 5).

Ignoring for the moment the morality of cultural piracy – some of Europe's greatest thinkers, such as Newton and Hume, put up no resistance when they learned that their work was shared with the public through piratical means – Europe's earliest *pyrates*, from the late 1600s to the 1800s, ignored everything from exclusive patents given through royal decree to common customs of registration. As a consequence, many sectors, but particularly in bookselling, used privilege and property rights to repress technological alternatives to "authentic" works. For example, English booksellers purchased rights to print from an author, had a royal patent, or belonged to an organization like the Company of Stationers. Johns (2009) describes the latter: "the Stationers' Company received its royal charter . . . in 1557 from Queen Mary. The company was to embrace all participants in the trade, binders, booksellers, and printers alike. . . . It had a remit to police its members to forestall seditious printing" (p. 24). Contained in Stationers' Hall was a registry book that the company used to determine who had registered a text first. The company also held court to decide between competing claims over the same book or similar enough texts. However, formal rules were not the only means open to the company. Employing tactics similar to those of Charles II, the company focused on associating the bookseller with the moral codes of a noble gentleman; his virtue was meant to provide a differential advantage in bookselling. When that tactic failed, authors would sometimes personally sign copies of their books to undermine false editions – at the extreme, Lawrence Sterne signed over 12,000 copies of *Tristram Shandy* (Johns, 2009, pp. 33–49).

Compared to the complexity of current intellectual property laws, the early methods of defending against piracy through ideas of honour and nobility seem embarrassingly unsophisticated. However, there is a clear connection with present techniques: back then, outsiders, renegades, anti-imperialists, and anti-monopolists – many of whom resided in Dublin, before English copyright laws were successfully applied to Ireland – were violating a major taboo of modern times by circumventing the reach of intellectual property law and custom (Johns, 2009, pp. 145–147). For the sellers of cinema, the unlawful reproduction of a film, in whole or in part, is perceived to be a drain on the power of related propriety claims. Furthermore, new technologies that allow the private citizen to watch a film at home must not subsequently create new avenues for illegal recording and copying – again, the technological creations of industry can threaten business if the latter does not put the clamp on the former. For example, before intellectual property rights caught up with Betamax, the major distributors that had hitherto relied on theatrical exhibition were hostile to Sony, Betamax's owner. As Maltby (2003) recounts, "Jack Valenti [the president of the MPAA] declared that [Betamax] was a parasite likely to kill moviegoing, and in 1976, Universal and Disney brought a lawsuit against Sony claiming that its Betamax machine encouraged infringement of copyright and arguing that its manufacture should be prohibited" (p. 192). Through this behaviour, Hollywood was involved in what Tim Wu (2010) calls the "Kronos Effect": "the efforts undertaken by a dominant company to consume potential successors in their infancy" (p. 25). When Betamax eventually succumbed to VHS, the latter was no longer perceived as a threat because the dominant business interests had by then adapted and incorporated home viewing through changes to copyright law.

4.4.3 The capitalization of mass culture

As an aspect of business, this power over the pace and direction of industry is connected to the common terms and symbols of modern finance. If capital is an index of strategic sabotage, as Bichler and Nitzan argue, the quantities of capital are a symbolic representation of a power struggle: "a conflict between dominant capital groups, acting against opposition, to shape and restructure the course of social reproduction at large. In this struggle, what gets accumulated is not productivity as such, but the ability to subjugate creativity to power" (Nitzan & Bichler, 2009, p. 218).

Bichler and Nitzan readily acknowledge that such claims about capital cannot be made trivially. So much of our common language about capital accumulation implies that the true foundation of magnitudes of capital lies in the realm of productivity. However, Nitzan and Bichler (2009) conceptualize captial *as* power with the help of Veblen, who was deeply sceptical that the quantities of capital could ever be measures of industrial production:

> If capital and capital goods were indeed the same "thing," [Veblen] asked, how could capital move from one industry to another, while capital goods, the "abiding entity" of capital, remained locked in their original position? Similarly, how could a business crisis diminish the value of capital

when, as a material productive substance, the underlying capital goods remained unaltered? Or how could existing capital be denominated in terms of its productivity, when technological progress seemed to destroy its pecuniary value? (p. 231)

According to Bichler and Nitzan, Veblen's distinction between business and industry carries over into the quantitative dimension of capital. The quantitative dimension of capitalist power is the "pecuniary capitalization of earning capacity. It consists not of [what is owned] . . . but of the present value of profits expected to be earned by virtue of such ownership" (Nitzan & Bichler, 2009, p. 231). In other words, strategic sabotage, according to Bichler and Nitzan, is the institutional backbone of capitalization. In this sense, capitalists are looking to the overall state of society in order to judge how expected earnings from strategic sabotage will eventually translate into actual earnings, what risk premium they should factor in and what should be considered the normal rate of return.

Later in this section we will investigate what the forward-looking characteristic of capitalization means for the social dimensions of mass culture. For now, let us pause to unpack the significance of defining capitalization as the power of ownership, instead of the so-called economic value of what is owned. As Bichler and Nitzan argue, neoclassical and Marxist approaches both interpret the meaning of capitalization with their respective assumptions that capital is a material-productive magnitude at its core. Assumptions of this type produce methodological problems that involve explaining how capitalization can either be a mirror-like reflection of productivity or entirely fictional, in relation to "real" capital. Instead of repeating Chapter 10 of *Capital as Power*, which is where the interested reader would find Bichler and Nitzan's critique of the productivity-capitalization relationship, we can see the *disconnect* between capitalization and the value of industry with an example from mass culture's graveyard: Blockbuster Video.

Older readers will remember the heights Blockbuster Video reached before it fell into bankruptcy. For much of 1990s and early 2000s, Blockbuster was *the* dominant firm in video distribution. Its blue-and-yellow stores numbered in the thousands, and they were everywhere in the United States (and in Canada, where I am from). As it was enjoying its significant market share of video rentals, Blockbuster was approached by a small start-up, Netflix, which tried to sell itself to Blockbuster for $50 million. Blockbuster not only refused, but it is reported that Blockbuster's CEO, John Antioco, also tried to contain his laughter at the meeting when the offer of sale was made (Levin, 2019).

Figure 4.4 plots the market capitalization of Blockbuster, Netflix and the S&P 500 – all rebased so January 31, 2006, equals 1. Figure 4.4 is a plot of financial qualities, but it is easy for the average moviegoer to read between the lines and recall what happened to Blockbuster after it refused to merge with a much smaller Netflix. As Netflix grew its DVD rental service and built a streaming service

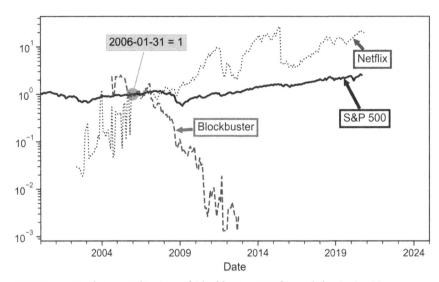

FIGURE 4.4   Market capitalization of Blockbuster, Netflix and the S&P 500

Source: Global Financial Data for the market capitalization of Blockbuster (BLIAQ1B), Netflix (NFLX) and the S&P 500 (SCSP500D).

Note: All series have been rebased, where the data point for January 31, 2006, equals 1.

(video-on-demand), Blockbuster was reporting losses and closing physical stores at an alarming rate. As Netflix became a "must-have" digital streaming service for younger audiences, the obsolescence of getting in your car and driving to your nearest Blockbuster Video store became a joke in John Mulaney's stand-up: "I was once on the telephone with Blockbuster Video — which is a very old-fashioned sentence".

Nevertheless, the fall of Blockbuster cannot be about *what* the firm owned. Why? Because for much of this story – before Netflix carried exclusive in-house titles – Blockbuster and Netflix virtually owned the same thing: non-theatrical distribution rights of film titles from the major Hollywood studios. If market value was tied to the productivity of these distribution rights, how could Blockbuster crash at the same time that Netflix soared in market value? The market value of Blockbuster was crashing because the strength of its strategic sabotage – the threat to withhold non-theatrical distribution rights of film titles for a price – was being undermined by a changing culture in movie streaming, for which Netflix was adapted and able to still command a price for its rentals. Furthermore, what Blockbuster owned was still technically valuable as industry; its rentals were still high-quality Hollywood films. Blockbuster was failing as a business, which simply is a measure of Blockbuster's ability to have future streams of income.

Figure 4.5 confirms that the capital of Blockbuster was not the same as its capital goods or intangible assets. Figure 4.5A plots the price-to-book ratios of

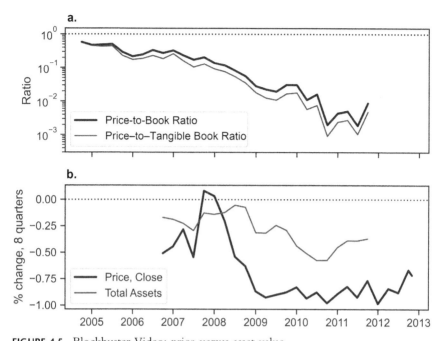

FIGURE 4.5   Blockbuster Video: price versus asset value

Source: Global Financial Data for the market capitalization and quarterly fundamentals of Blockbuster (BLIAQ1B).

Blockbuster, which is commonly used to judge if a stock is over- or undervalued with respect to the book value of its assets. Figure 4.5B demonstrates that the market value of Blockbuster fell faster than its assets, which might have decreased through liquidation sales, not devaluation. If future expected earnings (price) are tied to the productivity of its assets (book value), Figure 4.5 suggests that Blockbuster was technically "undervalued". Yet when we recognize the problems with this two-sided assumption about price reflecting productivity, it is less puzzling why the market value could deviate from the so-called productivity of what was owned. The market value of Blockbuster was a product of declining expectations about the ability of Blockbuster to strategically sabotage stores full of videos and DVDs *in the future.*

The disconnect between industrial productivity and capitalization does not disappear when we study the social dimensions of mass culture. Much of mass culture can be described as productive labour in a more sociological sense: people make, shape, consume and circulate meaning through their ideological and material activities, both inside and outside of work. However, there is a slight but crucial difference between the capital-as-power approach and frameworks that want to incorporate technology, labour and consumer activity into their theories of value. While the latter frameworks will commonly offer convincing reasons for a political economic theory of culture to include creativity, desire, meaning, and context in its concept of capital accumulation, they will also maintain that, ultimately, an expanded or inclusive concept of capital is still rooted in the productivity of its inputs.

Take, for example, the two-stage argument that splits the apparent difference between brand value and brand equity. Descriptions of brand value are, essentially, definitions of capitalization: Brand value is the

> financial valuation given to a branded product, service or company in terms of income, potential income, reputation, prestige, and market value. (Willmott, 2010, p. 525)

> In practice, income-based models typically use a discounted cash flow (DCF) of the value of brands, in which future cash flows are discounted to a "net present rate" using a discount rate intended to reflect the risk of those cash flows. (Moor & Lury, 2011, p. 442)

The next step in the argument is to claim that brand value is the process of monetizing brand equity, which is a complicated and sometimes obscure measure of a firm's immaterial wealth. In other words, brand value is the pricing of the future earning potential and risk of brand equity, which is composed of all the productive processes, both inside and outside the firm, that go into establishing brand loyalty and consumer preferences.

Many of the same social elements can be found in the capital-as-power approach. A noticeable similarity is the scope of capitalization:

> [W]e can say that in capitalism most social processes are capitalized, directly or indirectly. Every process — whether focused on the individual, societal or ecological levels — impacts the level and pattern of capitalist earnings. And when earnings get capitalized, the processes that underlie them get integrated into the numerical architecture of capital. (Nitzan & Bichler, 2009, p. 166)

However, an important difference lies in what capitalist ownership involves, or, more important, what it does *not* involve. An investment, whether it includes production in a factory, involves the use of an immaterial idea or relies on social knowledge or the behaviour of individuals in social settings, is simply the legal right to claim future earnings from ownership. For example, as an *industrial art*, filmmaking is an integrated composite of human knowledge and social activity. A film relies on the historical development of human knowledge about light, sound, storytelling, verbal and non-verbal communication and so on; it also draws from the development of ideas about style, setting and mood; and it can draw freely from the many sharable aspects of cinematic art: its methods, techniques, philosophies and even many of the ideas involved in making a film. When filmmaking is a business concern, many of these productive elements in art have *zero earning potential* because their use and application cannot be protected through copyrights or other means of exclusion. For instance, there is no copyright for the genre of horror or the idea that a good story involves a protagonist and an antagonist.

Thus, the capitalization of mass culture looks out into social dimensions of culture, but it does so with an eye to the claims of ownership that can actually be capitalized and bought and sold as commodities. When George Lucas made *Star Wars* in 1977 he, just like everyone else, was able to freely appropriate many myths and ideas that are in the public domain (Decherney, 2012, p. 17). The "stuff" that would make George Lucas rich were all of the copyrighted elements of *Star Wars*, which Lucas successfully registered under the "Star Wars Corporation".[7] First, we have the motion picture itself, which was initially owned by three parties: the Star Wars Corporation, Twentieth Century-Fox Licensing Corporation and General Mills Fun Group, Inc. We then have the elements that Lucas publicly registered as his property. Luke Skywalker, for instance, can be treated as an asset (now under Disney) because it is copyrighted as "Visual Material". This is the institutional mechanism of exclusion that allows owners to command a price from all of the Luke Skywalker imagery that does not fall under "fair use". There are also many other copyrighted elements, from the obvious (e.g., Han Solo, Darth Vader, Ben Kenobi) to the seemingly trivial (e.g., "X-Starfighter attacking Death Star", "Front view of Corellian starship", "Imperial storm troopers confronting Han Solo, Luke Starfiller[8] and Chewbacca the Wookiee", "Princess Leia Organa awards the heros [*sic*] of the rebellion").

When something in culture cannot be owned directly, capitalists will often calculate its indirect influence on earning potential. The "eye of capitalization", say Nitzan and Bichler (2009), looks everywhere, because the movements of society could influence the very circumstances that capitalists are trying to discount:

> Capitalists routinely discount human life, including its genetic code and social habits; they discount organized institutions from education and entertainment to religion and the law; they discount voluntary social networks; they discount urban violence, civil war and international conflict; they even discount the environmental future of humanity. (p. 158)

Investors in mass culture, whether their ownership is exercised directly though stocks or indirectly through hedge funds, investment portfolios or loans,[9] are also discounting social habits, especially those having to do with leisure time. The rituals of discounting the particular environment of leisure time are the same as those that discount other social environments, although the particular impact in each case may differ greatly. Work, unemployment, inflation, religion, social trends, war, piracy, technology and the presence of competing leisure activities – these are just a few things that could determine whether the customs and habits of consumers include a "healthy" dose of mass culture. The question for the forward-looking capitalist is whether businesses can deliver the goods they promise and whether people will pay to watch what is being sold. For instance, is the film industry sabotaged enough, are the habits of individuals predictable enough and is the general order of society stable enough to signal to the studio executive that it is prudent to green-light a $75 million budget for a motion picture about talking animals?

An equally important question for the "discounters" is how the changing state of the world can disturb the profitability of mass culture. What countries offer cheap labour? Are there tax incentives for producing culture in a certain country? How much security is needed to keep on-location work on schedule? Did MGM discount the risk of street rioting halting production of its TV series *Maya*, which was filmed in Srinigar, Kashmir, in the late 1960s? Did any executive or head of production from Twentieth Century-Fox in 1966 consider that the widening and damming of a small river in Castle Combe, England, for the purpose of filming *Dr. Dolittle*, would anger its residents to the point that two young Englishmen attempted to blow up the dam?[10] Taken from a recent annual report of Dream-Works Animation SKG, Inc. (2010), the following is a list of potential future risks identified by the company:

- laws and policies affecting trade, investment and taxes, including laws and policies relating to the repatriation of funds and withholding taxes and changes in these laws;
- differing cultural tastes and attitudes, including varied censorship laws;
- differing degrees of protection for intellectual property;
- financial instability and increased market concentration of buyers in foreign television markets;
- the instability of foreign economies and governments; and
- war and acts of terrorism. (p. 21)

DreamWorks' vested interest in the socio-political future of the world is not insignificant when nearly 49 per cent of its theatrical revenues come from outside the United States.

4.5 Conclusion

To our benefit, the influence of Marx pushed Garnham, Babe, Adorno and Marcuse to look for signs of institutional power in the production and distribution of mass culture. To our deficit, however, the insights of their analyses were ultimately undermined by the political economic foundations of Marxism, which

Chapters 2 and 3 show are shakier than they first appear. Marxist political economy makes too many problematic assumptions about the nature of capital. Contrary to what Marxist political economy assumes, economic processes in capitalism cannot be isolated from political power and prices are hardly straightforward reflections of productive labour time. Therefore, even the best Marxist analyses of mass culture still struggle to pinpoint the effect of power on capital accumulation, the goal of all capitalist investment.

The job of this chapter has been to prepare the theoretical grounds for Part II, which is where an alternative study of the political economy of Hollywood will be conducted with the capital-as-power approach. This preparation took some time, but the time spent was necessary to prevent certain problems from complicating our analysis. We want to explore various social dimensions of Hollywood cinema, but *without* having to arbitrarily decide which parts of culture are productive and which are not. We also do not want to inadvertently entangle our historical analysis of the business of Hollywood in deeper theoretical issues about what financial data means in terms of value theory. This entanglement sometimes happens when one assumes that, despite having no means to empirically test the claim, the general correspondence between prices and economic value is nevertheless true. A more common entanglement occurs when political economic research downplays the need to resolve theoretical issues about the measurement of economic value. Yet, as the unexplained correspondence between price and value moves further from the mind of the researcher, many qualitative, historical aspects of capitalist society are analysed without any inkling of the theoretical problems coming through the side door.

For example, the incorporation of Marxist theory in *Global Hollywood 2* confuses rather than strengthens its otherwise excellent study of the Hollywood film business (Miller, Govil, McMurria, Maxwell, & Wang, 2005). Its authors use the general framework of Marxist political economy to define a two-level project. First, Hollywood is bolstered by "corporate and state domination, with the US government instigating and facilitating capital accumulation generally and screen trade in particular". Second, films are "commodities whose value is derived from the labour that makes them" (Miller et al., 2005, p. 5). When combined, these two conceptual levels of *Global Hollywood 2* cover a great amount of historical detail: the involvement of the US government in Hollywood's global ambitions, international trade agreements (e.g., GATT), the power of copyright, "runaway production" (location shooting that only appears to have been filmed in the stated locale), the division of labour on a Hollywood film project, and the marketing and surveillance of consumer behaviour. Yet, as impressive as this scope is, the inclusion of the labour theory of value implies that labour time is the productive backbone of Hollywood's so-called economic dimension. And that implication is hard to support.

As an assumption that hangs over each page of *Global Hollywood 2*, the Marxist concept of value seeps from the background to the foreground, colouring the particular facts with a larger theory of capital. To be sure, the collage of well-researched historical details in *Global Hollywood 2* is not the problem. Rather, the nagging issue is the absence of any demonstration of how the manifold historical descriptions, which include prices and wages, connect to a concept of capital that, according to its own definition, denotes accumulation in quantities of labour time. Therefore, as historical details fly this way and that, the theoretical structure of *Global Hollywood 2* is unable to ultimately explain what is and is not a component in the engine of capital accumulation. Is it surplus value from labour alone, and if so, what is the correspondence between Hollywood's rate of profit and its rate of exploitation? What effects do the state, ideology and law have on the level of value produced in this sector? Labour is defined at the beginning of the book as the *de jure* source of value; however, by the time we reach the conclusion, we have travelled through a complex *de facto* story of how a film becomes a means for profit, and that story goes far beyond labour as such. The story of the Hollywood film business includes massive state investment, major diplomatic negotiations, copyright protection, monopoly restrictions, ideologies of pleasure and Americanism and so on (Miller et al., 2005, p. 363).

A keen reader might reply that *Global Hollywood 2* is doing what good Marxist political economy does well: it looks at all the historical conditions that underpin and surround capital accumulation. She may go on to reiterate the authors' point that they "blend disciplinary perspectives" because "historically, the best critical political economy and the best cultural studies have worked through the imbrication of power and signification. . . . Hollywood's cultural products travel through time, space and population" (Miller et al., 2005, p. 6). Yet if the political economy of Hollywood is this diverse, what is the purpose of stating in the introduction that only one universal quality, human labour, is the basis of value? Because of the book's rigour and breadth, we can say that *Global Hollywood 2* is trying to study the economic and power dimensions of capital accumulation in Hollywood. But if that is indeed the case, the labour theory of value causes undue friction. It relies on the assumption that an economic magnitude is distinguishable from political power.

For example, the authors of *Global Hollywood 2* note that the production of the Star Wars prequels took advantage of the nominal price difference between average wages in Hollywood and Australian film production ($635 v. $400–430 daily pay), but how is this presumed exploitation measured as socially necessary abstract labour time, and should we assume that Australian workers are therefore exploited more than their American counterparts? Similarly, the statement that "establishing scarcity through exclusivity is one of the enduring aims of copyright protection" is suggestive of accumulation-through-power (Miller et al., 2005, p. 227), but does this statement mean that legal institutions and state power are, far from being mere addendums, *directly* responsible for the capital accumulation of Hollywood? Or is copyright protection still just a mechanism of the capitalist superstructure, which only supports the mode of production rather than being integral to it? It is confusing to implicitly take away with one hand – if value is only rooted in labour – what the other hand offers explicitly – that copyright protection is a key function in profit seeking from cultural ideas and images.

If we commit to radical left politics, to which Marxism has contributed greatly, we should be prepared to overcome problematic assumptions that limit our research. The capital-as-power approach offers the advantage of openly affirming what Marxist political economy is forced to admit tacitly, namely, that, in the age of advanced capitalism, ideology, desire, signification, intellectual property rights, nationalism and many other political processes are just as important for accumulation as labour and machines are.

Notes

1 Readers of Garnham and Babe will notice that they present Marxist economics in very general terms. This is because they each perceive that cultural studies, as a group of scholars, does not touch the technical details of the labour theory of value. Rather, cultural studies raises concerns about the immovability of false consciousness and the bias of economic determinism.

2 Garnham and Babe are both using a common defensive strategy of Marxist theory. When something is of interest to post-structuralism (subjectivity, knowledge, language), Marxism often defends its relevancy by presenting itself as the better method to analyse the same phenomenon. Its methodology, so the argument goes, has a sharper blade for a social critique of power because it grounds various social phenomena in the same principles of historical materialism. For more examples of this argumentative strategy, see David McNally's (2001) critique of post-structuralist theories of language and John Sanbonmatsu's (2010) critique of postmodern subjectivity.

3 For a theory of how patronage can affect the form and content of artistic creativity, see Kempers (1994) for a historical analysis of Italian Renaissance art, from the thirteenth to the end of the sixteenth century.

4 If we were to extend our analysis of how the repressive characters of sublimation and desublimation are related, there would be two important steps. The first would involve Marcuse's crucial distinction between basic and surplus repression. This distinction is a corrective to the fatalistic character of Freud's metapsychology. The second step would consider Marcuse's theorization of non-repressive sublimation. Put simply, non-repressive sublimation is the idea that the pleasure principle is not automatically "redirected" to a substitute object or goal because sublimation could exist without "desexualization" (Marcuse, 1966, p. 208). For more on Marcuse's psychoanalytic theory and its relationship with political transformation, see Holman (2013); Horowitz (1977, 1987); McMahon (2011).

5 Otherness is not difference: "to say that figures are *other* (and not simply different) has a sense only if figure B can in no way derive from a different arrangement of figure A – as a circle, ellipse, hyperbole or parabola derive from one another and so are the same points *arranged* differently – in other words, only if no identitary law, or group of laws, is sufficient to produce B starting from A" (Castoriadis, 1998, p. 195).

6 One might argue that price increases are a reflection of Hollywood adding its value through quality, not quantity. Yet this argument circles back to the need for price to clearly reflect increases in utility, which is what Veblen critiqued in the first place. It is true that in periods of stagnation major studios spend a lot of money on making

blockbusters, but production of a high-quality blockbuster is still an outcome of strategic sabotage. Part II of this book provides empirical evidence of Major Filmed Entertainment using capitalist power to create a social environment that advantages its blockbusters over cinematic alternatives.

7   These examples of what aspects of *Star Wars* are protected by copyright were found in the United States Copyright Public Records (http://cocatalog.loc.gov/).

8   It is not a typo that Luke Skywalker is listed as "Luke Starfiller". Some of the Star Wars copyrights were registered as early as 1974.

9   For a clear but uncritical analysis of how an independent film is financed, before a major studio purchases the rights to distribute, see Wiese (1991).

10   The last two examples are taken from Dunne (1998, pp. 34, 129).

PART II

5
APPLYING THE CAPITAL-AS-POWER APPROACH TO HOLLYWOOD

5.1 Introduction

This chapter serves two purposes. First, it explains how the capital-as-power framework will structure our analysis of the Hollywood film business in greater detail. Second, this chapter explains why the rest of the project focuses on *risk* in the Hollywood film business. In the capital-as-power approach, risk is conceptualized as an elementary particle of capitalization: it is the *degree of confidence* that capitalists have about future earnings (of Hollywood cinema, in this case). In the interest of lowering risk and increasing their degree of confidence, Hollywood's business interests attempt to control, as much as possible, how new films will function in an already instituted order of cinema, which includes the creativity of filmmakers and the habits of moviegoers.

In contrast to Chapter 4, which presented the capital-as-power approach in a more conceptual form, the first part of this chapter will give a more technical explanation of how the capital-as-power approach is being applied to empirical research on the Hollywood film business. The description explains the methods of selecting Hollywood firms, using financial data, and measuring Hollywood's performance against relevant benchmarks. Translated into the language that will be used throughout Part II, we have a three-part series of research methods:

1 *The object of study:* Major Filmed Entertainment
2 *The logic of prices:* Capitalization and its elementary particles
3 *The measure of capital accumulation:* Differential accumulation

Following this explanation of research methods, the second part of the chapter begins the study of the effects of risk on the Hollywood film business.

DOI: 10.4324/9781003092629-7

5.2 Major Filmed Entertainment

Part II of this book describes and analyses the capital accumulation of the six major studios in Hollywood from 1950 to 2019: Columbia, Disney, Paramount, Twentieth Century-Fox, Universal, and Warner Bros. Table 5.1 presents each studio and its history of conglomerate parentage. The bottom of the table cites key sources in the gathering of this research.

When referring to these six studios as a group, I use the term *Major Filmed Entertainment*. There are three reasons why I use this category over other, more commonly used terms, such as *major film studios* and *Hollywood film distribution*.

First, the oligopoly of Hollywood film production and distribution can be challenging to study when, across decades, old companies evolve or new ones join the group of dominant firms. A historian of Hollywood studios might get nervous when they see a fixed term like *Major Filmed Entertainment*, but its usage is meant to group firms according to their shared objectives in capital accumulation. Thus, Major Filmed Entertainment is an abstraction that will sometimes seem distant from what we imagine happens on a film set or in a studio executive's

TABLE 5.1 Major Hollywood studios, 1950–2019

Studio	*Parents (period of ownership)*
Columbia	Coca-Cola (1982–1987)
	Columbia Pictures Ent./TriStar (1987–1989)
	Sony (1989–2019)
Disney	
Fox	News Corporation (1985–2012)
	Twenty–First Century Fox (2013–2018)
	Disney (2019)
Paramount	Gulf + Western (1966–1989)
	Paramount Communications (1989–1994)
	Viacom (1995–2019)
Warner Bros.	Warner Bros.-Seven Arts (1967–1969)
	Kinney National Company (1969–1971)
	Warner Communications (1972–1989)
	Time Warner (1990–2019)
Universal	MCA (1964–1989)
	Matsushita (1990–1995)
	Seagram Ltd. (1995–2000)
	Vivendi (2000–2011)
	GE (2004–2012)
	Comcast (2009–2019)

Relevant sources: For histories of the Hollywood film business and profiles of the major studios after the Paramount case of 1948, see D. A. Cook (2000); Langford (2010); Maltby (2003); Prince (2000); Wasko (1994, 2003). For details on the conglomeration and ownership structure of Hollywood, see Bagdikian (2004); Compaine and Gomery (2000); Kunz (2007); Thomas and Nain (2004).

office. Nevertheless, there is no incompatibility between the abstractness of the concept and a historical study like Christensen (2012), which seeks to know how each particular studio, such as MGM or Warner Bros., adopted its own set of aesthetic styles and corporate behaviours in the pursuit of profit. Rather, works like Balio (1993), Christensen (2012) and Langford (2010) are simply operating at lower levels of historical detail; abstracting up to a broader categorical term like *Major Filmed Entertainment* can be effective when the argument momentarily looks beyond particularities – for example the differences between the film styles of MGM and Warner Bros., or the differences between United Artists in 1930 and 1960.

Second, "Major Filmed Entertainment" is a language marker that helps remind the reader of the political economic assumptions that frame my empirical research on Hollywood's behaviour and performance. Some of the facts and data have been drawn from other sources in film studies and political economy, but I do not want my terminology to imply that there is an automatic agreement over the theoretical meaning of the data. For example, I refrain from calling Hollywood a "film industry", which is what many political economists will use to analyse the capitalist character of Hollywood cinema (Bakker, 2005; Crandall, 1975; Crane, 2014; Dante, 1990; De Vany, 2004; Litman, 1998; Pendakur, 2008; Wasko, 1982). Calling Hollywood a film industry is not automatically problematic, but its usage as an economic term will be confusing when the capital-as-power approach, *via* Veblen, rejects the price-productivity relationship and understands strategic sabotage to be business' *external* control of industry. When I refer to Hollywood's film industry – which I sometimes do – I am thinking of the technological and aesthetic capacities of film as an industrial art. This industrial art, in my mind, is not connected to a film business *a priori*.

Third, *filmed entertainment* is a term that reflects the scale of the available financial data from 1950 to 2019. The business of cinema has, in the last few decades, diversified its methods of gaining income – for example exhibition windows after theatrical exhibition (DVD, Blu-ray, internet streaming), intellectual property, franchising – and there are serious obstacles involved in trying to isolate the business of cinema in this age of conglomeration. At one end of the scale, we must still distinguish filmed entertainment operations from the different activities of Hollywood's corporate parents. For example, GE acquired NBC Universal from Vivendi in the early 2000s. For the period when GE had a full or partial stake in media entertainment (Comcast had a 51 per cent stake in NBC Universal from 2009 to 2019), this giant of corporate America was also investing in the business of appliances, aviation, gas, industrial motors, weapons and wind turbines, among others. Consequently, the market capitalization or net income of GE as a conglomerate gives us far too much noise for our purposes. At the other end of the scale, data for the film studios proper are not always available. "Major Filmed Entertainment" signifies that some of the data will sometimes include other filmed operations, like television or animation.

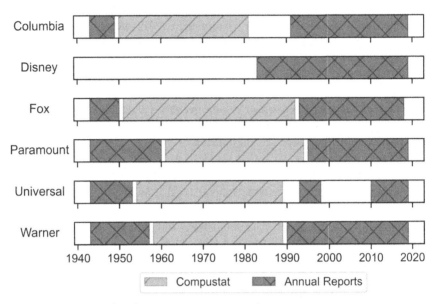

FIGURE 5.1 Major Filmed Entertainment: sources by year

Other researchers are aware of how the scale of data can create obstacles for empirical research on the financial aspects of Hollywood (Leaver, 2010; Wasko, 2003). In light of these obstacles, my empirical methods aim to be multi-sided. At the centre of my analysis is the "de-conglomerated" data on Major Filmed Entertainment. As is shown in Figure 5.1, data from annual reports begins in the mid-1940s, which gives smoothed time series (e.g., rolling averages) more runway. From around 1950 to the early 1990s, the source of data is Compustat, which is a Standard & Poor's database. The switch to annual reports in the early 1990s is an effect of when Compustat data on the Hollywood studios end: in the conglomeration wave that swept up Hollywood film studios in the 1980s (Kunz, 2007; Prince, 2000). Rather than continue the series with data on the conglomerate parents – which repeats the earlier problem in the example with GE – I have used the conglomerates' annual reports to extract data on each of their various business operations. The advantage of this method is that we can ignore the conglomerates' operations that are not relevant to specific arguments about Hollywood cinema. The disadvantage, however, is that our market capitalization data end when we switch from Compustat to annual reports.

I also use data on film releases, film attendance, theatrical grosses, opening theatres, ticket prices and other related facts. On their own, many of these facts will share the same shortcoming for our purpose: they do not provide information on profit. Yet they can supplement our core data on Major Filmed Entertainment. Like the parable of trying to discern the outline of an elephant through touch alone, the Hollywood film business is big enough to offer enough "touch points" – an array of perspectives that will sharpen our understanding of capital accumulation in the realm of cinema.

Therefore, while media conglomeration is certainly significant to a history of contemporary Hollywood and mass culture, our decision to focus specifically on film operations is purposeful. Film is still a distinct cultural commodity in capitalist society, and even when we limit ourselves to studying the role of capitalist power in Hollywood cinema we have more than enough research questions to juggle. Take James Cameron's 2009 blockbuster *Avatar* as an example. Seen from the heights of media conglomeration, *Avatar* is valued for being malleable intellectual property, which allows for its copyrighted material to be licensed and sold in fast-food chains, retail stores and amusement parks. Yet *Avatar* started as a film, and the film's function in profit does not become irrelevant when the pool of intellectual property claims widens; there are still relevant questions about what type of "superstructure" can be built on this film. For example, how does Cameron's ambitious usage of 3-D technology affect the film property's business performance? Were the style and content of *Avatar*-the-film instrumental or incidental to News Corp's ultimate interests in intellectual property and franchising? Answers to these *types* of questions can be answered with the capital-as-power approach, particularly at a broader level of film production and distribution. Let us turn now to capitalization, which is a key component in this approach.

5.3   Capitalization and its elementary particles

The concept of capitalization was first introduced in Chapter 4. Capitalization is the numerical architecture of capital. It is, according to Bichler and Nitzan, "the algorithm that governs and organizes prices" (Nitzan & Bichler, 2009, p. 153). In other words, capitalization is a generative force; it is the key logic that, denominated in prices, creates and re-creates the capitalist order.

The scope of capitalization widens when business enterprise attaches "income streams" to more social objects or processes. In fact, the formal universality of capitalization first interested neoclassical economics in the early twentieth century. Irving Fisher, for example, argued that every productive activity can be directly or indirectly capitalized because the logic of discounting expected future earnings applies to every claim on ownership that is treated as an "income-generating asset" (Nitzan & Bichler, 2009, p. 156).

In our case, capitalization is the lens through which the multifaceted, qualitative world of cinema, art and culture become, to Major Filmed Entertainment, objects and relations that need to be discounted to present prices. In other words, these qualities are transformed into what Marcuse describes more broadly as the "quantifiable qualities" of technological rationality (Marcuse,

1991, p. 136). Many of these qualitative aspects of cinema, art and culture are not owned by Major Filmed Entertainment directly, but the latter is trying to discount what it does own: claims of ownership whose expected income streams can be affected by the social composition of mass culture and the dynamics of consumption, leisure, pleasure and meaning in society.

According to Nitzan and Bichler (2009), this logic of capitalization can be deconstructed into its "elementary particles": earnings, hype, risk and the normal rate of return, which, like a treasury bill or a government bond yield, is a rate of return that "all capitalists believe they deserve" at minimum (p. 239).[1] The relationship between these variables can be presented this way:

$$K_t = \frac{E \times H}{\delta \times r_c} \tag{5.1}$$

Capitalization at any given time (K_t) is equal to the discounted value of future earnings (E) multiplied by hype (H), which measures the extent to which capitalists are "overly optimistic or overly pessimistic about future earnings" (Nitzan & Bichler, 2009, p. 189). The numerator is discounted by two variables: a rate of return that capitalists feel they can confidently get (r_c) and the risk coefficient (δ). Because risk is in the denominator, a smaller δ indicates a greater degree of confidence and therefore a larger capitalization, and a larger δ indicates the opposite. If, for instance, there is growing uncertainty about the size and pattern of a future stream of earnings, δ will increase and the asset in question will be discounted to a lower present price.

Because of the limitations to acquiring long-term data on the market capitalization of Major Filmed Entertainment (see Section 5.2), the key series in my analysis will be *operating income*. While the ideal would be to have a complete 60-year time series of market capitalization, we can use operating income to measure increases or decreases of elements within the capitalization formula. Over the long term, earnings are the main anchor of capitalization (Nitzan & Bichler, 2009, p. 186). We can also use operating income to measure risk. The second part of this chapter and the rest of Part II demonstrate that, in the case of Hollywood, risk (δ) is of crucial significance to its differential accumulation.

Figure 5.2 presents the operating income data of Major Filmed Entertainment. In Panel A we can see the raw data points of each firm in the group (for presentation purposes the log scale hides the rare occurrences of operating loses). Panel B presents annual and rolling averages of the data, which will often be referred to as "operating income per firm".

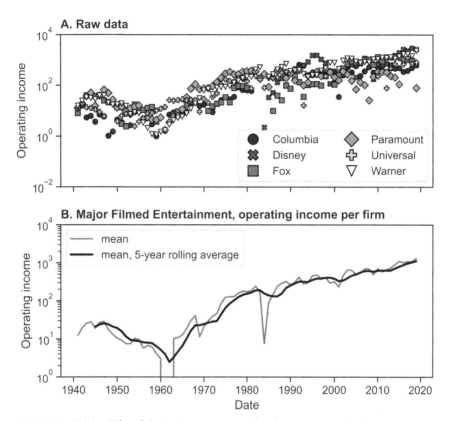

FIGURE 5.2 Major Filmed Entertainment: operating income, 1950–2019

Source: Compustat through WRDS for operating income of Major Filmed Entertainment, 1950–1992. Annual reports of Disney, News Corp, Viacom, Sony, Time Warner (Management's Discussion of Business Operations for information on their filmed entertainment interests) for operating income of Major Filmed Entertainment, 1993–2019.

5.4 Differential accumulation

Differential accumulation is rooted in capitalization. More specifically, it is rooted in the relative differences between capitalized properties. There is an implicit differential measure between any two magnitudes of capitalization. For example, on December 2, 2020, Apple's market capitalization ($2.093 trillion) was 1.7 times larger than Google's ($1.236 trillion), and Google's was 4.4 times larger than Disney's ($278.1 billion). Taken at a single point in time, these multiples are static measures of differential capitalization. Differential accumulation measures how differential capitalization changes over time. Treated as a dynamic process of redistribution, firms accumulate differentially when their capitalization rises faster than that of others and "their distributive share" becomes "bigger and bigger" (Nitzan, 2001, p. 230).

Similarly to how capitalization can be broken down into elementary particles, differential accumulation can be broken down into the elements of differential capitalization (Nitzan & Bichler, 2009, p. 327):

$$DK = \frac{K_a}{K_b} = \frac{\frac{E_a}{E_b} \times \frac{H_a}{H_b}}{\frac{\delta_a}{\delta_b}} \tag{5.2}$$

Like Equation 5.1, Equation 5.2 deconstructs capitalization into future earnings, hype, risk and the normal rate of return, which is effectively cancelled out because it is common to the capitalization of both the entity in question (a) and the benchmark to which it is compared (b).[2] By making each element the ratio of two entities, we have a platform to investigate the extent to which a firm or set of firms can accumulate differentially. The capitalization of K_a can rise faster than the capitalization of K_b through a rise in differential profit ($\dot{E}_a > \dot{E}_b$), a rise in differential hype ($\dot{H}_a > \dot{H}_b$) or a *decrease* in differential risk ($\dot{\delta}_a < \dot{\delta}_b$).

5.4.1 The differential accumulation of Major Filmed Entertainment

Since we are looking primarily at the longer-term trends of Hollywood cinema, hype (H), a mostly cyclical, shorter-term variable, will be kept hidden as a part of expected earnings (EE). Furthermore, our measure of differential accumulation has Major Filmed Entertainment in the numerator (set a in Equation 5.2) and a set called Dominant Capital in the denominator (b in Equation 5.2):

$$DK = \frac{K_M}{K_D} = \frac{\frac{EE_M}{EE_D}}{\frac{\delta_M}{\delta_D}}, \tag{5.3}$$

where M is Major Filmed Entertainment, and D is Dominant Capital. The set of Dominant Capital includes, for each year, the top 500 firms on the Compustat database, sorted by the market capitalization of all firms that are listed, but not necessarily incorporated, in the United States. This 500-firm set is meant to be similar to the S&P 500, which is a standard benchmark for the performance of large US-based corporations. As our study of Major Filmed Entertainment will rely on operating income data, so to will our measure of Dominant Capital – if it is to act as our benchmark. Figure 5.3 visualizes the construction of Dominant Capital's operating income per firm.

Would it be better to have filmed-entertainment firms in the denominator of Equation 5.2? There is no arithmetical barrier to plugging any firm or set of firms into a measure of differential accumulation. Thus, the method demands that we, the researchers, identify a good reason to use the differential-accumulation measurement in a particular way. Take, as a thought experiment, a piece of Major

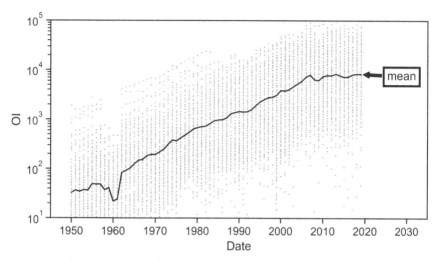

FIGURE 5.3 Dominant Capital: operating income, 1950–2019

Source: Compustat through WRDS. Top 500 sorted by the market capitalization each year.

Filmed Entertainment's historical performance: in 1996 the average operating income per firm of Major Filmed Entertainment was $504 million. For the same year, its average revenues per firm were $4.5 billion. Are these magnitudes large or small? Now consider other relevant questions. How would investors, who could always put money in sectors other than film and media, regard these numbers? How does Hollywood know if it is doing well? When is the financial performance of Major Filmed Entertainment cause for celebration, and when is it a reason for distress?

There are no universal answers to these questions. Instead, the *modus operandi* of actual capitalists is to find and use contextually relevant benchmarks for the performance of their investments:

> A capitalist investing in Canadian 10-year bonds typically tries to beat the Scotia McLeod 10-year benchmark; an owner of emerging-market equities tries to beat the IFC benchmark; investors in global commodities try to beat the Reuters/Jefferies CRB Commodity Index; owners of large US corporations try to beat the S&P 500; and so on. Every investment is stacked against its own group benchmark — and in the abstract, against the global benchmark. (Nitzan & Bichler, 2009, p. 309)

Relevancy, in this case, is defined by such factors as listed stock exchange and the size of the investment. As the oligopoly of Hollywood cinema, the size of Major Filmed Entertainment prevents small firms from being competitors in terms of

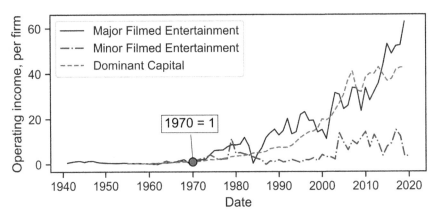

FIGURE 5.4 Dominant Capital: a benchmark for Major Filmed Entertainment

Source: Compustat through WRDS for firm data of Dominant Capital and "Minor Filmed Entertainment", and for operating income of Major Filmed Entertainment, 1950–1992. Annual reports of Disney, News Corp, Viacom, Sony, Time Warner (Management's Discussion of Business Operations for information on their filmed entertainment interests) for operating income of Major Filmed Entertainment, 1993–2019.

profits, revenues or other business indicators. Rather, Major Filmed Entertainment finds like-minded competition in the giant firms of their respective sectors. Their levels of accumulation are worthy benchmarks of the powerful.

Figure 5.4 illustrates that Dominant Capital is a more meaningful benchmark for Major Filmed Entertainment than what could be called "Minor Filmed Entertainment". The latter is not an organized collective of firms, but rather is a broad set of firms that operate in the following categories of the Standard Industrial Classification manual:

- 7812 Motion Picture and Video Tape Production
- 7819 Services Allied to Motion Picture Production
- 7822 Motion Picture and Video Tape Distribution
- 7829 Services Allied to Motion Picture Distribution

All three series in Figure 5.4 are rescaled so that 1970 equals one. Each series is the per firm average of annual operating income. The comparisons of operating income per firm demonstrate how, for the last 50 years, beating the average solely within the filmed-entertainment sector has became a meaningless goal for Major Filmed Entertainment. The average "Minor-Filmed-Entertainment" firm simply has not kept pace with the firms that dominate Hollywood cinema. Conversely, the average Dominant-Capital firm has not lost its relevancy as a benchmark; the trajectory of its operating profits is similar to Major Filmed Entertainment's.

5.5   The main objective of Part II: risk in the Hollywood film business

In light of what has been covered above, we can now outline the main objective of Part II in more detail. Our focus is on the role of risk in the differential accumulation of Major Filmed Entertainment. Risk does not tell the whole story of the capitalist character of Hollywood, but it is an elementary particle of the logic of capitalization. Risk is a partly subjective, partly objective factor that shapes the way a claim on future earnings is assessed. If capitalization discounts the size and pattern of a future stream of earnings, risk is the expression of the "degree of confidence capitalists have in their own predictions" of those earnings (Nitzan & Bichler, 2009, p. 208). Risk can also be expressed as a differential measure (e.g., $\frac{\delta_M}{\delta_D}$ in Equation 5.3), which lets us inquire how a firm or set of firms lowers its risk at a faster rate than others.

The decision to focus on risk is motivated by the relationship between the two series in Figure 5.5. The solid line plots the 5-year smoothed differential market capitalization of Major Filmed Entertainment from 1954 to 1993. Here, the average market capitalization of Major Filmed Entertainment is benchmarked against the average of Dominant Capital. As was mentioned when we first introduced the term *Major Filmed Entertainment*, the capitalization data for this group end at 1993; from this point onward, available data pertain to the market capitalization of Hollywood's parent conglomerates rather than the subsidiaries we are interested in. The semi-dotted series measures the 5-year smoothed differential operating income of Major Filmed Entertainment, which is likewise benchmarked against Dominant Capital. Unlike market capitalization, this series is available for the entire 1954–2019 period, since operating income for Major Filmed Entertainment can be obtained from their annual reports and Compustat. The juxtaposition of the two series shows that, for the years when there are data for both series, the differential earnings of Major Filmed Entertainment are insufficient to explain differential capitalization. Most significant, from 1980 to 1993, differential earnings declined while differential capitalization soared. The comparison of this difference unfortunately ends at this point in time, but Figure 5.5 demonstrates that differential capitalization depends not only on the *level* of earnings.

The study of risk also accounts for historical shifts in capitalist power. As Bichler and Nitzan suggest, capitalization is not a crystal ball in which one can see the future. Rather, it is a social ritual, one that attempts to estimate how a stream of income and its underlying social conditions will carry into the future (Nitzan & Bichler, 2009, p. 187). The difference between prophecy and estimation is significant. Social norms, values and behaviour can change, and business enterprise, which is trying to estimate this future, can never find an Archimedean point outside of society or safe from the winds of history. Consequently, there is

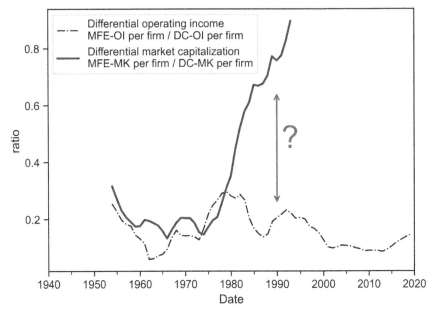

FIGURE 5.5   Differential capitalization and differential operating income of Major Filmed Entertainment

Source: Compustat through WRDS for market capitalization and operating income of Major Filmed Entertainment, 1950–1993. Compustat for operating income of Major Filmed Entertainment, 1950–1993. Annual reports of Disney, News Corp, Viacom, Sony, Time Warner (Management's Discussion of Business Operations for information on their filmed entertainment interests) for operating income of Major Filmed Entertainment, 1994–2019. Compustat for firm data of Dominant Capital, 1950–2019.

Note: Both series are smoothed as 5-year moving averages.

always "risk" that business estimates will turn out to be wrong. Moreover, risk can change as social actors, including capitalists, strengthen or weaken the continuity of established social relations.

As stated earlier, Bichler and Nitzan understand power as "confidence in obedience: it represents the certainty of the rulers in the submissiveness of the ruled" (Nitzan & Bichler, 2009, p. 398). Thus, if we translate into the more philosophical language of power, the capitalist degree of confidence $(\frac{1}{\delta})$ refers to the perceived duration and strength of obedience and the likelihood that future social behaviour will function for capitalist ends. For instance, capitalist confidence can increase when individuals have internalized the goals of a repressive society, when the persistence of fear, violence and poverty has actually helped social power acquire an "unshiftable weight" (Castoriadis, 1998, p. 109). Yet, however strong obedience may appear to be, it is always threatened by the possibility that individual or even social autonomy will resurface in the future. Even for the largest empires and the most repressive political regimes, there is never an absolute guarantee that social obedience will carry on indefinitely. Therefore, risk is the product of the inability of a ruling class to eradicate the potential for individual and group autonomy to resurface in the future.[3]

With respect to the forward-looking nature of the Hollywood film business, risk perceptions account for the possibility that the future of culture will be different – and perhaps radically different – from what capitalists expect it to be. This logic of capitalist accounting, while quantitative in expression (prices, income, volatility, etc.), is social in essence. For this reason, the risk perceptions of Major Filmed Entertainment cannot overlook any social dimension of cinema, be it aesthetic, political or cultural. The eye of capitalization searches for any social condition that could have an impact on "the level and pattern of capitalist earnings" (Nitzan & Bichler, 2009, p. 166).

As Grantham (2012) notes, this thorough evaluation of risk is evident at the level of film-project financing: "film risk is variable and the degree of risk is subject to structural considerations as well as the greater or lesser degree of 'riskiness' inherent in any project's subject matter, or associated with its writer, director, stars, and so on" (p. 200). But based on what was said earlier, Grantham's use of the word *inherent* is potentially misleading. Here, *riskiness* is a term of business, not art. We may be tempted to label a film "risky" if it challenges social taboos, or if, like Věra Chytilová's *Daisies* (1966), it uses the cinematic medium to critique political regimes. A filmmaker can also be said to be taking an "aesthetic risk" when they develop an untested cinematic style. However, indeterminate creativity in the realm of aesthetics or the development of political cinema can both exist separately from the logic of capital. In fact, it is Veblen's point that pecuniary value does not simply reflect political, cultural or aesthetic quality. Rather, when cinema is a business concern, vested interests flip the definition of *value*. Under their logic of capital, the potential of creativity, both anthropological and technological, are judged according to the terms of capitalist investment: a risky movie is one that fails not business's aesthetic criteria but its financial expectations.[4]

5.6   Our hypothesis about risk

With our focus on studying risk, we can assemble an overarching hypothesis for the rest of Part II:

Hypothesis

The drive to reduce risk – and the central role of strategic sabotage in this reduction – shapes Hollywood's orientation toward the social-historical character of cinema and mass culture. Major Filmed Entertainment uses its oligopolistic control of distribution to create what we can call an *order of cinema*. An order of cinema is the product of a cinematic universe — social relations and all — being valued as a deterministic social system. As an object of instrumental calculation, the orderliness of cinema is defined by the way various properties of cinema predictably function in the goal of differential accumulation.

Hollywood cinema can be treated as an order because cinematic creativity and social meaning are bound together – and in important ways shaped and controlled – by Major Filmed Entertainment's strategies to accumulate capital. "Risk" in this context reflects the degree of confidence investors have in this order of social relations actually generating predictable earnings. In other words, risk is the assessment of a three-part relationship among accumulation strategies, filmmaking strategies and the broader social consequences of cinema. Now, since risk perceptions are a major component of capitalization, reducing risk is a major driver of accumulation. This reduction, we will try to demonstrate, is accomplished by making the articulation and determination of an order of cinema ever more predictable.

The future is, of course, always unknown. Yet Major Filmed Entertainment, like other business enterprises, translates its control of industry and the historical trajectories of society into instrumental calculations about the future of its claims of ownership. If we break down the overall confidence of Major Filmed Entertainment into smaller building blocks of means and ends, we acquire a keener sense of how strategic questions about the control of social creativity will underpin the capitalization of cinema. For example, which film projects should be nurtured, developed and then green lit for production? Which film ideas should be rejected, and according to what criteria? Should creativity in filmmaking obey standards about form and content, and, if so, what should these standards be and how should they be instituted? What will happen to earnings if filmmakers are allowed to explore new ideas or experiment with untested filmmaking techniques? Will consumers welcome – that is, pay for – a political cinema that engages with social taboos or controversial subjects? Can Hollywood make them pay – and if so, how?[5]

In the contemporary era of the Hollywood film business, these and other questions about the artistic trends of filmmaking relate to the *financial risk of overproduction*. Veblen's concept of overproduction and its relationship with strategic sabotage in Hollywood will be covered in the next chapter. In the meantime, we can give context to the previously stated hypothesis. Historical changes to US theatrical attendance and the growing importance of international distribution both help explain why Major Filmed Entertainment shows preference for aesthetically limited production and a *habituated* audience, one that is ready and willing to keep gravitating around small sets of films, year after year. Within the capital-as-power approach, Major Filmed Entertainment's preference is expressed through historical evidence of a *depth strategy*, which often carries higher risk than a *breadth strategy*.

5.6.1   Looking for confidence in a shrinking pond

Few will be surprised when I say that a present-day moviegoer sees *fewer* films in theatres annually than a moviegoer did 50 years ago. What might surprise a reader is my belief that this historical change does not diminish the importance of theatrical releases in the capital accumulation of Major Filmed Entertainment. Technological changes in home entertainment have multiplied the opportunities for a moviegoer to watch a film outside of a theatre. As Figure 5.6 shows, physical formats (DVD, Blu-ray) and digitial streaming in recent years have summed to a greater share of revenues than theatrical exhibition's share. Nevertheless, particular theatrical releases still act as "tent-poles" by having big successes in theatres lift the level of non-theatrical revenues months later. Moreover, the decline of theatrical exhibition does not affect films equally. Blockbusters are still released in as many theatres as possible; medium- or small-budget films are the ones that desperately fight for marginal attendance numbers (Christopherson, 2013, p. 150).

Technological change does not make theatrical releases irrelevant, but rather forces us to take a different perspective on the shrinking "pond" of annual theatrical attendance. Figure 5.7 measures US theatrical attendance per capita from 1933 to 2019. After a sharp decline that was most likely caused by the advent

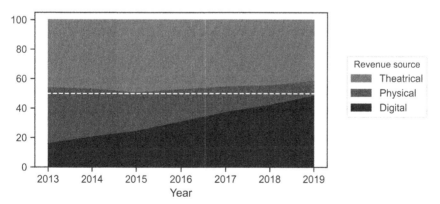

FIGURE 5.6   Global theatrical and home entertainment consumer spending, per cent shares of formats

Source: Motion Picture Association (previously Motion Picture Association of America; renamed in September 2019)

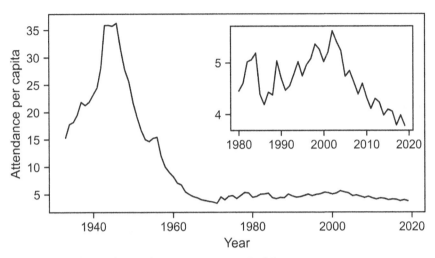

FIGURE 5.7 Theatrical attendance per capita, United States

Source: Finler (2003) for box-office receipts and ticket prices from 1933 to 1959; Bordwell (2006), 'Appendix: A Hollywood Timeline, 1960–2004,' for total attendance 1960–2004; www.natoonline. org/data/admissions/ for attendance 2005–19. IHS Global Insight for total United States population.

of television, American attendance per capita has stayed at roughly the same level since the 1970s. Since the 2000s there has been another decline, to a point where the average American is only seeing four films in theatres a year. In this context, the challenge for Major Filmed Entertainment might be to determine which four films the average moviegoer sees; and more specifically, to create a determinable order of cinema that keeps the spotlight directly on its most expensive films. Hollywood may certainly try to expand the market, pushing people to see more films in theatres. However, with US attendance per capita having remained nearly constant for over 50 years, the alternative strategy is for Major Filmed Entertainment to redistribute the market: to ensure that moviegoers see mostly their blockbusters (Cucco, 2009).

The actions of Major Filmed Entertainment confirm that this group of firms is, at minimum, adapting to a cultural environment where annual theatrical attendance of the average moviegoer is infrequent. Historically, attendance per capita has been in a reciprocal cause-effect relationship with Major Filmed Entertainment's pace of film production. Figure 5.8 shows the history of theatrical releases in the United States. As was first shown in Figure 4.3, the overall trend of Major Filmed Entertainment is to stagnate or decline its rate of theatrical releases. This push downwards has additional significance after the late 1970s. Relative to a total theatrical market that is still, as of 2019, in a continuing period of growth,

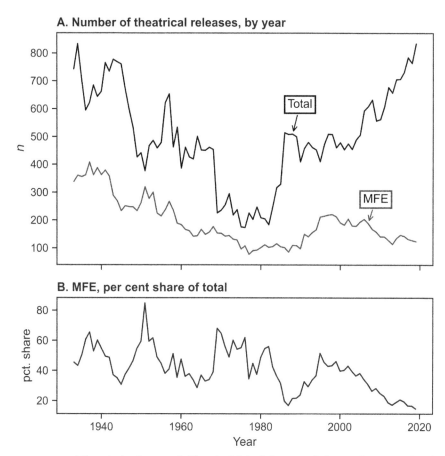

FIGURE 5.8   Theatrical releases: all films in United States and those of Major Filmed Entertainment

Source: Finler (2003) for U.S. theatrical releases from 1933 to 2002; MPAA/MPA Theatrical Market Statistics for total US releases from 2003 to 2019.

Note: For the purposes of simplicity, the film releases of the Motion Picture Association are labelled as Major Filmed Entertainment. See §5.2 for rationale and breakdown of Major Filmed Entertainment.

Major Filmed Entertainment has reached record lows in its per cent share of theatrical releases in the United States.

Digital technology and the internet support the strategy of redistributing theatrical consumption. For instance, Epagogix is a consulting firm that sells data analysis to the Hollywood studios. The firm uses a database of film scripts to capitalize the smallest details of any potential film project. After having broken down a client's script into separate elements, the database produces "values" for each element, as if the film were one big neoclassical production function. Malcolm Gladwell witnessed Epagogix's process in 2006:

> [Copaken, the co-founder of Epagogix,] started with the first film and had the neural network make a guess: maybe it said that the hero's moral crisis in act one, which rated a 7 on the 10-point moral-crisis scale, was worth $7 million, and having a gorgeous red-headed eighteen-year-old female lead whose characterization came in at 6.5 was worth $3 million and a 9-point bonding moment between the male lead and a four-year-old boy in act three was worth $2 million, and so on. (p. 143)

The *New York Times* covered a similar company named World Wide Motion Picture Group (Barnes, 2013). By running its own database and surveying the tastes of moviegoers, World Wide advises on the final construction of a Hollywood film. For example, it argues that it is financially risky for *any* film to have a bowling scene. Or, if you make a superhero movie, it is better for the bottom line that the protagonist is a "guardian superhero" rather than a "cursed superhero".

Google is doing something similar with the data it collects from searches. With a massive data set of potential moviegoers, Google understands that managing risk is a top priority in the capitalization of cinema. For example, a 2013 Google white paper begins with a problem scenario:

> It's Friday night and you're thinking about seeing a movie. Your thought process might sound a little like this: What's in theaters right now? What's that new movie my friend was just talking about a couple days ago? That trailer I saw for another film a few weeks ago looked interesting. Another movie review I read sounded promising . . . what should I see? (p. 1)

The "problem" is that leisure time is too open-ended. Google's solution, however, is more for the capitalist than the moviegoer who uses the internet to make a decision on Friday night. To help quantify the financial risk of moviegoer decision-making, Google tracks searches, YouTube views and advertisement clicks. It keeps data on searches for specific titles, especially big names like *The Dark Knight* or *The Avengers*. Google also analyses how the search criteria of potential moviegoers become less specific and more generic in slow periods between blockbuster films.

Google claims to lend confidence to Hollywood's future expectations in two ways. First, the data provided by Google can tell marketing teams how to adjust marketing strategies to "either capture the attention of the 'curious' moviegoer, or deepen audience engagement with a blockbuster title" (Google, 2013, p. 3). Second, and more significantly, Google states that internet data help Hollywood predict future movie sales. For instance, in the seven day window prior to a film's release date, if one film has 250,000 more search queries than a similar film, the film with more queries is likely to perform up to $4.3M better during opening weekend. When looking at search and click volume, if a film has 20,000 more paid clicks than a similar film, it is expected to bring in up to $7.5M more during opening weekend (Google, 2013, p. 5)

5.6.2   Hollywood abroad

Data from the Motion Picture Association indicate that Hollywood is now generating more revenues outside the United States than inside. Such a feat is inherently political. Contemporary Hollywood leverages US foreign power to make its biggest stars and films global phenomenons, particularly in countries that do not have the tools to protect or support their own domestic film culture. Through both the US government's opposition to the UNESCO convention, which aims to "protect and promote the diversity of cultural expressions", and the free-trade agreements that remove barriers to American film production, Hollywood major distributors have found political-economic opportunities to dominate the markets of such countries as Mexico, Canada, Australia and South Korea (Jin, 2011).

Hollywood's domination abroad is tied to Major Filmed Entertainment's contemporary drive to reduce risk. First, the stagnation of Hollywood film production limits the amount of titles that can be exhibited anywhere, and much like independent film production in the United States, national film cultures have been growing in recent years. Figure 5.9 is a sample of how national film productions compare to Major Filmed Entertainment's output. The thicker line in each panel is the 10-year per cent change of the country's national film production. The thin line, visualized in every panel, is the 10-year per cent change of Major Filmed Entertainment's film production. The comparison indicates that Major Filmed Entertainment roughly has a counter-cyclical strategy to the film production of other countries.

Second, Major Filmed Entertainment is not in a position in which *any* one of its films can become an international hit. There can be cultural barriers to the foreign success of certain American stories. Additionally, some countries have or want government policies to protect national film cultures against a Hollywood "invasion". By putting more weight on the international successes of a small handful of blockbusters, Major Filmed Entertainment can focus on its "best bets" for international success. It can also minimize the effect of barriers like quota policies, which stipulate restrictions based on number of imported films per year. For instance, when China opened its film market to revenue-sharing foreign distribution in 1994, it only allowed 10 imports per year. In spite of this restrictive situation, the handful of Hollywood films that were imported during this period did quite well; they were

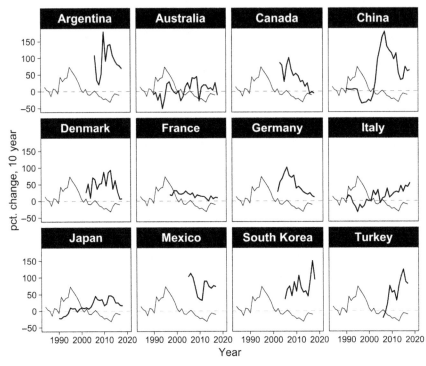

FIGURE 5.9 Major Filmed Entertainment versus the world: 10-year change in film releases

Source: Finler (2003) for US theatrical releases from 1980 to 2002; MPAA/MPA Theatrical Market Statistics for total US releases from 2003 to 2019. Screen Digest, UNESCO (http://data.uis.unesco.org/) and European Audiovisual Observatory - Film Market Trends (https://www.obs.coe.int) for national film releases of countries other than the United States.

Note: Linear fills were produced for missing data in the time series of Argentina (1998–2004), Mexico (2000–2004) and Turkey (1997–2004).

sometimes able to collectively claim as much as 70 per cent of China's box-office revenues per year (Su, 2011).

Third, Major Filmed Entertainment does not typically make specialty films for countries or regions of the world. Its preference is for a Hollywood blockbuster to have broad global appeal — even with examples of co-productions and the frequent use of location shooting.[6] Telling a story and creating appealing visuals that are popular "everywhere" requires many restrictions on the form and content of filmmaking — as we will see in later chapters. Conceptualized now as a perception of risk, the degree of confidence in international film distribution involves the uncertainty that the success of a film in some places – Los Angeles, New York, Tokyo, Lima, Beirut – will undermine success elsewhere – London, Melbourne, Istanbul, Cape Town. For instance, promotion and advertising are key factors of a theatrical-distribution strategy (Wasko, 2003), and there can be high risk if a studio is uncertain how much or how little promotion and advertising is needed for a film to be a big success in a foreign market. The benefit in reducing this type of uncertainty was recently demonstrated in the negative, when Disney promoted the Star Wars sequel trilogy (e.g., *Episode VII – The Force Awakens*) in China. The original Star Wars films were not previously exhibited in China, and its moviegoers did not grow up in an environment where, for generations of people, the Star Wars franchise was one of the centrepieces of popular culture. Thus, Disney added extra doses of promotion in China, but reports indicated that the effects of the extra promotion were still uncertain. For franchises the size of Star Wars, there might be few *certain* substitutes for the knowledge that an entrenched, dedicated fanbase will very likely make the next film a top-ranking success (Frater, 2018; Greenberg, 2016).

Figure 5.10 uses a proxy measure to take a snapshot of Major Filmed Entertainment's performance in international film distribution. The figure shows the average number of nationally produced films in that country's national box-office (e.g., average number of Ukrainian films in Ukraine's box-office top ten). The average is taken from UNESCO data from 2005 to 2017. In Figure 5.10A, countries are split by continent. Panel B shows the distribution of the average number of nationally produced films across all countries in the dataset. For parts of the globe, such as North America, Oceania and South America, the results in Figure 5.10 match our common ideas of national cinemas being unable to compete at the level of top-ranking theatrical exhibition. Some countries, such

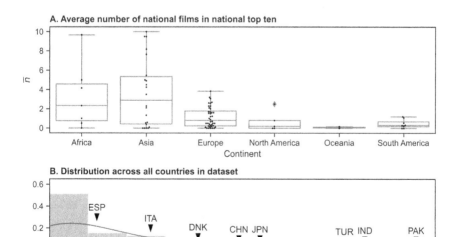

FIGURE 5.10   Box-office share, 2005–2017: Average number of national films in top ten box-office revenues, per national market

Source: UNESCO (http://data.uis.unesco.org/) for 2005–2017.

as Algeria, South Africa, Malaysia and Singapore, have virtually no national films in their respective top ten lists.

The exceptions to Hollywood's dominance in Figure 5.10 are potential battle-grounds of international cinema. National films in Europe have been able to take some of the top theatrical spots away from Hollywood (Buchsbaum, 2017). In Asia and Africa, the spread in the data is largest. China, where Hollywood's quick gains in the 1990s receded in the 2000s (Kokas, 2017; McMahon, 2020; Song, 2018; Wang, 2007; Yeh & Davis, 2008), is the biggest theatrical market to frustrate Major Filmed Entertainment's interests. Conversely, there are plenty of countries where Major Filmed Entertainment is overwhelmingly winning the fight for large shares of theatrical box-office grosses. The prize for these wins is a lowering of Major Filmed Entertainment's risk perceptions. Film consumption in countries where it is uncommon or rare for their domestic films to be in the national box-office top ten contributes to a more predictable global homogeneity: there is a greater likelihood that the top ten grossing films in such countries will be composed of the *same* Hollywood films (UNESCO Institute for Statistics, 2013).

5.6.3   The risk of depth

As we saw earlier, Major Filmed Entertainment has a history of stagnating its film output. The financial success of this stagnation depends on society at large. The trends of Hollywood cinema could take place in a social environment of general indifference, where few care about the future of cinema. But the actions of Major Filmed Entertainment could also meet waves of public resistance through film criticism, divestment and protest. This range of social effects is included in the risk perceptions of Major Filmed Entertainment because the behaviour of its firms could amplify the degree of sabotage in the "strategic sabo-tage" of cinema.

Major Filmed Entertainment tends to adopt what Nitzan and Bichler (2009) describe as a *depth strategy*. As one of the general means of differential accumulation, the strategies of depth involve stagflation (inflation + stagnant growth) and cost cutting. Accumulation through depth can trigger and fuel resistance from below because its methods of achieving higher earnings put greater stress on capitalism's social hierarchies and inequalities: a firm might attempt to sell a commodity with a bigger markup; a firm might try to depress industrial production below its techno-logical capacity to meet social needs; a firm might cut wages or lay off a part of its workforce. These strategies are all contentious and conflictual, making differential accumulation through depth often "uncertain" and "seemingly far more risky than breadth", the other general means of differential accumulation (Nitzan & Bichler, 2009, p. 19). By contrast to depth, *accumulation through breadth* seeks to increase the organizational size of a firm and involves green-field investment and mergers and acquisitions. The socio-political effects of breadth, at least on the surface, are far less confrontational and divisive.

Firms are not eternally bound to either depth or breadth. In fact, Bichler and Nitzan claim that depth and breadth, at least in the United States and the United Kingdom, tended to be counter-cyclical strategies in the twentieth century (Bichler & Nitzan, 2013; Francis, 2013; Nitzan & Bichler, 2009). And this alternation of depth and breadth, along with the pronounced differences between them, can help explain how Major Filmed Entertainment combines strategic stagnation and risk reduction to create and sustain an order of cinema. When running its depth strategy, Major Filmed Entertainment relies on the stability of the social relations that underpin its confidence. Stagnation can engender risk if a limited number of films no longer satisfies the desires and habits of moviegoers, or if people become tired of Hollywood concentrating on blockbuster cinema, at the expense of so many other possibilities in filmmaking.[7]

The goal of accumulation through depth is to increase the elemental power per "unit of organization" – for example, increase earnings per employee. In Hollywood's case, its strategy to accumulate through depth also involves increasing *earnings per film* during periods when the rate of film releases is stagnating or even decreasing. During these periods of stagnation, earnings per film become central to Major Filmed Entertainment's elemental power. An increase of this measure – used explicitly or not – represents Major Filmed Entertainment's attempt to have consumers gravitate to Hollywood's *limited* set of films. The place of earnings per film in the overall earnings of Major Filmed Entertainment can be presented algebraically:

$$\text{Earnings of MFE} = \text{films} \times \frac{\text{earnings}}{\text{films}} = \text{films} \times \text{earnings per film}. \quad (5.4)$$

Figure 5.11 is a representation of Major Filmed Entertainment's depth strategy. Measured against the CPI in the United States, Major Filmed Enterainment's "real" operating income *per film* has an upward trend. The biggest wave of accumulation through depth occurred between the early 1960s and the late 1970s, a period which contains the beginning and end of New Hollywood cinema. The depth strategy also has a clear role in Major Filmed Entertainment's ability to differentially accumulate. The strongest period of accumulation-through-depth is also Major Filmed Entertainment's biggest wave of differential accumulation since 1950. Conversely, Major Filmed Entertainment's differential operating income per film experienced a decline in the 1980s and 1990s – only to see a small bounce-back in the 2010s.

Figure 5.12 demonstrates that accumulation-through-depth is likely achieved through stagflation. In each panel, differential operating income is plotted against the 25-year per cent change of a relevant variable. The first two variables – number of films released and number of employees in film production – are proxy measures of unemployment, whereby a negative growth rate signals the

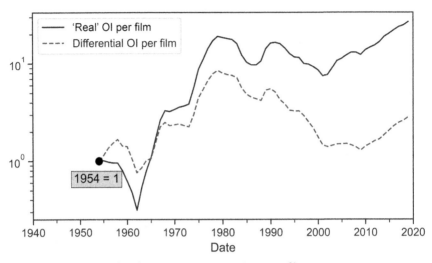

FIGURE 5.11   Major Filmed Entertainment, earnings per film

Source: Compustat through WRDS for operating income of Major Filmed Entertainment, 1950–1992. Annual reports of Disney, News Corp, Viacom, Sony, Time Warner (Management's Discussion of Business Operations for information on their filmed entertainment interests) for operating income of Major Filmed Entertainment, 1993–2019. Finler (2003) for US theatrical releases from 1933 to 2002; MPAA/MPA Theatrical Market Statistics for total US releases from 2003 to 2019.

Note: Differential measure is the operating income per firm of $\frac{\text{Major Filmed Entertainment}}{\text{Dominant Capital}}$. See §5.4 for an explanation of using differential measures.

shrinking of opportunities to be employed in a major Hollywood film project. In both Panels A and B, we can observe how the stagnation of output contributes to differential operating income. The third panel plots ticket price inflation. Its *positive* correlation to differential operating income demonstrates that the biggest 25-year increases in ticket prices have generally produced the biggest gains in differential accumulation.

What about the breadth strategy? As mentioned earlier, the Hollywood film business is free to pursue either a depth or breadth strategy. With respect to the behaviour of Major Filmed Entertainment, the availability of data makes the measures of breadth more indirect. Nevertheless, we can perceive the limits of Major Filmed Entertainment's breadth strategy with data on mergers and acquisitions in the media-entertainment sector and green-field investment in film theatre construction.

According to Nitzan and Bichler (2009), many economic theories of mergers and acquisitions are entangled with problematic assumptions about the scale of technological efficiency, the cost of "in-house" production or the existence of rational profit maximization. Bichler and Nitzan argue we can solve the "mystery" of why mergers and acquisitions occur by seeing amalgamation as a key process to boost differential earnings through power.

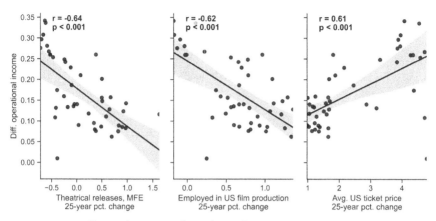

FIGURE 5.12   Differential earnings through stagflation

Source: Compustat through WRDS for operating income of Major Filmed Entertainment, 1950–1992. Annual reports of Disney, News Corp, Viacom, Sony, Time Warner (Management's Discussion of Business Operations for information on their filmed entertainment interests) for operating income of Major Filmed Entertainment, 1993–2019. Finler (2003) for US theatrical releases from 1933 to 2002; MPAA/MPA Theatrical Market Statistics for total US releases from 2003 to 2019. Finler (2003), boxofficemojo.com, www.natoonline.org/data/ticket-price/ for average theatrical ticket prices, United States.

The historical trajectories of mergers and acquisitions are more complicated than its theoretical conceptualization, in part because amalgamation often moves in waves. Hollywood film studios have themselves been consumed by multiple waves of megers and acquisitions (Bagdikian, 2004; Kunz, 2007). While this suggests the occurrence of some accumulation through breadth, the strategy might be limited if the media entertainment sector is now consuming firms at a global level. Nitzan and Bichler (2009) explain the problem with recurring waves of amalgamation:

> amalgamation is akin to eating the goose that lays the golden eggs. By gobbling up takeover targets within a given corporate universe, acquiring firms are depleting the pool of future targets. Unless this pool is somehow replenished, mergers and acquisitions are bound to create a highly centralized structure in which dominant capital owns everything worth owning. (p. 347)

Figure 5.13 demonstrates there is a slowdown of amalgamation within media entertainment. The figure uses data from the Institute for Mergers, Acquisitions and Alliances, which has breakdowns by business sector. The figure plots the data of "Media & Entertainment" as a ratio to the average across all sectors, which is used as a proxy for differential breadth. As we can see in both panels, the relative trends to amalgamation in media entertainment, measured by dollar

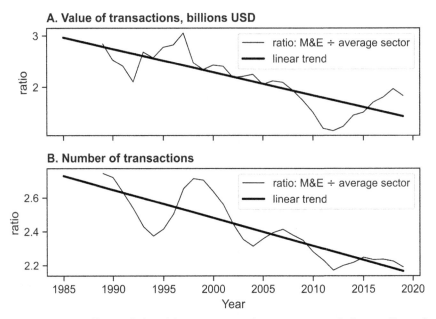

FIGURE 5.13 Differential breadth: mergers and acquisitions of the media and entertainment sector

Source: Mergers and acquisitions by industrial sector from Institute for Mergers, Acquisitions and Alliances (IMAA).

value or number of transactions, are downward. Opportunities for mergers and acquisitions could return in the future, but the relative declines in size and number are indicators that, for the time being, big amalgamations – which make big gains in power by fusing "previously distinct earning streams" (Nitzan & Bichler, 2009, p. 342) – are in the past.

When we think of the technological variety of media platforms for Hollywood film distribution (e.g., theatres, DVD, Blu-ray, digital streaming, TV, etc.) there appears to be an open frontier for green-field investment. But if there are now multiple paths to consumer attention, what is stopping Hollywood from increasing its film production? I believe the answer is found in theatrical distribution. Our minds can easily imagine that multiplatform distribution allows for any film to be inches from the hands of consumers, but theatrical attendance remains, for better or worse, Hollywood's key battleground for cinema attention. Consequently, Hollywood will rely on green-field investment only if it is likely that theatrical moviegoing can grow in tandem.

Figure 5.14 shows that, like amalgamations in media entertainment, the big jumps in theatrical attendance are in Hollywood's rear-view mirror. Panel B

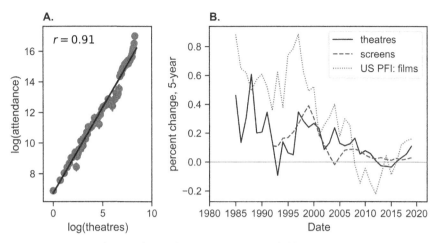

FIGURE 5.14   Can theatrical attendance grow? Green-field investment in US theatres and number of screens

Source: boxofficemojo.com for theatrical grosses and total theatres of individual films. Finler (2003), boxofficemojo.com, www.natoonline.org for average theatrical ticket prices, United States. https://www.natoonline.org for number of screens (as of March 2020) and number of total theatres, indoor and drive-in (as of March 2020). IHS Markit for National Income and Production Accounts, Nominal Private Fixed Investment in Intellectual Property Products, Entertainment, Literary and Artistic Originals: Theatrical Movies.

plots 5-year rates of change for three time series about the US market: number of theatres, number of screens and nominal value of private fixed investment in theatrical films. The growth rates of all three series have declined since 1980 – and in many cases during the same years. The positive correlations of the three series in Panel B (theatres ~ screens: +0.65, screens ~ PFI: +0.68 and theatres ~ PFI: +0.56) affect our perspective on Panel A. The latter plots the log-log correlation of attendance and total theatres for all US releases from 1983 to 2019. On its own, the very strong relationship between attendance and theatres is not surprising – to get lots of people to watch your film, you need lots of theatres to accommodate for popular demand. However, the same strong correlation is a financial and engineering challenge if you want to *increase* your attendance. In this case, the growth of attendance involves boosting the growth rate of theatre construction, which has been historically trending downwards.

5.7   Conclusion

This chapter has set the stage for the rest of Part II. Having moved step by step through some of the more technical details of the capital-as-power approach, the following analysis of risk reduction has a theory to operate within.

The rest of Part II researches the role of risk in the Hollywood film business in two ways. First, we are interested in the quantitative dimension of Major Filmed Entertainment's risk reduction strategies. From this perspective we look to find empirical evidence of what Major Filmed Entertainment has been able to achieve in the film sector. Moreover, measures of differential risk can explain the intensity of Major Filmed Entertainment's behaviour – it seeks a high degree of confidence in its ability to redistribute income faster than others, including other dominant capitalists and society at large. Second, sections of Part II seek to understand how the aesthetic and social dimensions of cinema were affected by Major Filmed Entertainment's push to reduce risk. By linking our study of differential risk to a historical and theoretical study of Hollywood cinema, we can connect Major Filmed Entertainment's financial goals to the strategic sabotage of social creativity.

Notes

1 The normal rate of return can fluctuate, but, according to Bichler and Nitzan, this rate is perceived as "normal" because state power has made this a universal condition of business – for example, government bonds guarantee a return that capitalists can then seek to beat through private investment. In fact, the normal rate of return is a foundation for strategic sabotage: if your firm cannot make a "reasonable profit" – that is, something as least as high as the "normal" rate – limit production or shut down. For more on the power underpinnings of the normal rate of return, see (Nitzan & Bichler, 2009, pp. 243–248).

2 The entities K_a and K_b do not necessarily have to be single firms; they can be the total or average capitalization of a set of firms.

3 While Spinoza (2007) did not use the same terms, we can find the germ of this idea in his *Theological-Political Treatise*: "A person's judgment, admittedly, may be subjected to another's in many different and sometimes almost unbelievable ways to such an extent that, even though he may not be directly under the other person's command, he may be so dependent on him that he may properly be said to be under his authority to that extent. Yet however much skillful methods may accomplish in this respect, these have never succeeded in altogether suppressing men's awareness that they have a good deal of sense of their own and that their minds differ no less than do their palates" (§20.2).

4 According to Jonathan Rosenbaum, film journalism helps perpetuate the idea that a movie's quality is signified by its financial success. He points to a recent worrying trend in film journalism that conflates two business terms – *turkeys* (bad movies) and *bombs* (financial disasters). This conflation perpetuates a sort of shorthand for the general audience, where a film must be a turkey because the financial data tell us it was a bomb (Rosenbaum, 1997a).

5 If these questions seem to hint at a theory of consumer sovereignty, the first part of Chapter 7 argues that it is problematic to put consumer sovereignty at the heart of an analysis of risk in the Hollywood film business.

6 For example, analysts of American cinema in China identify that Hollywood's main alternative to the quota system is co-production with a Chinese studio (Curtin, 2016; O'Connor & Armstrong, 2015). Co-production appears to be a suitable option because foreign investment can still take place, and Chinese partners can help tailor stories to the expectations of Chinese audiences. From a broader political economic

perspective, the difference between Chinese co-productions and Hollywood's typical behaviour as a global enterprise is a matter of power. Hollywood does use film labour and production studios all around the world (Curtin, 2016) and post-production of digital media can be done virtually anywhere. However, the extension of a film production network does not, by itself, transfer or dilute the rights of private ownership. A major Hollywood studio can have location scouts in London, shoot in Bulgaria or hire a film crew in Tunisia, but Hollywood's power remains unchanged because the studio has retained ownership of its claim on future income (McMahon, 2015; Nitzan & Bichler, 2009; Veblen, 2004). This retention of control is why global opportunities to work on Hollywood film projects are concentrated in location-shooting and post-production; the costs of these jobs are being cut in the interest of Hollywood, as countries and regions around the world compete to offer financial incentives, tax breaks and cheap labour (Miller et al., 2005).

7 When Hollywood is having a good year – controversy-free and lots of ticket sales for its biggest films – public resistance appears as an unlikely event. Yet, like Machiavelli's prince, Major Filmed Entertainment must pursue its own particular goals but without losing the hearts and minds of its "people" (Machiavelli, 1999).

6

THE RISK OF AESTHETIC OVERPRODUCTION

6.1 Introduction

The capitalist structure of Hollywood might not extinguish every flame of creativity from its film projects, but the interests of business leave scars and bruises on the aesthetic dimension of Hollywood cinema. Contemporary filmmaking is organized such that Major Filmed Entertainment can use its position in film distribution to exercise power over the pace and direction of creativity. This group and the other involved business interests, like banks that offer financing and firms that are looking for licensing and merchandising opportunities, stand between film production and the market (Wasko, 1982). Thus, when creativity is perceived to be "too risky", Major Filmed Entertainment is able to act. Some film projects, on account of their subject matter or style, can be effectively withheld from the market because no major firm will purchase the rights to distribute them. A film project may be able to find financing but under a contract that stipulates conditions about form, content, budget, cast, crew, and so on. A film can be produced, but management will have a role in the direction and pace of creation. And if business interests are still sceptical about their investment in potentially chaotic artistic creativity, the right of film ownership often includes the right of "final cut" – that is, the right to modify a film before it is released but after the director presents their final version (Bach, 1985).

But must the dominant Hollywood firms purposefully stand between the professional filmmaker and the moviegoer? Is the answer to this question binary, or is there an issue of extent here? To what degree should the business of film distribution shape and limit the social creativity of filmmaking? How is that degree of control determined?

DOI: 10.4324/9781003092629-8

This chapter analyses the structure of Hollywood film distribution through the lens of risk. In both its technical and conceptual senses, risk is relevant to the study of how Hollywood, as a business, utilizes social creativity. The conventional wisdom is that cinema is a very risky business enterprise, which means that even the biggest Hollywood firms are uncertain about their financial success (a point that is elaborated in Chapter 7). Yet, Major Filmed Entertainment appears to have devised strategies to reduce the possibility that the future of culture will be radically different from what capitalists expect it to be. This making of order does not eliminate risk entirely. Rather, from the perspective of capitalization, the industrial art of filmmaking and the social world of mass culture can be transformed into an *order of cinema*, in which film projects are weighable and calculable in terms of future expectations. Under such historical conditions, estimations of a film's social significance can, with a degree of confidence, be incorporated into the capitalization formula. Furthermore, certain strategies affect risk perceptions as much as they affect earnings: the repetition of genres, sequels, remakes; the cult of movie stars; the institution of false needs and wants through the sales efforts of business; and the dual ability to make movies resonate with established desires and to ready the industry of filmmaking for potential changes in social desire. All of these strategies schematize the social relations of cinema (Adorno, 2004d). Social habits, attitudes and values, in this environment, become things that can fit into a "knowable" distribution, which then can be quantified as risk (δ).

In the interest of lowering risk, Major Filmed Entertainment attempts to predetermine how new films will function in an already instituted order of cinema, which includes the creativity of filmmakers and the habits of moviegoers. For instance, if a particular studio is trying to determine, with some degree of certainty, the potential theatrical attendance for a new romantic comedy, there is a benefit if the larger social relations of cinema in which this comedy is embedded – both the creation and consumption of films – are determinable because they are orderly. And if the social relations of cinema are determinable because they are orderly, Hollywood's biggest distributors can then select and capitalize upcoming film projects with a greater degree of confidence.

The first part of this chapter analyses how the pace and direction of social creativity has a bearing on Major Filmed Entertainment's degree of confidence, which refers to the ability of capitalists to make predictions about future earnings. It also examines how Major Filmed Entertainment strategically calibrates its effect on the social creativity of cinema – how it controls the pace and direction of filmmaking but without suffocating it completely.

The second part argues that the repetitive, habitual qualities of Hollywood cinema are a defense against the possibility of *aesthetic overproduction*. Importantly, the term *overproduction* is being used in the same way that Veblen uses it. Aesthetic overproduction is the language of business, not art; it occurs when aesthetic decisions undermine the profitability and capitalization of a film, regardless of how these decisions look in the light of aesthetic, cultural and political judgement.

The third part presents examples of Major Filmed Entertainment limiting the threat of aesthetic overproduction. The examples vary in content and approach, but the combination of them is meant to mitigate some of the empirical challenges to observing the threat of aesthetic overproduction. For instance, there is no "smoking gun" in Major Filmed Entertainment's hand; the effects of its control need to be estimated or deduced from general behaviour in the production and distribution of Hollywood cinema.

6.2 The capitalist desire for an order of cinema

The base layer to an order of cinema is automatically created under capitalism. At any given time, the composition of the cinematic world can be stratified according to the quantities of a universal language: price. For example, one can go to a website like boxofficemojo.com and arrange the world of cinema according to box-office gross revenues, where the biggest theatrical grosses are at the top and the lowest are at the bottom. The same financial stratification is implied when a film is capitalized. When a film is given an expected theatrical revenues plateau (e.g., $20 million, $70 million, $300 million), the Hollywood film business is making an estimate about the future popularity of the film (Litman, 1998, p. 44). This financial estimate automatically positions a film among other films. The meaning of $200 million expected revenues, for example, is relative, as it depends on how other contemporary film projects are capitalized (McMahon, 2013, 2015).

A more substantial concept of order includes the social actors and institutions that can, to differing degrees, have an effect on the financial stratification of films. There are firms that try to boost their investments through advertising and public relations. There are film critics and media personalities who can extol some films and criticize others. There are consumers who prefer certain types of films over others, or maybe they want to use their leisure time for something other than cinema. This more substantial concept of order also includes the form and content of films. The films at the top of the financial pyramid may touch on common themes or adopt similar cinematic styles. The financial order of cinema may also be stratified according to how society values the political function of art. If people expect art to be more entertaining than confrontational, it could be difficult or impossible for politically contentious subjects, like abortion, or traumatic human behaviour, like genocide, to be top performers financially.

This more substantial order of cinema frames the risk perceptions of Major Filmed Entertainment. When some aesthetic qualities of cinema are perceived as riskier investments than others, Hollywood has a financial interest to be strategic about which expressions of human creativity it will affirm and which expressions it will mould, shape, modify or even reject. This same strategy manifests itself when some film projects are given bigger budgets than others – some ideas, regardless of their artistic value, will never be profitable if production costs grow to the size of a Hollywood blockbuster. Hollywood also needs to account for the possibility that the behaviour and attitudes of moviegoers can change. A popular film might inspire a wave of sequels or copycats – but is mimicking past financial successes always an effective strategy?

Plenty of examples illustrate how the social dimensions of film affect the risk perceptions of Major Filmed Entertainment. Some examples are found in the annual reports of the relevant firms. Time Warner, the owner of Warner Bros. from 2003 to 2018, lists risk factors relating to filmed entertainment and leisure time:

> [Time Warner] must respond to recent and future changes in technology and consumer behavior to remain competitive and continue to increase its revenues. . . . [Time Warner] faces risks relating to increasing competition for the leisure and entertainment time and discretionary spending of consumers, which has intensified in part due to technological developments and changes in consumer behavior. . . . The popularity of [Time Warner's] content is difficult to predict, can change rapidly and could lead to fluctuations in the Company's revenues, and low public acceptance of the Company's content may adversely affect its results of operations. (Warner, 2011, p. 13)

This "public acceptance of content" is important. If a film property is to be valued as an asset, its form and content must be evaluated – even before the film is made – in the light of social meaning (Vogel, 2011, pp. 99–106). For example, on account of its style and subject matter, a film property may lose its relevance (i.e., pecuniary value) as social meaning changes with the passage of time:

> … [W]ar epics, for instance, might be very popular with the public during certain periods but very unpopular during others. Some humor in films is timeless; some is so terribly topical that within a few years audiences may not understand it. In addition, because everything from hair and clothing styles to cars to moral attitudes changes gradually over time, the cumulative effects of these changes can make movies from only two decades ago seem rather quaint. (Vogel, 2011, p. 101)

The changing values of cultural and political meaning are not simply external factors that stand outside the reach of corporate strategy. Rather, a firm's labour force can be so innovative and original that its creativity undermines the pecuniary value of older assets: they are suddenly "out-of-date" because artistic labour has inaugurated a new cultural environment (Earl & Potts, 2013).

On the problem of treating a film as a long-lived asset, Prince (2000) is correct to argue that part of the uncertainty relates to the technological changes in distribution (theatre, VHS, DVD, etc.). "Determining the profitability of a given film", writes Prince, "can be an elusive undertaking because so many revenue sources figure into this determination" (Prince, 2000, p. xx). However, part of the reason that so few films are freely released into the public domain, regardless of technological changes, is that every significant shift in social-historical relevance gives Major Filmed Entertainment another opportunity to recapitalize its old film property. The tragic death of an actor can make their filmography popular again; a new channel of TV distribution, like Turner Classic Movies, can open future income streams for films that have been overlooked for decades; or, genres, like science fiction and musicals, can suddenly rebound in fashion. These examples contextualize the valuation of film libraries, which are often key assets in the mergers and acquisitions of media conglomerates (Kunz, 2007; Vogel, 2011).[1] Indeed, *Casablanca* is an asset (currently for AT&T), and would expectations about its future earnings not incorporate its mythological position in popular histories of cinema? How would one recapitalize *Casablanca* if the American Film Institute, in its next round of publishing lists of great American films, knocked this film down in rankings or removed it completely from "AFI's 100 Years . . . 100 Movies"?

Although changes to the order of cinema occur infrequently, they can be so abrupt that great uncertainty surrounds the capitalization of film property. One such abrupt change was the transition from silent film to sound in the late 1920s. For example, uncertainty over whether silent films would still have a place alongside "talkies" forced Albatross, a medium-sized French company, to temporarily stop all film production, as it was unable to price its own property:

> We have not been able to do it [assess the book value of completed films], because the sudden shock that shudders through the motion picture markets because of the apparition of sound film, makes every estimate, even approximately, impossible, especially for the older films. At present, most foreign countries have stopped nearly completely to buy them. We must put on hold all film production until the situation becomes clear. (Conseil d'Administration, April 25, 1929, quoted in Bakker, 2004, p. 64)

The uncertainty caused by the advent of sound cinema had a less severe effect on the studios that actively developed sound technology than it did on Albatross, but it affected them as well.[2] Because the aesthetics of sound cinema were still too open-ended during its nascent period, the major studios agreed to place a temporary moratorium on their own research and development. To really pursue sound cinema as a business enterprise, Hollywood studios first needed to decide if they were going to export American "talkies" in English, or whether they would be more accommodating to the languages of other countries.[3] Just as significantly, they did not yet know what a sound film should even look like (Hanssen, 2005, p. 102). Music and sound effects could be retrofitted onto films that were originally silent; a film could be released in two versions, one silent and another in sound; or a film could be silent for the majority of its running time, except for a few scenes that have dialogue or singing (e.g., *The Jazz Singer*).

Certain journalists have been fortunate enough to witness how the risk of social significance manifests on a film set or the studio lot, when studio executives, producers and directors argue over the form and content of film projects. In Lillian Ross's *Picture*, a book that serialized her reporting on the filming of *The Red Badge of Courage*, we find the recurring theme of the conflict between creativity and risk.[4] Many of the daily struggles over filming *The Red Badge of Courage* were the consequence of MGM's uncertainty about whether Americans in 1951 were even interested in seeing a film version of an 1895 book about the American Civil War (Ross, 2002). John Gregory Dunne spent one year investigating the workings of Twentieth Century-Fox in 1967 (Dunne, 1998). One of Dunne's stories is crass yet illustrative of how even the smallest details of a film can become subject to risk perceptions. Dunne describes a meeting at which Twentieth Century executives were talking about the studio's plan to distribute *Tony Rome* in Israel. The film, a detective story starring Frank Sinatra, is heavy on American slang. Two people in the meeting, Harry Sokolov and Stanley Hough, were concerned that much of the dialogue would not resonate with an Israeli audience. Richard Zanuck, who at the time was executive vice president in charge of worldwide production, worried less about the translation of English dialogue to Hebrew. He felt it was always possible to "dub it in local slang". As Dunne (1998) then notes, Owen McLean, the head of casting, remained uneasy about a scene he feared was *untranslatable*: "there was a scene in the picture based on the double-entendre of an old woman calling her cat a 'pussy'" (p. 154).

Uncertainty about the effectiveness of a *double-entendre* is not an insignificant concern. In fact, a PricewaterhouseCoopers report gives us a sense of how a sudden shift in what is considered funny or entertaining can create real financial problems for those who are on the hook for a film's costs. A change in the world of cinema can cause a "pre-release" write-down, which happens when the costs of the film become larger than its future expected earnings. As the report states, "pre-release write-downs generally occur when there is an adverse change in the expected performance of a film prior to release". Of the five examples about what can adversely change the future expectations of an individual film, four relate to the social relations of cinema:

- "Market conditions for the film that have changed significantly due to timing or other economic conditions";

- "Screening, marketing, or other similar activities that suggest the performance of the film will be significantly different from previous expectations";
- "A significant change to the film's release plan and strategy"; and
- "Other observable market conditions, such as those associated with recent performance of similar films" (PricewaterhouseCoopers, 2009, p. 26).

6.3 The threat of aesthetic overproduction

Major Filmed Entertainment's control of film distribution is not simply about the level of future earnings. Confidence, or low-risk perceptions, derives from Major Filmed Entertainment's ability to be the ultimate arbiter of the future of cinema. If Major Filmed Entertainment is unable to stand between the filmmaker and the consumer, the administered relationship between the aesthetic dimension of cinema and established social meaning breaks down, risk perceptions rise and capitalization tanks.

Risk perceptions cannot overlook the aesthetic dimension of cinema because each decision about film design has an effect on the overall degree of confidence. Nitzan and Bichler's (2009) argument about the eye of capitalization explains why a film's many qualities – for example, its genre, style, story, cast, director, production quality – and its possible resonance with established cultural and political attitudes would all be "integrated into the numerical architecture of capital": many dimensions of cinema can impact "the level and pattern of capitalist earnings" (p. 166). The Hollywood film business may or may not succeed in creating an order of cinema through the control of filmmaking – that is yet to be determined empirically – but, according to its own logic, it must translate the political, cultural and aesthetic qualities of cinema into the quantitative and forward-looking logic of capital.

A film project is translated into the logic of capital in its germinal stages, well before the first day of filming. Expectations about future earnings are being discounted to present prices when some scripts are sold while others are ignored, when some projects are properly developed while others sit idle, and when some projects are produced while others never make it out of "development hell".[5] As Wasko (2008) points out, in contrast to popular belief, "Hollywood films do not begin when the camera starts rolling, but involve a somewhat lengthy and complex development and pre-production phase during which an idea is turned into a script and preparations are made for actual production followed by post-production" (p. 43). A project begins as a film concept, usually in the form of a full script in its first draft. If approved by management, the project then goes into development, which is still far from the production stage (Wasko, 2008, p. 45). In development, the film concept is polished, the script is edited and re-edited, sometimes even rewritten completely, and producers and agents start talking about the film's possible "players" (main cast and director).

Risk perceptions permeate all along the line because a calculation of the expected earnings of cinema must work with, and sometimes in spite of, another logic: the logic of art. More specifically, the Hollywood film business must determine how it will strategically sabotage the creativity of those for whom cinema is primarily an art form. Such a characterization of social creativity is not meant to suggest that every artist or moviegoer is critical of the creative limits that are imposed by business.[6] Instead, the industrial art of filmmaking, with all of its aesthetic qualities, puts the Hollywood film business in a particular business–industry relationship, with specific features that cannot be ignored. The ways and means of any particular business–industry relationship depend on the type of industry being controlled by business.

The freedom of cinematic art to evolve in unforeseen ways can potentially threaten the financial goals of Major Filmed Entertainment. Creativity is a wild animal, and Major Filmed Entertainment wants to harness it in order to develop, finance, produce and distribute the "right" set of films. In this sense, "right" and "wrong" both refer not to aesthetic standards but to earnings. Fundamental to capitalist investment is the confidence that, if needed, Hollywood firms are able to steer social creativity in new directions *but with investors never losing control*.

If we imagine for argument's sake that the control of social creativity is unnecessary for capitalist ends, it will seem that film studios make bad films because they lack "creative" labour. Instead, however, the repetitive, even cautious, quality of Hollywood's imagination indicates that the film business aims to keep creativity in the film industry within a limited bandwidth. In its own way, a 2003 article in *The Economist* recognized that unharnessed artistic creativity troubles the Hollywood film business. The article characterized the business–industry struggle in Hollywood as that between "suits" and "ponytails":

> That the [film] industry tends over time to swing too far in favour of the ponytails, only to swerve back too far in favour of the suits, shows how hard it is to find a middle way. Devising a habitat in which creativity can flourish, yet within tight operational constraints: there lies a sequel for the entertainment industry worthy of a Hollywood blockbuster. (Anonymous, 2003)

Of course, there are historical examples of business dictating that filmmaking travel in one direction when it should have, in financial hindsight, encouraged cinema to go in another direction. For instance, the popularity of *The Sound of Music* (1965) was mistakenly taken as a sign that the major studios should say "Yes!" to more campy musicals when, outside of Hollywood, American youth and civil rights groups were rejecting discriminatory laws, old political institutions and conservative cultural attitudes. To be sure, eventually Hollywood would come to its business senses and enthusiastically embrace the student, civil rights and anti–Vietnam War movements of the 1960s, but not before releasing a long string of unpopular musicals: *Camelot* (1967), *Doctor Dolittle* (1967), *Chitty Chitty Bang Bang* (1968), *Hello, Dolly* (1969), *Paint Your Wagon* (1969), *Star!* (1968), *Sweet Charity* (1969) and *Darling Lili* (1970). The financial failure of *Darling Lili* was particularly bitter: in an explicit attempt to re-exploit *The Sound of Music*, *Darling Lili* stars Julie Andrews, who plays a singing spy in the First World War (D. A. Cook, 2000, p. 12).

Overall, business decisions about the form and content of Hollywood films are haunted by the spectre of *aesthetic overproduction*. Two things about the concept of aesthetic overproduction should be noted immediately. First, the term is my own tailoring of Veblen's generic concept of "overproduction". Second, overproduction applies "not to the material, mechanical bearing of the situation, but to its pecuniary bearing" (Veblen, 2006c, p. 215). Thus, overproduction does not mean that the material and intellectual capacities of a workforce are overtaxed, nor does it mean that a community is physically or mentally unable to consume what is in supply. Overproduction is a "question of prices and earnings"; it refers to a level or type of production that is inexpedient purely on "pecuniary grounds". Aesthetic overproduction is itself a consequence of how the business accounts of art "are kept in terms of the money unit, not in terms of livelihood, nor in terms of the serviceability of the goods, nor in terms of the mechanical efficiency of the industrial or commercial plant" (Veblen, 2006c, p. 85). Thus, regardless of what a film project could mean in political terms, or regardless of the potential for creative film design to strengthen the social importance of cinema, film projects are, like other assets, "capitalized on the basis of their profit yielding capacity" (Veblen, 2006c, p. 85).

In the case of Hollywood cinema, the threat of aesthetic overproduction cuts across the spatial and temporal divisions between film production, distribution and exhibition.[7] Indeed, the business interests of Hollywood might glimpse the spectre of aesthetic overproduction well before a film is completed and distributed. For instance, the brevity of Hollywood "pitch" meetings, which determine whether a film project will even get funds for production, is a pre-distribution hurdle that many film ideas have to clear (Elsbach & Kramer, 2003). What is said or left unsaid during a pitch meeting can foreshadow the uncertainties of acquiring, developing, producing and then distributing a project that is potentially too "weird" or "complex" for an audience (Mamet, 2007; Wyatt, 1994). Conversely, the financial failures of distribution can go back upstream and define aesthetic overproduction for those readying new film projects. The infamous failure of *Waterworld*, for instance, serves as a sober warning for those who think a new project has all the "right" elements for high grosses – for example, big movie star, lots of action, expensive and elaborate sets.

The threat of aesthetic overproduction tells us a few things. First, the autonomous creation of new social significations is, in general, antithetical to capitalist interests. Again, the potential for artists to openly redefine the meaning and ends of art does not threaten cinema as a cultural-political activity – free from the repressive demands of business enterprise, cinema could support a political project of open, democratic cultural creation (Holman & McMahon, 2015). Yet the unpredictability and openness of artistic creation can undermine the instrumental calculation of expected future earnings. The capitalization of film falls apart if either the *telos* of a film or its relationship to an already-instituted social imaginary is obscure to the point of being non-determinable.

Second, Major Filmed Entertainment has a real incentive to sustain a form of cinema that is conservative because it is repetitive and formulaic. Even if there is a technological/anthropological capacity for the art of filmmaking to go well beyond the "limits" that are imposed in Hollywood cinema, guideposts like the star system and film genres help keep everybody involved from veering too far off the well-beaten path. To be sure, these guideposts are not meant to suffocate all forms of artistic innovation; film production requires large amounts of creative and technical skill. Rather, genre and the Hollywood star system "save" filmmakers the trouble of yearning for, and then abandoning, unconventional filmmaking techniques that could jeopardize distribution with one of Hollywood's dominant firms (Rosenbaum, 2000). This foreclosure of alternatives through institutional norms is a defence against the first point, the potential for autonomous creation. By obeying its own instituted formulas of filmmaking, Hollywood reinstitutes the "canonical and vacuous tautology" that is, according to Castoriadis, hidden within many notions of creativity. Social institutions often define the ends of human activity in such a way that "the new is no more than the actualization of a possible which was given (to whom?) from the start" (Castoriadis, 1984a, p. 234). For Castoriadis, this version of creativity is less threatening to an established social order because the radical creation of new forms is denied. Rather, human imagination is limited to imitative production; the scope of creativity is bounded by an already existing Form or Idea (Castoriadis, 1998, p. 197).

Third, the repetitive nature of mass culture, of which Hollywood is a central part, is about more than ideology. Risk perceptions partly determine the level of capitalization, and confidence about the size and pattern of expected earnings is likely to increase if moviegoers had a predilection for only a narrow range of film types. The threat of aesthetic overproduction is a strong reason why the Hollywood business has a vested interest in effectively "pre-selling" new films through stylistic repetition. When Hollywood repeats itself, the "new" already has, in the eyes of a habituated moviegoer, a familiar, pre-digested quality (Maltby, 2003). This cycle of repetition also explains why independent filmmakers will sometimes vocalize their opposition to having films appeal to the sensibilities of the average audience. Making films "for only themselves" or "for nobody" is a form of symbolic resistance to all that is implied when Hollywood says it makes films to "please an audience" (Ortner, 2013, pp. 51–53).

Fourth, if the underlying identity between creation and consumption is firmly rooted in capitalist power, Hollywood gains additional flexibility about what types of films it will make. As Adorno recognized, the ideology of mass culture can become "as internally antagonistic as the very society which it aims to control" (Adorno, 2004e, p. 181). In the last few years, for example, Hollywood has demonstrated that it has no problems showing rape, poverty, racism and violence on the silver screen. As long as these cinematic representations of an unjust reality have a determinable relationship to the habits and attitudes of an audience, the cultural representation of social contradictions is not antithetical to the goal of profit. Mass culture's weak impact on real social contradictions is consistent and, therefore, predictable with respect to risk perceptions.

6.4   Limiting aesthetic overproduction with capitalist power

We can conclude this chapter with examples where, I believe, Major Filmed Entertainment is using capitalist power to limit the threat of aesthetic production. When expressed as this type of threat to financial expectations, the potential of an artist to create new social significations is translated into a risk calculation. Thus, these examples of limiting, standardizing and regulating creativity illustrate how the actuality and potentiality of human creation are entangled in the business-industry relationship that Veblen originally conceptualized (Veblen, 2004, 2006c). In the conceptual language of Adorno (2004a), this entanglement is a product of administration and culture having incompatible goals, whereby the former is instrumental and the latter is not.

The examples share the same theme: Major Filmed Entertainment and its cooperative institutional partners stand as barriers to the creation, autonomous or otherwise, of (radically) new social significations. This barrier is not 100 per cent effective, but Major Filmed Entertainment also does not want to extinguish the "fires" of artistic creativity entirely. Instead, the barriers to autonomous creation are creating a general social dialectic of institutional power and human creativity.

At certain moments in its history, Hollywood will ease its control of industry if the alternative of increasing control is too costly. In these moments Hollywood firms appear to be performing creative destruction, which Schumpeter thought monopolies would need to perform on a regular basis. For example, the creativity of what many scholars call "New Hollywood" (Berliner, 2011; Bernardoni, 1991; M. Harris, 2009; Kirshner, 2012; Langford, 2010), a period from roughly 1968 to 1977, could be labelled "creative destruction". Because of falling profits in the 1960s, the largest Hollywood firms purposefully gave young filmmakers autonomous creative control – from project approval to final cut. Filmmakers such as Hal Ashby, Robert Altman, Peter Bogdonovich, John Cassavetes, Francis Ford Coppola, William Friedkin, Sidney Lumet, Arthur Penn and Bob Rafelson were encouraged to supersede old Hollywood fare with political themes and a New Wave style.

More often, however, Major Filmed Entertainment's relationship with human creativity demonstrates the falsity in the assumption that Hollywood can only meet the demands of society when it allows the best and brightest talent to stretch their creative capacities to the fullest. At minimum, the relationship between the qualities of film production and the needs and wants of film consumers is mediated by capitalist institutions. There are also many instances that demonstrate both Hollywood's ability and financial desire to *stagnate* social creativity in cinema. Thus, the effect of Hollywood on the social relations of cinema can advantage its investments, while simultaneously disadvantaging the pursuit of business and art with alternative methods. Hollywood's power over filmmaking, in this sense, is not about the productivity of labour. Neither is it necessarily the case that Hollywood has to perform creative destruction over and over again.

6.4.1   When Hollywood gets repetitive: genres

The effects of capitalist power can be observed in the repetitiveness of Hollywood cinema. The use of film genres in Hollywood, for example, is much more than a philosophy of aesthetic forms; it is an industrial technique that can sometimes, in the Hollywood system, act as a form of structural constraint on the scope of creativity (Neale, 2000). A new film project in Hollywood will usually obey the divisions that prevent some genres from being mixed together – "horror western" anyone? The same film project might, like so many other Hollywood films before it, insert a romantic element into the story because this type of mixture is considered standard. A new film, situated within a particular genre, might also be pressured to affirm the tropes and clichés of that genre – so as to conform to what audiences have been conditioned to expect.

Some readers may now be thinking of notable exceptions in Hollywood cinema. Nevertheless, we can disagree about particular differences between Hollywood films, but we can still think together about structural pressures and its effects on art. Is it in Hollywood's financial interest to be repetitive and formulaic? Is the injection of small changes into well-used aesthetic formulas or styles the best that Hollywood can do creatively? Are instances of repetition a function of business strategy, or does Hollywood overuse formulaic filmmaking techniques when it lacks innovative alternatives?

With respect to the institutional habit of using genre, we can investigate Major Filmed Entertainment's tendency to combine genres in pairs. In the mathematics of combinations, this combination of pairs would be expressed as nC_2 or $\binom{n}{2}$, where n is the number of choices of genre. Since a filmmaker or screenwriter can technically choose any set of genres – to say nothing about the ability of

TABLE 6.1   Combinations of genres from example

Film	Genre 1	Genre 2
Spaceballs	Adventure	Comedy
	Adventure	Sci-fi
	Comedy	Sci-fi
Crocodile Dundee II	Action	Adventure
	Action	Comedy
	Adventure	Comedy

TABLE 6.2   Tally of combinations from example

Combination	Tally
Action–Adventure	1
Action–Comedy	1
Adventure–Comedy	2
Adventure–Sci-fi	1
Comedy–Sci-fi	1

people to create new genres — we can take a slightly different approach with Internet Movie Database (IMDb) data. By gathering IMDb's list of genres for a series of films, we can tally the number of different combinations in Hollywood's actual set of releases. In other words, this perspective observes the empirical output of Hollywood's creative range within genre combinations.

As an illustrative example of the method being used, let us begin with just two films in 1987: *Spaceballs* and *Crocodile Dundee II*. IMDb lists ["Adventure", "Comedy", "Sci-fi"] as the genres of *Spaceballs* and ["Action", "Adventure", "Comedy"] for *Crocodile Dundee II*. Table 6.1 shows the number of pairs we can produce when the order of choices is not important (such is not the case with permutations). Table 6.2 tallies the combinations and shows that, in this set of two films, "Adventure–Comedy" is the most popular combination.

Figure 6.1 follows this method but for a large set of films from 1983 to 2019. In this set are 1,334 films, and each one is above the 75th percentile in opening-theatre rank of its year. As will be explained in more detail in the next chapter, this approach to selecting films for analysis – which is slightly different than selecting films by gross revenue – is related to the risk perceptions that relate to Major Filmed Entertainment needing to decide about opening-theatre size before theatrical revenues begin to flow. The edges in Figure 6.1 visualize the total occurrences of each pair of genres. To minimize clutter – there are 168 different pairs in the data set – I set the line width of each edge between two genres to be the tally, divided by one hundred and rounded to one decimal point. For instance, the line between "Action" and "Adventure" is thickest (3.8 pt) because there are

376 films that have this pair of genres. Other edges are invisible because they occurred fewer than 5 times – for example, "Crime–Western", "Animation–Horror", "Biography–Romance".

As a visual representation of Hollywood's repetitiveness, Figure 6.1 has limits. For instance, films that only have one genre listed on IMDb are excluded. Additionally, the simple counting of genre combinations cannot tell us about any qualitative differences between films that share the same combinations. Nevertheless, Figure 6.1 highlights patterns in Major Filmed Entertainment's use of genre. If the genres in the figure were Hollywood's only choices for film production, only 66 per cent of possible pairs are being used (168 out of 253 or $\binom{23}{2}$ possible combinations). Moreover, a constellation of genres accounts for the majority of the

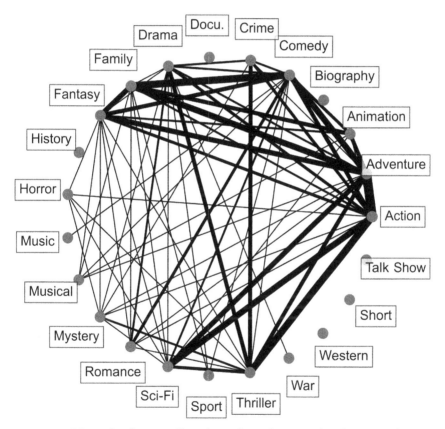

FIGURE 6.1 Network of genres, films above the 75th percentile of opening theatres, 1983–2019

Source: IMDb.

Note: Films with only one listed genre are excluded from the visualization.

data set: [Action, Adventure, Animation, Comedy, Crime, Drama, Family, Fantasy, Sci-Fi, Thriller]. This constellation of genres is a suitable representation of the films that typically open in lots of theatres at once.

How does this type of repetition come about? In his sardonic language, playwright, screenwriter and film director David Mamet argues that corporate structure reinforces formulaic repetition in Hollywood film production. For instance, there are the hierarchical relationships between script readers and their bosses:

> The entry level position at motion picture studios is script reader. Young folks fresh from the rigours of the academy are permitted to beg for a job summarizing screenplays. These summaries will be employed by their betters in deliberations.
>
> These higher-ups rarely (some, indeed, breathe the word "never") read the actual screenplay; thus, the summaries, called "coverage", become the coin of the realm.
>
> Now, like anyone newly enrolled in a totalitarian regime, these neophytes get the two options pretty quickly — conform or die. Conformity, in this case, involves figuring out what the studios might like (money) and giving them the illusion that the dedicated employee, through strict adherence to the mechanical weeding process, can provide it. The script reader adopts the notion that inspiration, idiosyncrasy, and depth are all very well in their place but that their place has yet to be discovered and that he would rather die than deviate from received wisdom.
>
> The mere act of envisioning "the public", that is, "that undifferentiated mass dumber than I", consigns the script reader to life on the industrial model. He or she now is no longer an individual but a field boss, a servant of "industry". . . . Deprived of the joys of whimsy, contemplation and creation, they are left with prerogative. So script coverage is brutal and dismissive. (Mamet, 2007, pp. 77–78)

Mamet came to his opinion about Hollywood's corporate structure by his first-hand experiences in writing, producing and directing for Major Filmed Entertainment. Interestingly, Mamet's (2007, p. 78) critique of Hollywood for demanding conformity is actually *rationalized* by the "creative instability hypothesis" of Earl and Potts (2013). For Earl and Potts, the perceived risks of human creativity make it rational for business managers to remain within the aesthetic mainstream and to only allow the creative envelope to be pushed with conservative hesitation. Similarly to Mamet's view that there is a lot of creative talent that Hollywood ignores or is hesitant to hire (Mamet, 2007, p. 79), Earl and Potts admit that the issue of creative instability is not about a deficit of ingenuity and creativity in labour. Rather, artistic novelty, complexity and even playful experimentation are business risks because they can exacerbate competition in the form of "overshooting". Overshooting is the "other side" of "Schumpeterian competition" (Earl & Potts, 2013, p. 153), whereby demand is destroyed by Hollywood allowing its creative labour too free a hand in innovation and complexity – all of which Earl and Potts acknowledge can be good for art (Earl & Potts, 2013, p. 154).

From the standpoint of Adorno's critical theory, Earl and Potts are trying to rationalize the so-called necessity of business needing to separate its instrumental goals in cultural creation from the truth of art. Once separated, strategic sabotage is a "beneficial" approach to reducing risk in mass culture. For example, management's strict control of employee creativity is a mitigation against the so-called risks of consumer attention. Consumer attention, according to Earl and Potts (2013), is assumed to be an independent variable that requires business to be conservative about what it can control, the creativity of its employees:

> [I]t is to be expected that a product will be rejected if consumers cannot "get into" it because it requires too much skill in discerning patterns in, and construct meaning from, the flow of information associated with it. If products are highly complex, many potential customers may fail to give attention to them after initially failing . . . to discern plot, theme, melody and so on. The human tendency to make evaluations relative to prior reference points and to suffer from loss aversion will limit the willingness of customers, as well as suits and creatives, to take risks with products that seem to be straying too far from familiar territory. (p. 161)

A conservative approach to complexity makes sense, but only because Earl and Potts refer to the behavioural psychology of consumers in a very matter-of-fact style. With a low estimation of each consumer's cognitive capacities, they create a situation that appears unavoidable; under these circumstances, the rational manager *must* control social creativity.

In their version of management mitigating consumer risk through its control of producer creativity, Earl and Potts ignore the ways in which dominant firms could have a hand in shaping the social environment from which consumer attention sprouts. For instance, does the global presence of Hollywood cinema have no effect on consumer predilections for types of films? Are some films or film project ideas deemed too alien, confusing or weird by virtue of how Hollywood cinema socializes and habituates our film-watching skills? Earl and Potts claim that "consumers can develop their skills in appreciating creative products by successfully trying more challenging works" (Earl & Potts, 2013, p. 161) – but does this aesthetic education take place in a vacuum, or is it the sole responsibility of the consumer? Does Hollywood have a hand in affecting the production, distribution and exhibition of "challenging" cinema?

By ignoring these type of questions, Earl and Potts (2013) come to the conclusion that the business and creative sides of modern entertainment share the same "rational" perspective about art, creativity and risk: "In working out how far the creative envelope should be pushed, both suits and creatives will, if acting rationally, take account of the need to ensure that the product that is offered aligns with the consumption capabilities of potential customers" (p. 161). Fortunately for us, the problematic assumptions that built this conclusion are easy to find. As we consider the role of power in the Hollywood film business, we can see how Earl and Potts's argument has internalized all of the social conditions necessary to make creativity appear to be "naturally" or "inherently" risky. Moreover, Earl and Potts are speaking of risk in pecuniary terms, which does not reflect, following Veblen's arguments about capital and overproduction, the risk of creativity for anyone other than the people profiting from the investment.

6.4.2 When Hollywood gets repetitive: casting

Ridley Scott's *Exodus: Gods and Kings* is a telling example of Hollywood rationalizing its so-called inability to widen the boundaries of its creativity. In this case, the boundaries concern Hollywood's tendency to reserve roles for its biggest stars, even when a big star appears unfit for the role in question.

Much of the pre-release journalism on *Exodus* concerned the contentious decision to cast white Hollywood actors in the story of Moses opposing the Pharaoh and leading the Israelites out of Ancient Egypt (Anonymous, 2014; Child, 2014; Palmer, 2014). Christian Bale, who was cast to play Moses, became a *de facto* spokesperson for the film and attempted to diffuse some of the criticism. Bale's defence of the casting decisions inadvertently reveals how these decisions were not made for a lack of historically available alternatives: "I don't think fingers should be pointed, but we should all look at ourselves and say, 'Are we supporting wonderful actors in films by North African and Middle Eastern filmmakers and actors, because there are some fantastic actors out there'" (Anonymous, 2014). The obvious rationale for not casting fantastic North African or Middle Eastern actors instead of Bale and other white Hollywood actors is rooted in the financial goals of Hollywood – even Bale acknowledged this. However, such a rationale not only downplays the racist element of this story; it actually obscures how Hollywood's *modus operandi* transforms a controversial choice about casting into a so-called rational business decision. For instance, when Scott defended his film with the argument that he had to assemble the "best possible cast . . . on a budget of this scale [\$140 million]", he admitted to Hollywood's interest in profit but glossed over the main reason why narrow-minded casting decisions are the so-called best business strategies.

If we start to ask follow-up questions about the aesthetic decisions of the film, it becomes clearer that the size and influence of Hollywood in modern cinema has a hand in making these decisions become instrumentally rational under specific historical conditions. Is it *necessary* for a film about the book of Exodus to cost $140 million? Is it necessary that, for the sake of entertainment, Moses bear a sword rather than a staff, or that the Red Sea be made red from man-eating crocodiles sent by God? Is it necessary that Moses be portrayed as an atheistic warrior — where God might be the hallucinatory consequence of a concussion – rather than the eventual lawgiver of God's commandments? If the answer to each question is "no", we actually catch a glimpse of how the casting of Bale fits into a larger political economy of power. Hollywood is bending the curvature of modern cinema in such a manner that there is a financial disincentive for it to cast a film about Moses more appropriately, even when Bale claims this is what he would personally hope for: "To me that would be a day of celebration. For the actors it would be wonderful. It would be a wonderful day for humanity, but also for films and for storytelling in general" (Anonymous, 2014).

My cynical side thinks Bale is being disingenuous with his hope for better casting in the Hollywood blockbuster he stars in. However, the issues of repetitive or narrow casting in Hollywood are more institutional than they are individual. We can use IMDb data, once again, to demonstrate the extent of Hollywood's repetitive casting in films above the 75th percentile in opening-theatre size. Major Filmed Entertainment must certainly assess the risk of casting in this set of films, as their wide theatrical openings need to cover distribution and advertising costs by generating lots of revenues as fast as possible. *Exodus*, for instance, is above the 75th percentile in opening-theatre size in its year of release, and we just saw Bale and Scott defend casting in relation to the film's expensive budget and the need for a star to generate blockbuster-level sales.

Table 6.3 helps me explain my method of gathering casting data. For each film, I gathered the first 20 actors on the cast list. With respect to actors having enough dialogue or screen-time for their roles to be memorable, a Hollywood film is rarely 20 actors deep. However, a long list of actors can achieve two things at once. First, it can account for the possibility that an notable actor is unexpectedly lower on IMDb's cast list. Morgan Freeman's role in *Batman Begins* is a good example. In Table 6.3 Morgan Freeman is 12th on the list. There could be many reasons why he is 12th on the list, but the important thing is that his cameo-like role in the film would have been excluded with more a selective slice of IMDb data. Second, a lengthier list of actors gives us data to investigate if repetition in casting occurs further down the list, with actors who are not stars in the public's mind but who have secured roles in a Hollywood film. For instance, Table 6.3 includes actors with smaller speaking roles in *Batman Begins*: Mark Boone Junior as Arnold Flass, Linus Roache as Thomas Wayne, Larry Holden as district attorney Carl Finch, Colin McFarlane as Gillian B. Loeb and Emma Lockhart as Young Rachel Dawes. Does the possession of these roles in *Batman Begins* increase the likelihood that an actor will have roles in other films above the 75th percentile in opening-theatre size?

TABLE 6.3 Example of casting data from IMDb

Year	Title	Title ID	Actor	Actor ID
2005	*Batman Begins*	372784	Christian Bale	288
2005	*Batman Begins*	372784	Michael Caine	323
2005	*Batman Begins*	372784	Liam Neeson	553
2005	*Batman Begins*	372784	Katie Holmes	5017
2005	*Batman Begins*	372784	Gary Oldman	198
2005	*Batman Begins*	372784	Cillian Murphy	614165
2005	*Batman Begins*	372784	Tom Wilkinson	929489
2005	*Batman Begins*	372784	Rutger Hauer	442
2005	*Batman Begins*	372784	Ken Watanabe	913822
2005	*Batman Begins*	372784	Mark Boone Junior	95478
2005	*Batman Begins*	372784	Linus Roache	730070
2005	*Batman Begins*	372784	Morgan Freeman	151
2005	*Batman Begins*	372784	Larry Holden	390227
2005	*Batman Begins*	372784	Gerard Murphy	614283
2005	*Batman Begins*	372784	Colin McFarlane	568801
2005	*Batman Begins*	372784	Sara Stewart	829815
2005	*Batman Begins*	372784	Gus Lewis	1600560
2005	*Batman Begins*	372784	Richard Brake	104114
2005	*Batman Begins*	372784	Rade Serbedzija	784884
2005	*Batman Begins*	372784	Emma Lockhart	1439087

The IMDb data show that Major Filmed Entertainment is (a) repetitive in its casting and (b) that this repetition is unequal across the distribution of actors in the dataset. Figure 6.2 shows two distributions of film count per actor. Panel A shows the top 20 actors, sorted by total count of roles between 1983 and 2019. Readers will likely recognize all or some of the names in Panel A. The panel also shows signs of racial and gender inequalities in Hollywood casting: the majority of the list is white, actors of Asian descent are missing and there is not a single woman in the top 20 (the first five female actors outside the top 20 are Julia Roberts [16 films], Sandra Bullock [15], Angelina Jolie [15], Halle Berry [15] and Carla Gugino [15]). As Yuen (2016) demonstrates through interviews with actors of color trying to secure roles in Hollywood, racial discrimination in casting limits opportunities in different ways – for example, perceiving actors of color to be "too foreign" or not American enough in demeanor and accent, typecasting by ethnicity or skin color, and restricting acting opportunities to a narrow range of stereotyped characters. The unfairness of the biggest female stars having fewer film counts than men is not surprising when systemic gender discrimination and the role of power in distributing roles to women might be one of Hollywood's biggest open secrets – especially after the testimonies of many in the #MeToo movement. This prevalence of gender discrimination is also institutional rather

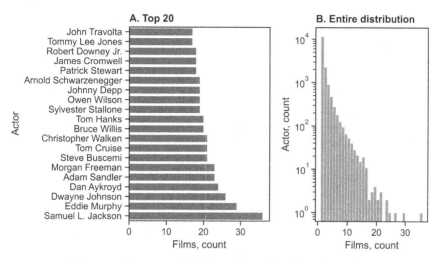

FIGURE 6.2 Film count by actor, films above the 75th percentile of opening theatres, 1983–2019

Source: IMDb.

than being about "bad apples" in the workplace. Erigha (2019) demonstrates how Black women are repeatedly disadvantaged in securing creative roles in Hollywood filmmaking, such as directing and screenwriting. The interviews of Simon (2019) with Hollywood talent agents revealed the degree to which the job of talent representation advantaged white men; many of the prominent positions in talent agencies were held by white men and their shared beliefs that "good" masculine traits were necessary for strong job performance created exclusive networks of patrimonial mentoring, affected who was promoted to talent agent, and enabled talent agents to openly complain about the so-called emotional instabilities of their female clients.

Panel B in Figure 6.2 dispels the belief that *any* role in a wide-release film will lead to other roles in big Hollywood films. There are 16,154 actors in the data set, and roughly 60 per cent will only have *one* appearance in this set of films from 1983 to 2019. Because of this power distribution in film count per actor, elite status can be reached with only a few films to one's name. Christian Bale, for example, is listed in the data set six times: *Batman Begins, The Dark Knight, Terminator Salvation, Public Enemies, The Dark Knight Rises, Exodus: Gods and Kings*. This is actually a fraction of Bale's filmography – the data set is not counting his numerous (serious) roles in smaller theatrical releases – but what is counted in the figure puts Bale above the 95th percentile of the data set. The actors in Panel A are all in the 99.9th percentile.

To see if repetitiveness of casting has changed over time, Figure 6.3 is built from rolling windows of data. Five-year windows of casting data are created first and then the film count is computed for each actor. This avoids actors with long careers skewing measurements of recent years – for example, the cumulative film counts of Eddie Murphy or Samuel L. Jackson would beat any newcomer, whose career started in the mid-2010s. The y-axis of each panel in Figure 6.3 measures the inequality of every 5-year distribution as a Gini coefficient, where 0 is perfect equality and 1 is perfect inequality. The x-axis in Panel A selects the top ten actors in each window and calculates the mean of their film count. Panel B plots on its x-axis the number of films released by Major Filmed Entertainment, smoothed as a 5-year rolling average.

Figure 6.3 is interesting for at least two reasons. First, rising inequality in the figure is, in this case, an effect of Major Filmed Entertainment being more repetitive with its top-tier A-list actors. For example, in the period from 1983 to 1987, Dan Aykroyd was first with six films and the top ten actor average was 4.7 films; in the period from 2015 to 2019, Dwayne Johnson was first with 11 films and the top ten actor average was 7.5 films. Second, there is a curious nonlinear path in Panel B. From 1983 to 2009, there is a tight correlation between the increase in the number of films and the increase in inequality in casting. The inflection point

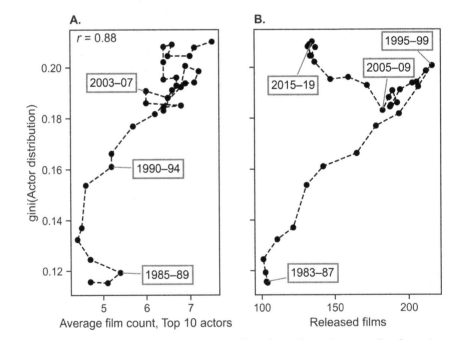

FIGURE 6.3   Inequality in actor distribution, films above the 75th percentile of opening theatres, 1983–2019

Source: IMDb for cast lists of films. Boxofficemojo and MPA for number of films released by Major Filmed Entertainment.

at 2009 puts the relationship on a new trajectory, whereby there is increasing inequality as the number of films *decrease*. Additional work will be needed to explain why the inflection point occurs around 2009. For now, I can make a hypothesis by drawing from Leaver (2010), who conceives of actors and their agents as a group that fights *against* film distributors for claims on film earnings. A-list actors cannot control the number of films released by Major Filmed Entertainment, the x-axis in Figure 6.3B. Yet they have agents who can fight against new opportunities to cast actors more equitably. If casting decisions in the mid-2000s were about to follow the historical patterns of Hollywood casting since the 1980s, the decreases to film output signaled to A-list actors and their agents that the future might be "too equal".

6.4.3   When Hollywood defines what is good cinema

On the question of who judges the quality of a film, it is easy to start with a notion of subjectivity and say the ultimate judge of a film's quality is the individual moviegoer. As individual moviegoers, this is often what we think we are doing: we have the autonomy to "decide for ourselves" if a film is good or bad. Picturing each moviegoer as having a separated, independent experience with a film makes sense on a physical level – a film's images and sounds are being perceived with *my* eyes and ears. The reality of film criticism, however, is misunderstood if we imagine the social world of cinema to be simply composed of individuals exercising independent judgement. Major Filmed Entertainment, for example, is actively shaping this social world. What effect does this have on our conceptions of a good film?

As a social institution with considerable investment in the financial future of cinema, Major Filmed Entertainment is adept at promoting *one-dimensional* definitions of good cinema. A one-dimensional definition of good cinema, which I am conceptualizing with the critical theory of Marcuse (1968b, 1968d, 1978, 1991), does not include the aesthetic and technological potentials of cinema. Rather, a one-dimensional definition is more positivist in character, as the characteristics of good cinema are defined more immediately, according to what is actually being watched. The actual realities of film consumption are important to Hollywood because inequalities in the distribution of films limit the "existing reality" of the average moviegoer, whose perspective on cinema is much narrower than what is technically available in film libraries, universities and the collections of film lovers. Thus, the potential of cinema does not simply live in the mind, as pure theory; it includes films that are neglected in common ideas of what people think the film medium can achieve.

The starkest examples of a one-dimensional definition of good cinema are found in Hollywood's advertisements. With a perverse hope that the audience has cultural amnesia, Hollywood will tell you that its next film is promised to be a cinematic experience of the highest quality. Yet the one-dimensional definition of good quality comes from more than the superlatives of film advertising. Hollywood's definition of good cinema is institutional at its core. The behaviour of Major Filmed Entertainment, for example, affects such factors as the level of public access, availability of alternatives and the strength of cultural education.

Film critic Jonathan Rosenbaum shares this concern about the institutional barriers that protect Hollywood's position in definitions of good cinema. From his experience as a film critic, Rosenbaum (2000) presents a long list of examples where the Hollywood film business affects the way film journalism can explore the histories and geographies of film art. Often excluded from the category of "good" cinema are films that editors think will be too alien to their readership. The independent, avant-garde or just plain weird might find some amount of journalistic coverage, especially in the age of the internet, but Rosenbaum's experience at film festivals, the *Chicago Tribune* and his guest television appearances on Chicago Tonight all reveal there is an underlying inequality in attention. Not only does mainstream journalism choose to stay within the boundaries that Hollywood helps define, but film critics also turn into pseudo-marketers:

> Consider what might happen if Roger Ebert couldn't find a single movie to recommend on one of his weekly shows. Or let's assume that this has already happened once or twice. How much freedom would he have to assign a thumbs-down to everything three or four weeks in a row without getting his show canceled? And for all the unusual amount of freedom I enjoy at the *Chicago Reader*, how long could I keep my job if I had nothing to recommend week after week? For just as Communist film critics were "free" to write whatever they wanted as long as they supported the Communist state, most capitalist film critics today are "free" to write anything as long as it promotes the products of multicorporations; the minute they decide to step beyond this agreed-upon canon of "correct" items, they're likely to get into trouble with their editors and publishers. (Rosenbaum, 2000, p. 54)

Rosenbaum's criticism is similar to what Adorno said about the power of scale in modern advertising: large capitalist firms can advertise their products to such a degree that we come to associate the quality of an object with the amount of advertising or publicity it gets. This power of scale also binds the profession of film criticism to a business that is not in the habit of admitting to the quality of what lies beyond its own boundaries. For instance, the journalistic conspiracy of silence regarding Bela Tarr's seven-hour-long *Sátántangó* was, according to Rosenbaum, a means of ignoring hard truths about the institutional repression of aesthetic potential. If other film critics, like Rosenbaum, thought the film's long shots and extremely slow pace excellently captured the philosophical themes of nihilism and authoritarianism, it would challenge, even in some small way, the rationale of the mainstream film business (Rosenbaum, 2004, p. 48). If its length of seven hours is not excessive in terms of art, the high quality of *Sátántangó* shakes the illusion that Hollywood's shorter films are the reflection of universal laws about the duration of good films. Additionally, the film reveals that there is an implicit business risk to artists making great films: "If great films invent their own rules", writes Rosenbaum (2004, p. 48), Bela Tarr demonstrates that one can create a type of masterpiece that cannot be covered in the national media.

Rosenbaum gives another relevant example (Rosenbaum, 2000, pp. 91–106). In his opinion, the American Film Institute (AFI) betrays its mandate to honour "the most outstanding motion pictures" because its acts of honouring American cinema hardly ever stray from the films of major Hollywood studios. This produces an ideological echo in the AFI's lists of "top" films. Some of the listed films are outstanding in their own right, but the AFI uses its institutional power to tell people what they already think – that *Casablanca*, *The Wizard of Oz*, *Gone with the Wind*, *E.T.*, *The Godfather* and *Star Wars* are outstanding films in the history of cinema. As should be the case in film journalism, so should it be the case with the AFI: neglected films in independent, alternative or foreign cinema should be pulled out from under the shadows of Hollywood rather than get pushed deeper into the darkness. Even though the AFI is only concerned with American cinema, Rosenbaum claims that it is not difficult to produce much more representative lists of what has been outstanding in all of its history.

6.4.4   When Hollywood defines the limits of cinema

Rosenbaum's critical views of Hollywood's dominance rely on interconnected arguments: that the aesthetic qualities of mainstream Hollywood are overvalued and that alternatives like *Sátántangó* are undervalued. I agree with Rosenbaum, but I also recognize that the argument is dependent on how one rates his ability to judge film quality. Consequently, I think we can corroborate a part of Rosenbaum's argument in way that relies less on his likes and dislikes of specific films in the history of cinema.

Rosenbaum's argument presents Hollywood as an institution that can influence the chances of critics and consumers wandering outside the boundaries of Hollywood's familiar territory. It is unlikely we can clearly delineate this territory at the scale of individual films; at this small scale, subjective predilections and differences in personal experience create many opportunities to move the line that defines what is included in "mainstream Hollywood". We can, however, investigate whether a larger set data on Hollywood cinema spreads across the sample space of a measurement. In probability theory, a sample space is the set of all possible outcomes of an experiment. For example, the sample space of drawing a single card from a 52-card playing deck is the set of all single cards in the deck: $\{A\heartsuit, 2\heartsuit, 3\heartsuit, \ldots \}$.

As Hacking shows, the same physical object (e.g., deck of cards, coin, film) can be the starting point of a broad range of experiments in probability, ranging from simple trials to complex ones that incorporate conditionals into the results. Thus, the definition of a sample space is determined by the "chance set-up", which is Hacking's (1965) phrasing to explain how a "device or part of the world" is used to conduct trials:

> A piece of radium together with a recording mechanism might constitute a chance set-up. One possible trial consists in observing whether or not the radium emits radiation in a small time interval. Possible results are "radiation" and "none". A pair of mice may provide a chance set-up, the trial being mating and the possible results the possible genetic make-ups of the offspring. The notion of a chance set-up is as old as the study of frequency. (p. 12)

Our chance set-up starts with the following question: if I randomly select a film from a group of films, what is the expected Motion Picture Association (MPA)[8] film rating (G, PG, PG-13, R)?

Why should we investigate the expected MPA film rating? The MPA film-rating system is most frequently seen from the perspective of the consumer, who understands the rating system as information about much or how little "objectionable" content is in every theatrically released film. From a different perspective, however, one can understand the MPA film-rating system to be one of Hollywood's non-governmental means to control the creation and distribution of artistic creativity. For example, artistic labour is channeled into ranges of subject matter, language and imagery by the requirement that a North American theatrical release must have a MPA film rating.[9] Moreover, there is a ceiling that "adult-themed" films can bump against: the "X" or NC-17 rating. This is technically the fifth rating, but it is virtually a taboo rating to all major theatre exhibitors (Lewis, 2002). Thus, the film directors in Hollywood are effectively tethered to four "acceptable" tiers before anything is shot. As Lewis (2013) notes, contracts oblige directors to "deliver their film as G, PG, PG-13 or R" (p. 43). Film directors must also appeal or agree to the changes the MPA's Classification and Rating Administration says are needed to approve the final cut of the film for theatrical release.

The history of the MPA rating system and its political economic character are outside the scope of this project; Lewis (2002) and other writers have identified many of the political economic reasons for Hollywood developing its own system of "self-censorship" (Balio, 1993; Decherney, 2012; Maltby, 1983; Powdermaker, 1950; Rosenbaum, 2000), which perhaps had its most controversial period with the "studio system" and the Production Code Administration (PCA); (Bordwell, Thompson, & Staiger, 1985; Maltby, 1993; Schatz, 2008; Trumpbour, 2002). With respect to the question of probability earlier, Rosenbaum's critiques and the political economic factors of the MPA are related to the outcome of a random sampling of *actual* theatrical films. The institutional power of the MPA is the capitalist power of Major Filmed Entertainment. Consequently, when we randomly draw a PG-13 or R-rated film, we can use the trial to investigate if the inequality of theatrical film distribution is affecting the likelihood of the result.

Figure 6.4 presents the distribution of all the films that are included in our investigation. In total there are over 11,000 theatrical releases in the dataset. To account for the presence of re-releases, only the first appearance of each unique IMDb film ID is kept in the data set. For example, *The Polar Express* was originally released in 2004, but it had limited re-releases for the next 15 years. We can use the distribution in Figure 6.4 to calculate the probabilities of randomly selecting a film rating from the entire population: G (0.028), PG (0.159), PG-13 (0.275), and R (0.536).

Figure 6.4 shows that R-rated films are the majority rating in the entire population. With data from 1985 to 1996, De Vany and Walls (2002) investigated if an abundance of R-rated films has had any effects on the business of Hollywood. Their paper argues that this output of so many R-rated films is a mistake for business interests. Hollywood might be pressured to cater to filmmakers who gravitate to the R rating out of desires for creativity and prestige, but De Vany and Walls (2002) believe the views of studio executives should change: "An executive

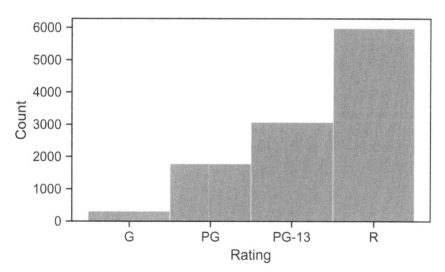

FIGURE 6.4 Film count by rating, 1983–2019

Source: IMDb.

seeking to trim the 'down-side' risk and increase the 'upside' possibilities in a studio's film portfolio could do so by shifting production dollars out of R-rated movies into G-, PG-, and PG13-rated movies" (p. 426). However, De Vany and Walls might be preaching to the converted. When we introduce the inequality of film distribution as a variable, we can see how the R-rated film does not dominate the *core* of Hollywood theatrical distribution. Rather, R-rated films, which are numerous as a group, are marginalized in the wide-release strategy, which is key to blockbuster cinema.

De Vany and Walls (2002) overlook this point because their analysis implies that Hollywood is responsible for all of the films in their data set – they often describe it as the set of films in Hollywood's "portfolio" (p. 438). It is very likely that all of their films are distributed by American firms; it is also likely that many of the films are "inside" Hollywood as they are distributed by a major studio or one of its subsidiaries. However, the general usage of "Hollywood" minimizes Rosenbaum's critique and also obscures the realities of some films getting much more corporate attention than others (Ulin, 2010). By using opening theatre rankings, we can group films by their relative places in the annual distributions of opening theatres (e.g., the film with a ranking of 4 was the fourth-largest opening of its year). This ranking is very important in determining the distribution of promotional and advertising budgets across a film-release schedule. The low-ranking film, for instance, is released into the world on small advertising campaigns; they rely on word-of-mouth behaviour to make the audience grow. The high-ranking film in opening theatres has an entirely different birth. They enter the theatrical market across entire countries and receive aggressive levels of promotion and advertising (Cucco, 2009).

Table 6.4 outlines how bins of films are created from the population. For each year, films are labeled according to the percentile of their opening theatre ranking. There are five labels: Blockbuster, Major, Medium, Limited, Very limited. The second row of the table indicates where, on average, the cut between bins is made. For example, the average cut between "Major" and "Medium" occurs at 89.8, which makes the last "Major" film 89 in rank and the first "Medium" film 90. Data on average number of theatres shows that there is an exponential relationship ($y = 87.3e^{0.72x}$) between the increase in category and the increase in the average number of opening theatres.

TABLE 6.4 Binning films by opening theatre rank

Category	Blockbuster	Major	Medium	Limited	Very limited
percentile	0.9–1	0.8–0.89	0.6–0.79	0.3–0.59	0–0.29
inner cut, mean	44.8	89.8	178.4	310.8	
op. theatres, mean	3073.3	2027.8	577.1	77.9	2.1

Each category of films has its own sample distribution of ratings. A measure of proportional representation can be calculated with a ratio between the distribution of ratings in each sample and the distribution of ratings in the entire population. For example, 17.6 per cent of the films in the "Major" category are PG rated. In the entire population, 15.9 per cent of the films are PG rated (see Figure 6.4). This means there is a slight over-representation of PG-rated films in the "Major" category (17.6/15.9 = 1.1). Conversely, a ratio less than 1 signals an under-representation, proportional to the entire population of films in the data set.

Figure 6.5 plots the proportional representation of each rating for each category. From this perspective, the abundance of R-rated films looks different. There is a visible under-representation of R-rated films in the "Blockbuster" and "Major" categories. Consequently, the more likely outcome for the R-rated film is to have a limited release of some type. Figure 6.6 helps demonstrate that the influence of opening theatre rank on film rating has a historical trend. For the plot in Panel A, the average film rating was taken from a random sampling of 1 million draws. A numerical average was produced by making the G-to-R scale a numerical scale from 1 to 4. The random sampling occurred on each year (e.g., 1 million samples from the "Blockbuster" category in 1983, 1 million for 1984, etc). The time series in Panel A show the "Blockbuster" category hovering around PG-13. The other categories have averages closer to 4, the R rating. Panel B of Figure 6.6 indicates that deviations from the averages are also reducing over

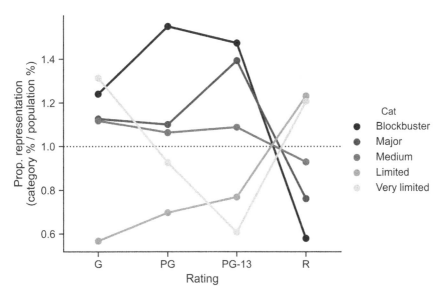

FIGURE 6.5 Proportional representation of MPA film ratings, by category, 1983–2019

Source: IMDb.

Note: See Table 6.4 for method to bin films into five categories.

time. This suggests that the MPA rating system is more entrenched, whereby there is less variance in the ratings-release relationship.

There are some limits to how this experiment can be connected to Rosenbaum's argument. For instance, our perspective is too broad to see the reasons why any film receives its MPA rating. Moreover, the approach risks suggesting that R-rated films are "outside" Hollywood, when it is also entirely possible that a radical alternative to a Hollywood film contains no R-rated content. Nevertheless, opening-theatre rank is a helpful method for seeing trends in the distribution of our social attention. If blockbuster cinema is Hollywood's main territory, it has issues of over- and under-representation within. The film released nation-wide and with lots of advertising and promotion is, relative to other releases, more likely to be PG-13 or below. The R-rating, which includes many films that receive this rating for how they address social issues of race,

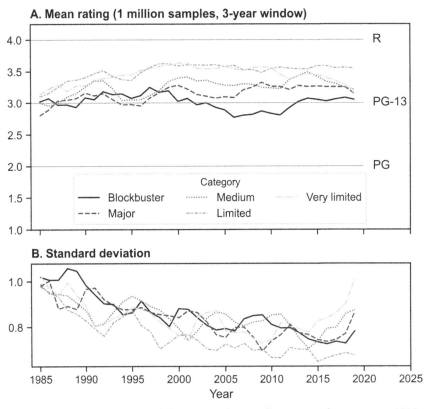

FIGURE 6.6 Mean and standard deviation of MPA film ratings, by category, 1983–2019

Source: IMDb.

Note: See Table 6.4 for method to bin films into five categories.

gender and sexuality (e.g., *12 Years a Slave*, *Brokeback Mountain*, *Carol*, *Do the Right Thing*, *Moonlight*, *Revolutionary Road*), are on the margins by virtue of their likelihood of *not* receiving wide-release distribution strategies and lots of corporate attention *in advance* of the theatrical run.

The preceding examples help us transform theoretical claims into more concrete arguments about the threat of aesthetic overproduction. In the next chapter, we demonstrate how Major Filmed Entertainment has managed to systematically decrease its risk, both absolutely and differentially.

Notes

1 For a selection of important film library transfers between 1957 and 2010, see Vogel (2011).

2 In a partnership with Western Electric, Warner Brothers was developing a "sound-on-a-disc" system in 1926. The Fox Film Corporation, which was to merge with Twentieth Century Pictures in 1935, was the first to develop a means of putting sound on film stock (Hanssen, 2005, p. 90).

3 As Kristin Thompson (1985) notes, "In early 1928, Louis B. Mayer declared that he was not worried [about the language problem]; he assumed that the popularity of American films would lead to the use of English as a universal language" (p. 158)

4 Ross intelligently focuses on Gottfried Reinhardt, the producer of the *The Red Badge of Courage*. Being half-artist and half-manager, the struggle between art and commercial interests was acute for Reinhardt. In 1951, with the film yet to be released, and with MGM growing anxious over the film's expected profitability, Reinhardt described his experiences in the food chain of managers and artists:

> [Louis B. Mayer, the head of MGM,] says to me the picture is no good because there is no story. I tell him we are adding narration to the picture, but he says narration won't help what isn't there. L. B. is a dangerous man. If you're his enemy, he destroys you. If you're his friend he eats you. . . . I don't know why it is; every time I go to lunch, I have to run into L. B. Today, on my way to lunch, he came at me like a battleship: "Mr. Reinhardt!" Then he told me the same things all over again. "Why don't you want to make a hit? Why don't you want to make money for the studio?" Today I said to him, "When John Huston [the director of *The Red Badge of Courage*] comes to me and says he wants to make a picture, I am honored. You hired him. I didn't." He didn't hear me. He talks about the picture as though it were refrigerators. (Ross, 2002, p. 210)

5 A project is in "development hell" when "a script is in development but never receives production funds" (Wasko, 2008, p. 53). In his "how-to" book about film financing, Michael Wiese (1991, p. 32) estimates that Major Filmed Entertainment produces one film for every 50 projects that remain forever in purgatory.

6 As was visible in Powdermaker's anthropological study of different jobs in Hollywood, there is a mixture of attitudes about the aesthetic value of Hollywood film production. Some of the interviewees seemed not to care about the ideals of art at all. Rather, fame was their main concern. For others, especially screenwriters who had originally hoped to become successful novelists, Hollywood cinema was perceived more as a mediocre art form (Powdermaker, 1950).

7 The spatial and temporal divisions between production, distribution and exhibition are, nevertheless, still relevant to strategic sabotage. In this regard, Hozic's (2001) analysis of how the control of film production significantly changed when filmmaking started to move from studio lots to location shooting is relevant.

8 For the purposes of readability, I am using the most recent name of the trade association. The Motion Picture Association of America (MPAA) was renamed to MPA in 2019. The acronym "MPAA" was first used in 1945. From 1922 to 1945 it was named "Motion Picture Producers and Distributors of America" (MPPDA).

9 Our focus is limited to the MPA rating system only for the purposes of the experiment. Countries around the world have their own national or regional rating systems (Biltereyst & Winkel, 2013). Some rating systems are not tiered according to different levels of sex, profanity and violence. In China, for example, there is no tiered rating system, and state censors use general criteria to determine if all films, both domestic and foreign, adhere to "the principles of the Chinese Constitution and maintain social morality" (O'Connor & Armstrong, 2015, p. 9). Consequently, state censors can ban a film from theatrical exhibition if it is deemed to offend China's "general audience" (Langfitt, 2015).

7

THE RISE OF A CONFIDENT HOLLYWOOD

7.1 Introduction

This chapter presents my empirical research on Major Filmed Entertainment's success in reducing risk from 1950 to 2019. This development will mostly be presented graphically, in a series of figures that give us a better sense of how and to what extent Major Filmed Entertainment has increased its degree of confidence by lowering risk in the capitalization of cinema. As stated in Chapter 5, our overarching hypothesis is that any increase in confidence about the order of cinema is a significant factor in Major Filmed Entertainment's drive to accumulate differentially.

Due to the scope of the project and the lack of long-term data on the prices, revenues and profits of VHS, DVD, Blu-ray and other forms of digital distribution,[1] much of our detailed analysis will focus on Major Filmed Entertainment's strategy of distributing blockbuster-type films for large theatrical openings – that is, "saturation booking". As will be shown, the twin-engine strategy of saturation booking and blockbuster cinema has been a success for Major Filmed Entertainment. First, Major Filmed Entertainment has been using, from the early 1980s to 2019, the saturation-booking strategy more effectively: Hollywood is getting better at predicting which films will effectively use opening theatres to outperform their cohorts. Second, changes to the volatility of consumer habits have also benefited the blockbusters of Major Filmed Entertainment; the consumption of the most popular films is becoming increasingly less volatile. Third, the duration of saturation booking, measured by how many days the average film is in theatres, is shortening, and this reduction advantages blockbuster films over those films that receive a lower number of opening theatres – that is, "platform releases".

DOI: 10.4324/9781003092629-9

The evidence provided in this chapter offers an important empirical foundation on which we can theorize Hollywood's aesthetic preferences in the contemporary period. Indeed, it is curious that long after the collapse of the studio system in 1948, visible boundaries on the form and content of Hollywood cinema continue to persist (Bordwell, 2006; Langford, 2010). Independent-film distribution is no longer suffocated by the uncompetitive strategies of "block booking"[2], and the art of film production is no longer bounded by the moral standards of the Production Code. It also appears that the social relations of Hollywood cinema, on both the business and consumer sides, are, technically, much more free: Major Filmed Entertainment has the moral and political freedom to make more types of films, and consumers, likewise, have the freedom to explore parts of cinema that would have been marginalized or non-existent under the distribution methods of the classical studio system.

But as we delve under this surface, we will see how capitalist power continues to shape the art of filmmaking and its potential, and specifically, how this transformation has brought about a substantial reduction in risk. The drop in risk from 1950 to 2019 parallels the sector-wide transition from American New Wave cinema (higher risk) to the narrowed strategy of blockbuster, high-concept cinema (lower risk). While many of the qualitative details of this transition will be presented only in Chapter 8, the quantitative research in the current chapter establishes that the evolution of Hollywood's aesthetics in the contemporary age is the result of strategic sabotage. Therefore, Major Filmed Entertainment today has the same political economic goal it had when it relied on the studio system, the MPPDA (the original version of the MPA), the Production Code and the PCA – to control the social creativity of filmmaking for pecuniary ends.

7.2 Challenging assumptions about risk

To begin a more precise analysis of historical risk reduction in Hollywood, it is useful to challenge the popular assumption that risk in the Hollywood film business is perpetually or "inherently" high. This assumption sometimes appears in the form of an aphorism – for example, William Goldman's oft-quoted phrase that, in the Hollywood film business, "[n]obody knows anything". This assumption can also appear in sophisticated economic models (De Vany, 2004; Litman, 1983). Regardless of how it appears, this assumption of perpetual high risk in Hollywood makes mainstream theories of Hollywood economics run into one very significant problem. Essentially, mainstream approaches tend to ignore the historical development of risk. In its place is an ahistorical concept, which is used to set systemic risk at an "inherently" high level. Thinking that risk in Hollywood is fixed puts blinders on our research, making it difficult to think how the particular techniques of Major Filmed Entertainment, such as the repetition of genres, sequels and remakes, the cult of movie stars and the institution of false needs and wants, can affect the level of risk or change the social environment about which risk perceptions are made.

The ahistorical concept of risk is produced when mainstream approaches move from the particular to the universal, when specific risk-reduction strategies in Hollywood become components of a general risk environment (De Vany, 2004; Litman, 1983; Nelson & Glotfelty, 2012; Pokorny, 2005). At the level of specific strategies, many theoretical arguments acknowledge that the Hollywood film business can actively reduce risk. Some theorists, for example, consider how famous movie stars, with their perceived ability to draw consumers to some movies rather than others, are employed to reduce financial risk (Elberse, 2007; Hadida, 2010; Ravid, 1999). Others point to the blockbuster method of filmmaking, which is argued to be Hollywood's style of choice because it is also a way to reduce risk (Denisoff & Plasketes, 1990; Litman, 1998; Ravid, 1999). The tone of these theories change dramatically, however, when they take a wider view and incorporate their fundamental assumptions about economics and capitalism. At a macro level of analysis, strategies of the Hollywood film business are suddenly ineffective in reducing the *overall level of systemic risk*. The star system and blockbuster cinema can only mitigate the risk inherent in the greater business environment. They cannot significantly curtail it.

Why the odd disconnect? Confusions about the ability of Hollywood to reduce risk often stem from an author's use of neoclassical economics. Neoclassical theories of risk in the Hollywood film business tend to put individual, autonomous consumer sovereignty at the centre of their analysis. When placed at the centre, consumer sovereignty is the ultimate *extraneous* risk to business strategies; a consumer might "form attachments to specific film 'markers' such as stars and genre" and might even "seek a degree of familiarity in their film consumption experience" – but, nevertheless, "consumer tastes in film are ultimately unpredictable" (Pokorny & Sedgwick, 2012, pp. 188–190). Consumer unpredictability, on its own, is certainly a relevant factor to a film business. However, confusions about risk grow because neoclassical approaches, particularly the competitive branch of neoclassical economics, elevate consumer sovereignty and ignore the role of power in Hollywood's business strategies. For instance, to suggest that, in the film business, economic actors are in a state of perfect competition and too small to change the historical circumstances of risk (De Vany, 2004, p. 270), the sizes of the dominant firms in Hollywood have to be ignored. One also has to ignore questions about the abilities of dominant firms to affect the ideologies of its consumers. If Hollywood has ways to manipulate consumer attention, it is hardly straightforward to argue that the sovereign consumer is an unalterable arbiter, possessing the "economic" freedom to always be fickle when the next film is released (Garvin, 1981, p. 4).

Authors who rely on consumer sovereignty do not use the assumption the same way. Small differences in emphasis or interpretation produce nuances in neoclassical theories of risk in Hollywood. Between authors, these nuances can be very important; for our purpose the nuances are not as significant as the fundamental assumptions that push these theories in the *same* direction. Thus, the following subsections look at different examples of authors *concluding* that the contemporary Hollywood film business is condemned to high risk.

7.2.1 Passive risk mitigation

When Hollywood's level of risk is impervious to historical transformation, risk-reducing techniques can only do so much. One consequence of this assumption is that the capitalist's remaining option is to reduce risk passively, through portfolio investment. As Bichler and Nitzan point out, the mathematics of an argument about portfolio diversification – "it causes the price volatility of the portfolio as a whole to be smaller than the average volatility of the individual assets" (Nitzan & Bichler, 2009, p. 204) – is not a problematic issue in itself. Rather, the problem relates to the notion that capitalists use portfolio diversification because they cannot actively shape the world to favour their pecuniary interests.

Pokorny and Sedgwick (2012), for example, see portfolio investment as mitigation for the instability that exists at the "atomic" level of individual film projects:

> [A]ny film production strategy based on the success of single, one-off film projects is doomed to failure. Rather, a more sensible strategy for a rational profit-maximizing film producer is to produce a wide range of films annually, in the hope that at least some of these will produce profits that will compensate for the losses that a large proportion of these films will inevitably generate. That is, we could characterize the successful film studios/distributors as constructing diversified annual portfolios of films, diversified according to production budget and genre, and allocation of stars, directors and screenwriters. The issue, then, is not so much which of the films in the portfolio are profitable, but simply that the portfolio itself is profitable. (p. 190)

Pokorny and Sedgwick's recommendation for portfolio diversification makes some sense, but the bad outcome of non-portfolio investment is less relevant to a Hollywood studio than an individual who is unable to alter the risk of what is being bought and sold. When Hollywood holds claims of future streams of income from cinema, it is hardly sitting on its hands and accepting that the risk of each asset is fixed. How do we know this? Pokorny and Sedgwick's argument about diversification is fusing two things: a portfolio of assets, which is component of business, and a "portfolio" of people and things, which are controlled by Hollywood and in the interest of profit. Consequently, the "one-off film project" might be high risk, but, in the hands of someone who has the power to control the people and things of the film industry, its financial future is not inevitably "doomed to failure". In fact, if the risk of an individual film project is beyond the reaches of a capitalist, why is there so much corporate interference in the production of film projects? Would it not be simpler to mitigate the risk of film project with more portfolio investment strategies?

As we will see in another subsection, a possible response to my critique would claim I am mistaken about the "location" of risk. Hollywood studio heads and executives have undoubtedly meddled in the creation of cinema, but the risk is not "inside" Hollywood but "outside" its walls. *Consumer unpredictability*, on its own, appears to be a reasonable consideration for *any* business. However, there is a clear tendency for studies of Hollywood economics to exaggerate the power of consumer unpredictability, to a point where film-business strategies appear to never possess any capitalist power. On this assumption, the world of cinema can never be made to have machine-like regularity when the sovereign consumer is an unalterable arbiter, possessing the "economic" freedom to always be fickle when the next film is released (Garvin, 1981, p. 4).

With respect to Pokorny and Sedgwick's argument, consumer sovereignty eventually makes the capitalist nothing more than a passive investor in a portfolio of cinema. But a neoclassical theory of consumer sovereignty stumbles because it must come down to earth, to a world populated, from around 1900 onwards, by trusts, trade associations, giant corporations, conglomerates, active governments and other social institutions that would have an effect on consumer behaviour. Also, the association of inherent risk with consumer sovereignty must treat consumer behaviour as a series of "revealed preferences", even though, as Galbraith (1997) notes, the hyperactivity of capitalist firms in marketing, advertising, and branding makes it difficult to find the sovereign consumer among society's creators of wants: "So it is that if production creates the wants it seeks to satisfy, or if the wants emerge *pari passu* with the production, then the urgency of wants can no longer be used to defend the urgency of the production. Production only fills a void that it has itself created" (p. 125).

7.2.2   Risk in Hollywood is infinite

If consumers are unpredictable, how severe is this force of unpredictability? For some, the permanent autonomy of consumers reveals an "inherent" level of risk that is so high that *ex ante* predictions are actually impossible. According to De Vany (2004),

> revenue forecasts have zero precision, which is just a way of saying that "anything can happen". . . . The "nobody knows" principle . . . is revealed in the infinite variance and scale-free form of the probability distribution. When the probability distribution is scale free it has no characteristic size and there is no typical movie. If variance is infinite, the prediction is impossible; one can only say that the expected revenue of a movie is X plus or minus infinity. (p. 260)

"Plus or minus infinity" – we need to pause on this point. It is significant because it technically demolishes the capitalization of cinema. How, for instance, can you discount future earnings if δ equals $\pm\infty$? What is leading De Vany to argue risk in Hollywood is this extreme?

According to De Vany (2004), "the confidence interval of [a] forecast is without bounds" (p. 71) because moviegoer behaviour is stochastic but with an important twist:

> Movie fans imitate one another to some extent. They also share information with one another about their likes and dislikes. This means that a consensus about movies grows over time as the audience explores movies. The process of discovery and convergence to a consensus is part imitation, part communication. As the consensus begins to converge, so does the way the audience distributes itself over movies.
>
> The Bose–Einstein process is a stochastic version of this part-imitation, part communication process. As it evolves, the probability that n people will be drawn to a movie depends on the number who saw it before. The probability of a growth in revenue depends on the level of revenue already earned. This implies that the movies with the largest revenues have the largest expected growth which produces a nonlinear feedback in demand. (p. 9)

Word-of-mouth behaviour, so goes this type of argument, is an unpredictable, inherent risk of consumer sovereignty; it can stop a "hit and run" strategy dead in its tracks (Cucco, 2009, p. 223). For the first few weeks, it may be possible for Hollywood to attract audiences simply through promotion and advertising, even for its bad films. But after that, according to De Vany, an "uninformative information cascade" reaches it limit and the chaos of word-of-mouth communication takes over. This latter process, De Vany maintains, always makes the future success of a theatrical release extremely uncertain; your unknown film can become a hit and your expected hit can become a flop when people start to talk.

De Vany's arguments are unsatisfying because they are embedded in a framework that assumes that the Hollywood film business is eternally subject to this extremely high degree of uncertainty. It is probably true that Hollywood has experienced great uncertainty – for instance, Chapter 6 has an example about the uncertainty of firms during the nascent period of sound cinema. But is Hollywood doomed to live in a permanent state of extreme risk, such that the variance of expected revenues is always infinite? De Vany (2004) thinks so, as this is part of his conclusion to *Hollywood Economics*:

> Anyone who claims to forecast anything about a movie before it is released is a fraud or doesn't know what he is doing. The margin of error is infinite.

That does not mean that he won't ever get it right, only that he seldom will and only because of sheer luck. (p. 275)

By contrast, it is helpful to briefly consider the concept of history that is at the core of the capital-as-power approach. For Nitzan and Bichler, societies are historical because human beings have the ability to change the foundations of a social order through active creation. Nitzan and Bichler (2009) capture this point with the verb–noun *creorder*: "Historical society is a *creorder*. At every passing moment, it is both Parmenidean and Heraclitean: a state in process, a construct reconstructed, a form transformed. To have history is to *create order*" (p. 305). This concept of history draws from the philosophy of Cornelius Castoriadis, who offers us the term *social-historical*. For Castoriadis (1998), the hyphenation of social and historical signifies that it is

> impossible to maintain an intrinsic distinction between the social and the historical, even if it is a matter of affirming that historicity is the "essential attribute" of society or that society is the "essential presupposition" of history. . . . It is not that every society is necessarily "in" time or that a history necessarily "affects" every society. The social is this very thing – self-alteration, and it is nothing if it is not this. The social makes itself and can make itself only as history. (p. 215)

The capital-as-power approach is, therefore, open to the investigation of the social-historical development of risk. Capitalist power may never be able to make the business of culture risk-free, but we put up barriers to our own analysis if we assume that risk in Hollywood is inherent because it is also ahistorical. Moreover, we have reason to be skeptical that Major Filmed Entertainment cannot integrate a degree of confidence into the capitalization of cinema. There are infamous examples of expensive flops in the history of cinema, but the logic of capitalization can still function as a social ritual that accounts for the uncertainties of the future. As Frank H. Knight argues, we need to see the gradations and differences in economic uncertainty. Some uncertainty, for example, "is easily converted into effective certainty; for in a considerable number of such cases the results become predictable in accordance with the laws of chance, and the error in such prediction approaches zero as the number of cases is increased" (Knight, 1921, p. 46).

7.2.3   There was power, but now there is none

Consumer sovereignty and the ideas that spring from this concept are, as noted by Leo Lowenthal, born from the "false hypothesis that the consumer's choice is the decisive social phenomenon from which we should begin further analysis" (Lowenthal, 1961, p. 12). At an even more fundamental level, the false hypothesis of consumer sovereignty is rooted in problematic assumptions about the analytical separation of economics and politics in capitalism. By digging down to this assumption – which we challenged in Chapter 2 – we reach the source of a recurring temptation: treating the financial statistics of movies as transparent indicators of economic rationality. Certainly, film revenues rely on consumers opening their wallets and giving money to Hollywood. Yet, this simple fact can lead someone to split politics and economics, which allows aspects of capitalist power to disappear from view. For instance, if sovereign consumers create hierarchies of taste, it follows that both the popular, financially successful movies and those that die lonely deaths from under-consumption are "deserving" of their respective fates in a free market. The people are not simply opening their wallets; they are speaking as rational, economic film critics.

Take, for example, Barry Litman's *The Motion Picture Mega-Industry*. Trying hard to balance theory and historical fact, Litman seeks to recognize the existence of both consumer sovereignty and monopoly power. On one hand, he states that

> effective consumer demand directs supply and strong "consumer sovereignty" prevails. This is clearly the case in the motion picture marketplace where movie patrons register their dollar votes directly for the kinds of movies they prefer, and the differential box office rewards create the financial incentive for the next round of motion picture investment. (Litman, 1998, p. 4)

This theoretical position on the sovereignty of consumers is maintained, on the other hand, in a study of the organizational power of Hollywood's major film distributors. To determine whether consumer sovereignty has been undermined by such power, Litman (1998) takes an "industrial organization approach", which

> begins by examining the product and structure of an industry in its basic components – demand, market concentration, barriers to entry, vertical integration, conglomerates, and so on in order to gain an overall picture of the distribution of current market power and the chances for de-concentration in the future. (p. 5)

To balance these two conflicting perspectives about the character of capital accumulation, Litman argues that the history of the business of Hollywood can be split into two periods: the period of organizational power and the subsequent period of the sovereign cultural consumer. For Litman, the twilight of Hollywood's monopoly power was the late 1940s. Price fixing and "excess" profits were enjoyed up until 1948, when the US Supreme Court decided on Hollywood's vertical integration of film production, distribution and exhibition in *United States v. Paramount Pictures*. After the Supreme Court's ruling that the major film studios would be required to sell their stakes in film exhibition, a new day dawned:

> With vertical disintegration and the end of block booking and franchising, assured access to theatres was no longer guaranteed: films would have to compete according to their intrinsic quality. This naturally opened up the market for independent producers and distributors whose products would now be judged according to merit rather than percentage. (Litman, 1998, p. 15)

In my view, Litman's temporal division is more the product of his theoretical leanings than historical facts. Decades of monopoly power in the film business did not dissuade Litman from making consumer sovereignty the first principle in his study of Hollywood cinema and modern capitalism. To be sure, *United States v. Paramount Pictures* is frequently cited as marking the end of Hollywood's classical studio system (Hanssen, 2005; Langford, 2010; Maltby, 2003). Yet we are beyond facts when we argue that people have been free to register their "dollar votes" since 1948 (Litman, 1998, p. 4). Litman's characterization of the end the classical studio system assumes that legal regulation rinsed off political contaminants from an economic system that is, at its core, atomistic and competitive. Similar to Olson (1982), Litman assumes that there is nothing about politics and institutional power that can change the meaning of capital; the economy, even when contaminated by external non-economic factors, is strictly defined as a rational determination of nominal prices that behave according to "real" utility. Monopolies can affect consumer demand, or they can erect arbitrarily high barriers to entry on the supply side, but their effect on the revealed preferences of consumer sovereignty does not, in this picture, change the definition of what the capitalist economy "truly" is.

In this sense, the idealization of consumer sovereignty obscures aspects of capitalist power in our current social-historical state. Either the power of the Hollywood distributors fades and becomes a thing of the past – this first scenario implies, to paraphrase Marx, that there has been power, but there is no longer any (Marx, 1990, p. 175) – or, like an eternal flame, consumer sovereignty survives in all circumstances, even when a business sector continues to be dominated by a set of giant firms. Like the stoic in Hegel's *Phenomenology of Spirit*, the second version of consumer sovereignty is indifferent to the very social structures that determine whether an individual can be free in the first place (Hegel, 1977, §197ff.). Neither version is convincing to our analysis of Hollywood and risk. The free, individual determination of needs and wants – the purported principle behind consumer sovereignty – is an idea that is actually radically democratic at its core: it implies individual autonomy. And as Marcuse (1991) explains, capitalism is effective at repressing autonomy while simultaneously offering a great deal of individual choice:

> Under the rule of the repressive whole, liberty can be made into a powerful instrument of domination. The range of choice open to the individual is not the decisive factor in determining the degree of human freedom, but what

can be chosen and what is chosen by the individual. The criterion for free choice can never be an absolute one, but neither is it entirely relative. Free election of masters does not abolish the masters or the slaves. Free choice among a wide variety of goods and services does not signify freedom if these goods and services sustain social control over a life of toil and fear – that is, if they sustain alienation. And the spontaneous reproduction of superimposed needs by the individual does not establish autonomy; it only testifies to the efficacy of the controls. (pp. 7–8)

Thus, while there is no direct, physical coercion to buy and consume commodities for pleasure and relaxation, the ability of capitalists to create a realm of leisure time through power – the apparent sanctuary of the private individual – should cause us to rethink the ability for consumers to be external, unalterable factors of financial risk in media and entertainment.

7.3   The risk reduction of Major Filmed Entertainment

The history of Major Filmed Entertainment's risk reduction is easier to analyse with evidence in front of us. Figure 7.1 presents an updated version of my index for the volatility of Major Filmed Entertainment's earnings per firm. The figure is presenting *ex post* risk. For each year, I compute the per cent rate of change of earnings from its five-year trailing average. Second, I measure, for each year, a trailing 15-year standard deviation of the computed rates of changes. Thus, the larger the standard deviation, the greater the volatility in the earning growth rates of Major Filmed Entertainment's previous 15 years.

With data going into the late 1940s, the time series in Figure 7.1 shows us that the troublesome period was from the late 1960s to the last years of the 1970s, when risk spiked and stayed high. After the 1970s, risk steadily declined and continued to decline to 2019. The level of risk in 2019 is also lowest in the period from 1950 to 2019. The annotations in Figure 7.1 are meant to introduce us to the film history that overlaps this reduction in risk. We might not know the contribution of each film to this decline – and there are many other important films in the history of Hollywood cinema – but the coincidence of significant risk reduction occurring after the twilight of "New" Hollywood is unlikely an accidental one.

The next step is to historicize this process. How did Major Filmed Entertainment manage to reduce its risk so systematically from the 1970s to 2019? This dominant oligopoly reduced risk with two important techniques: saturation booking and blockbuster cinema. As much as these two techniques are well-known characteristics of contemporary Hollywood, the risk perceptions of Major Filmed Entertainment relate to their successful application. For instance, Hollywood must decide how many big-budget films it will produce or finance — all in the hopes that each one will become a hit at the box office. Moreover, executives, managers and

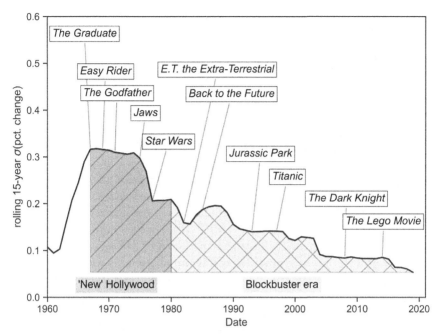

FIGURE 7.1 Volatility of earnings per firm, 1943–2019

Source: Annual reports of Columbia, Paramount, Twentieth Century-Fox, Universal, and Warner Bros. for operating income, 1943–1955. Compustat through WRDS for operating income of Major Filmed Entertainment, 1950–1992. Annual reports of Disney, News Corp, Viacom, Sony, Time Warner (Management's Discussion of Business Operations for information on their filmed entertainment interests) for operating income of Major Filmed Entertainment, 1993–2019.

producers must, in the interest of future income, ask questions that underpin the capitalization of film projects. For instance, what type of film can reach the highest revenues plateau? Does it matter if a film opens in ten theatres, 100 theatres or 1,000? Which stories or ideas will get big production budgets? Which film projects should go to blockbuster levels and open in more than 3,000 theatres? Because there is not 100 per cent certainty about the future behaviour of moviegoers, these questions all relate to risk management. Furthermore, a wide-release strategy is not simply designed to accumulate big revenues; it is designed to accumulate them *as quickly as possible* (Elberse, 2013).

The rest of the chapter will examine the historical progression of Major Filmed Entertainment's risk reduction in more quantitative detail. The analysis will first demonstrate that, since the early 1980s, Major Filmed Entertainment has been able to make progressively better predictions about its saturation-booking strategy. Second, we will account for the positive relationship between blockbuster cinema and saturation booking. And finally, a collection of figures will show the extent to which Major Filmed Entertainment's continuous use of saturation booking and blockbuster cinema is changing the order of cinema.

7.4 Predictable saturation booking

Saturation booking is a distribution-exhibition strategy that gives a film a "wide" release by simultaneously exhibiting the film in as many theatres and on as many screens as possible. Saturation booking starts on opening day, continues on opening weekend, and remains in place for as long as the film is popular in cities and towns all over the country. This wide-release strategy is not simply designed to accumulate big revenues; it is designed to accumulate them as quickly as possible. For example, the 2001 film *The Mummy Returns* opened in 3,401 theatres in the United States and earned 90 per cent of its domestic theatrical revenues in its first five weeks. By contrast, *O Brother, Where Art Thou?* opened in five theatres in the same year, and only eventually grew to a maximum of 847 theatres. It took four months to earn 90 per cent of its domestic theatrical revenues (which were almost five times smaller than the box-office gross revenues of *The Mummy Returns*).[3]

The sector-wide institution of saturation booking has modified Major Filmed Entertainment's orientation to risk and the social world of cinema. In other words, even if Major Filmed Entertainment has always sought to control the creation and consumption of films for pecuniary ends, the nature of the saturation-booking strategy compelled Hollywood to add another consideration to its predictions about the expected earnings of a film. Saturation booking is not applied to every film. The Hollywood film business must now decide, on the basis of what it thinks will be popular, which films will be given wide theatrical releases. The tiered exhibition system of classical Hollywood may be no more (e.g., a film completes its exhibition in "first-run" theatres before going to "second-run" and so on; Waterman, 2005), but some contemporary films will only ever get "platform" releases, which means they will open in a small number of theatres, usually in select cities (New York, Los Angeles, etc.). Moreover, not every cinematic premise or idea is suitable for the blockbuster style, and since saturation booking gives the widest releases to Hollywood's biggest, most expensive blockbusters, not every film is deemed suitable for the saturation-booking strategy.

Therefore, a confident decision about a distribution strategy is a confident judgement about how a film will rank relative to its cohorts. For example, there is historical evidence that top-ranking films, sorted by revenues, have been able to outperform other films by a wide margin. In addition, for each decade since the late 1940s, the share of all box-office revenues that go to the top 1 per cent of films, ranked by revenues, has grown. Mark Weinstein (2005) describes this phenomenon:

> In the late 1940s, the top 1 percent of films represented 2 percent to 3 percent of studio revenue; by the early 1960s, this had tripled, to an average of about 6

percent. This trend has continued in recent years. In 1993 the world-wide revenues for the top 1 percent (two films) of 163 major-studio released films were 13.8 percent of the total. (p. 252)

We can infer, along with Sedgwick, that this widening gap between the revenues of the top films and the rest of their cohorts began when Hollywood "became increasingly focused on the production of 'hit' films", which require large sums of money for "production values" and "visual and audio innovations" (Sedgwick, 2005, p. 187). This widening gap, however, carries its own risk perceptions. While platform releases can sometimes become popular and pull in revenues that few business experts and marketing strategists originally expected, wide-release films are designed to dominate the top tier. The difference between wide releases and platform releases is decided upon, and a wide release is typically paired with a large advertising and promotion budget. Thus, investor confidence in Major Filmed Entertainment might drop if unknown films become popular while the wide releases that are advertised *ad nauseam* repeatedly underperform.[4]

To investigate the risk perceptions of saturation booking, I use opening theatres as a proxy for future expectations. Opening theatres stand as a proxy for future expectations because *the decision about the number of opening theatres is made before a stream of box-office revenues actually begins to flow.* In other words, a decision about release strategy is based on financial expectations about what will happen to each film on its opening weekend and onwards. Furthermore, as I established above, the biggest hits earn an above-average share of revenues, which in turn relates to the ways films can generate big revenues from a wide theatrical release.

The key point to our examination of risk is that not every high-grossing film is the product of a wide-release strategy. A platform release can, over time, become popular and consequently earn a relatively high level of gross revenues. For example, *Schindler's List*, which opened in only 25 theatres, ended up the ninth-highest grossing film of 1993. But Major Filmed Entertainment does not want to wait for its wide releases to eventually become popular; it wants to hit the iron when it's hot. It wants to open a select number of films in a large number of theatres – often 1,500, 2,000 or even more – and to gross as much income as it can and sooner rather than later. This strategy, though, requires Major Filmed Entertainment to be very confident in its particular choices, and the question is where this confidence comes from.

Historical data on opening theatres enable us to compare the differences in opening strategies (films sorted by opening theatres) and the outcome (films sorted by theatrical gross revenues). We can show an example of how this comparison works with a series of tables. In Table 7.1, we use data from boxoffice-mojo.com to rank the very top films by their box-office gross revenues. The table also provides the number of opening theatres for each film. Table 7.1 is interesting for a few reasons. What first stands out is *Platoon*, which only opened in six

TABLE 7.1 Films released in 1986, ranked by box-office gross revenues

Film	Box-Office Gross Revenues	Opening Theatres
Top Gun	$176,786,701	1,028
Crocodile Dundee	$174,803,506	879
Platoon	$138,530,565	6
The Karate Kid Part II	$115,103,979	1,323
Star Trek IV: The Voyage Home	$109,713,132	1,349
Back to School	$91,258,000	1,605
Aliens	$85,160,248	1,437
The Golden Child	$79,817,937	1,667
...	...	...

Source: www.boxofficemojo.com for US theatrical gross revenues and opening theatres.

TABLE 7.2 Films released in 1986, ranked by opening theatres

Film	Box-Office Gross Revenues	Opening Theatres
Cobra	$49,042,224	2,131
Police Academy 3: Back in Training	$43,579,163	1,788
Raw Deal	$16,209,459	1,731
The Delta Force	$17,768,900	1,720
The Golden Child	$79,817,937	1,667
Friday the 13th Part VI	$19,472,057	1,610
Back to School	$91,258,000	1,605
Poltergeist II: The Other Side	$40,996,665	1,596
...	...	...

Source: www.boxofficemojo.com for US theatrical gross revenues and opening theatres.

theatres but eventually went on to become the third-highest grossing film of 1986; this success makes *Platoon* a good example of a highly successful platform release. The second and perhaps more important point is that there is no one-to-one match between revenue rankings and opening-theatre rankings. For example, the two top-grossing films – *Top Gun* and *Crocodile Dundee* – did not have the two widest releases of that year. Even on this abridged list, we can see five films that had wider releases in 1986.

Table 7.2 offers a different view of the same year. It sorts films released in 1986 not by box-office revenues, but by opening theatres. Aside from two films, *Back to School* and *The Golden Child*, none of the films in Table 7.2 appears in Table 7.1. The films in Table 7.2 had the widest releases in 1986, but only two of them were able to even reach the $50 million plateau. The table also does not have any of the five films that broke the $100 million barrier, which is what separates the five biggest films of 1986 from the rest of their cohorts.

TABLE 7.3 Rankings in 2007

Ranked by Gross Revenues	Ranked by Opening Theatres
Spider-Man 3	*Pirates of the Caribbean: At …*
Shrek the Third	*Harry Potter and the Order …*
Transformers	*Spider-Man 3*
Pirates of the Caribbean: At …	*Shrek the Third*
Harry Potter and the Order …	*Transformers*
I Am Legend	*Fantastic Four: Rise of …*
The Bourne Ultimatum	*Ratatouille*
National Treasure: Book of Secrets	*Bee Movie*
…	…

Source: www.boxofficemojo.com for US theatrical gross revenues and opening theatres.

Taken together, Tables 7.1 and 7.2 compare the top-performing films (ranked by gross revenues) to what Hollywood expected the top-performing films to be (ranked by opening theatres). In this case, Hollywood's expectations *via* opening theatres were inaccurate; the largest grossing films came not from the largest openings, but from "below", from opening release strategies that were closer to platform releases. To quickly dispel any doubt that this uncertainty is unalterable, let us look at Table 7.3. It reproduces for 2007 an abbreviated version of Tables 7.1 and 7.2. As we saw, only two films appear in both tables for 1986 – *Back to School* and *The Golden Child*. As Table 7.3 demonstrates, five films appear in both rankings for 2007. Furthermore, the *same five films* of 2007 occupy, although in different order, both top five spots. The benefits of increased predictability at the box-office pay off: in 2007 the gross revenues of the top 10 per cent of films accounted for roughly 75 per cent of all US box-office revenues. Moreover, risk reduction in 2007 extends further down the list of film rankings. For example, of the 50 widest releases of 2007, 39 films or 78 per cent, went on to become part of the 50 biggest grosses of 2007.

Predicting financial success based on opening-theatre strategies is more likely in 2007 than in 1986. Figure 7.2 provides a more detailed picture of the earlier example. The figure analyses the dependence of revenue rank on theatre rank. For each year from 1982 to 2019, films are sorted and ranked by opening theatre size, where the largest opening is first and so on. Each film is given a rank for its position in opening theatre size and then for its position in yearly gross revenues. If, for instance, a film had a theatre rank of 1 and a revenue rank of 6, the film would be the first largest opening of its year and would have achieved the sixth largest gross revenues.

Even if a few wide-release films still do poorly, confidence about the wide-release strategy comes from greater predictability overall, whereby the largest openings will, in general, become the highest ranked films. The four panels in Figure 7.2

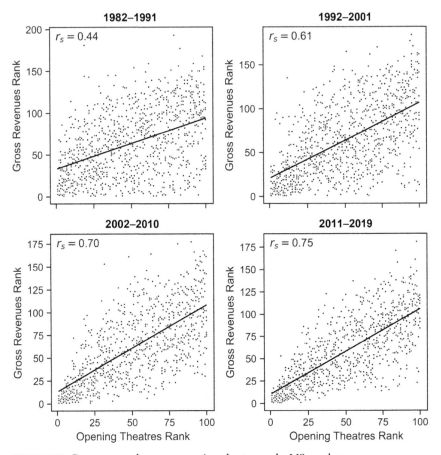

FIGURE 7.2   Revenue rank versus opening theatre rank, US market

Sources: www.boxofficemojo.com for yearly gross revenues and opening theatre sizes of individual films.

show that Major Filmed Entertainment has had a boost in its confidence about saturation booking. Each of these panels isolates a period of years and plots the hundred widest releases against their revenue rankings. In the most recent period – the panel in the bottom right – the relationship is tightest; this would translate into higher confidence that the widest releases will become the biggest hits.

Figure 7.3 plots annual Spearman correlations of the data in Figure 7.2. A Spearman correlation is better suited than a Pearson correlation because the measurement involves two ordinal variables: revenue ranking and theatrical ranking. As the figure shows, the correlation between revenue rank and theatre rank has been rising since the 1980s. Moreover, Panel B illustrates how the 25 widest

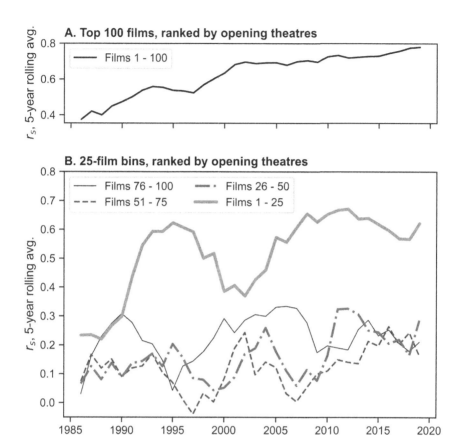

FIGURE 7.3 Spearman correlation between revenue and theatrical ranks

Source: www.boxofficemojo.com for yearly gross revenues and opening theatre sizes of individual films.

releases are doing the heavy lifting. Overall, these films are achieving strong cor-relations between their revenue rank and theatrical rank.

The evidence in Figures 7.2 and 7.3 corroborates some of the research of Elbrese, who also concludes that opening theatres data can show that there is an increasing success to the blockbuster strategy (Elberse, 2013). Yet I differ in my political-economic interpretation of why opening theatre size is a good predictor of theatrical revenues. Elbrese consistently uses gambling metaphors in her writing because the working assumption is that blockbusters are risky and that executives make high-stakes bets. Problematically, this assumption does not include the broader political-economic power of the firms involved. By ignoring Major Filmed Entertainment's ability to influence the circumstances of saturation booking, one creates the illusion that big-budget films succeed or fail on their own

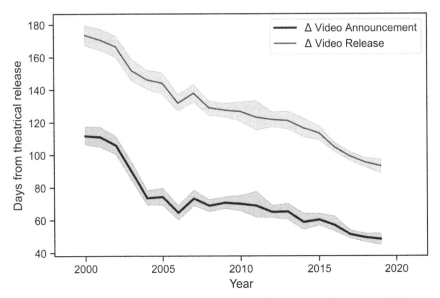

FIGURE 7.4 Average US theatrical release window for major studios, 2000–2019

Source: "Video Windows Grosses MAJOR" from https://www.natoonline.org/data/windows/.

feet. This illusion disappears when we look at how Major Filmed Entertainment uses its institutional power to shape the social environment of saturation booking.

For example, Major Filmed Entertainment has been, in negotiations with theatre owners, shortening the theatrical release window in two ways: the average number of days a film is in theatres and the average number of days before a film is released in a video format (DVD, Blu-ray, streaming). In Figure 7.4, National Association of Theater Owners data are used to approximate the average size of Hollywood's theatrical release window. The series "Video Announcement" is the average amount of days between opening day and the day when video release plans are announced – a signal that theatrical release is winding down, or even finished. The series "Video Release" measures the entire period between opening day and the beginning of the video window.

This shortening of the theatrical release window is partly attributable to internet piracy and bootlegging. By releasing its video formats at a quicker pace, Major Filmed Entertainment is attempting to distribute each product before piracy does too much damage to theatrical revenues. Piracy notwithstanding, this shortening of the theatrical release window cuts the word-of-mouth factor off at the knees. After a film has already been in theatres for a few weeks, and as the din of manufactured media buzz fades, there is only a small interval in which word of mouth can put a film on a new, possibly unexpected, financial trajectory. As Cucco

(2009) notes, this weakening of the word-of-mouth factor actually *advantages* a saturation booking strategy, which is the hallmark of blockbuster cinema:

> The expectation of [film] quality can be a risk as far as revenues are concerned, especially when speaking about blockbusters. This is why these films have been widely released on the opening weekend for almost 30 years now. By showing the film in many theatres at the same time, the number of people who watch a movie without reading reviews or hearing opinions beforehand increases. (p. 223)

Just as important, the quickening of theatrical release disadvantages films like *O Brother, Where Art Thou?*, which was mentioned earlier in this section. In the last few years, a theatrical run is roughly a month shorter than it was at the start of the millennium. A shorter run is not a concern to any film that, with the help of lots of promotion and advertising, will accumulate large revenues at the start of this theatrical run. But for a platform release like *O Brother*, its attendance grows slowly and "organically" (translation: without much studio support). The successful platform release depends heavily on *positive* word of mouth to generate a wave of excitement in the middle of its theatrical run.

In addition to the historical changes in theatrical window size, there is rising inequality in both the distribution of theatrical revenues and opening theatre size. Figure 7.5 plots the yearly Gini coefficient, a common measure of inequality, of theatrical revenues and opening theatres from 1980 to 2019. Panel A covers all films released in the United States. It demonstrates that the rising inequality of theatrical revenues is positively correlated with the rising inequality in the distribution of opening theatres between films. This correlation between two forms of rising inequality in theatrical exhibition is directly related to Hollywood's objective of risk reduction. The rises in inequality occur in a similar fashion and at the same time as the series in Figure 7.3A, which indicates there has been a steady increase in the chance for the widest releases to end up also being the largest in terms of gross revenues. Figure 7.5B looks at inequality above the 75th percentile of each year, ranked by opening theatre size. Interestingly, Panel B shows a change in the early 2000s. Before the 2000s, there was virtually no inequality in the theatre distribution of the widest releases (a Gini coefficient of 0 is perfect equality). Since the 2000s, however, Major Filmed Entertainment is even treating its biggest projects differently; some are getting even more opening theatres and this is translating into a greater annual share of theatrical revenues.

7.5   The blockbuster effect

Blockbuster cinema, which first emerged in the 1970s, is different from "event" films of the past. Hollywood films before the 1970s, no matter how big in

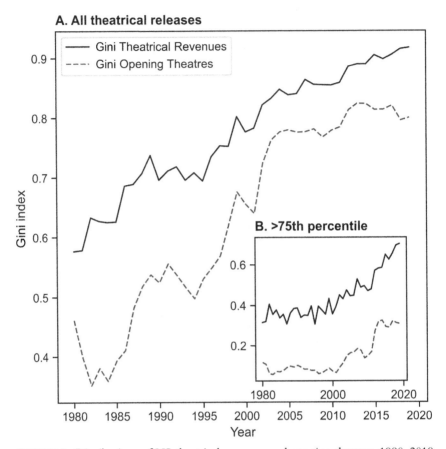

FIGURE 7.5 Distributions of US theatrical revenues and opening theatres, 1980–2019

Sources: www.boxofficemojo.com for yearly gross revenues and opening theatre sizes of individual films, 1980–2019.

production value and grand in scale or imagination, did not get wide releases through simultaneous exhibition — saturation booking was only used for exploitation and pornographic films. Instead, a pre-1970 Hollywood film moved through a tiered system that staggered the exhibition schedule. "First-run" theatres – movie theatres in metropolitan centres – would get the film first.[5] Only when the "first-run" was complete would the film move on to the second tier, and so on down the line. The actor and director Tom Laughlin broke this convention in 1971. By using the saturation-booking method for his own Hollywood film, *Billy Jack*, Laughlin helped usher out the classical system of exhibition, which still carried on after the 1948 Supreme Court decision forced Major Filmed Entertainment to divest its movie-theatre holdings.

The relevance of blockbuster cinema to the risk perceptions of saturation booking can be understood dialectically. Like the self-reflective movement of Reason in Hegel's philosophy, a more effective use of the saturation-booking strategy was an eventual solution to the early shortcomings of saturation booking in the 1970s.[6] Look beyond the two most obvious financial successes of the 1970s – *Jaws* and *Star Wars* – and there are examples of this decade having qualities that undermined the interests of Major Filmed Entertainment. First, if blockbusters were to be high-octane fuel for the big engine of saturation booking, Major Filmed Entertainment would need to learn how to design enough "must-see" films for the top financial tier. This lesson was first taught in 1976, the year that was sandwiched between *Jaws* and *Star Wars. Jaws* created a new pecuniary standard for high-grossing films, and in this environment, the great financial success of *Rocky* – the highest-grossing film in 1976 – was, as Cook (2000) describes, "puzzling and unnerving" (p. 52). *Rocky* was a low-budget project that featured, at the time, a cast of unknown actors. Its unexpected success twisted the knife in the side of designed-to-be-blockbuster films like *King Kong* (1976) and *The Deep* (1977), two films that could not repeat the financial success of *Jaws* (D. A. Cook, 2000, p. 44).

Second, if the blockbuster style was going to be a mainstay for years to come, Major Filmed Entertainment needed the "right" type of creativity. Spielberg and Lucas were certainly proving their worth early on, but many of their contemporaries in the late 1970s were making *auteur*/blockbuster hybrids that proved to be incompatible with the wide-release strategy. On the one hand, the production costs of films like Kubrick's *Barry Lyndon*, Peckinpah's *Convoy*, Friedkin's *Sorcerer*, Coppola's *Apocalypse Now*, Scorsese's *New York, New York*, and Cimino's *Heaven's Gate* were far too big for a small-release strategy to be profitable; on the other hand, the form and content of these films were also too esoteric to ever reach the revenues plateau of a *Jaws* or a *Star Wars*.

Figure 7.6 helps illustrate the transformation from the 1970s to the current era of Hollywood cinema, 1980 to 2019. The figure is a proxy for the consumer habits of American cinema. It presents the volatility of attendance for both the top three and top five films per year. Volatility is computed in two steps. For both the top three and top five films per year, the annual growth rates of total attendance are computed from the 1940s to 2019. The two series in Figure 6.5 are measures of, for each year, a 20-year trailing standard deviation of these growth rates.

Interestingly, the volatility of attendance in the 1970s, the first decade of blockbuster cinema, was similar to that of the 1960s and even the mid-1950s – two periods when saturation booking was not yet a Hollywood strategy. Thus, we can surmise that, even if the release of *Jaws* in 1975 was the first big success of saturation booking, the related degree of confidence had not yet begun to increase. To be sure, having single-handedly pulled in around 128 million attendances in the United States, *Jaws* was an example to be mimicked

immediately. Wyatt (1994) describes the saturation-booking strategy that followed on its heels:

> Following *Jaws*, high quality studio films developed even broader saturation
> releases; in 1976, *King Kong* (with a 961 theater opening); in 1977, *The
> Heretic: Exorcist II* (703 theaters), *The Deep* (800 theaters), *Saturday Night
> Fever* (726 theaters); in 1978, *Grease* (902 theaters) and *Star Trek–The
> Motion Picture* (856 theaters) continued to expand the pattern of saturation
> release and intense television advertising. (p. 112)

Despite this flurry of wide releases, however, Figure 7.6 illustrates that there is still
a difference between the 1970s – a decade when blockbuster cinema was still in
its infancy – and the contemporary period from 1980 to the present – a time
when blockbuster cinema has become Hollywood's predominant style. The two
series – "Top Three Films" and "Top Five Films" – both start their decline in
the 1980s and reach their lowest levels in the 2000s. By 2011, the 20-year trailing
standard deviation for the attendance of the top three films was 48 per cent less

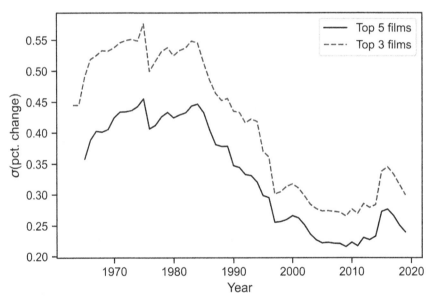

FIGURE 7.6 Volatility of US theatrical attendance: top three and top five films

Source: Bradley Schauer and David Bordwell, 'Appendix: A Hollywood Timeline, 1960–2004,' in
Bordwell (2006). For years not covered in Schauer and Bordwell, see www.boxofficemojo.com for
yearly gross revenues of individual films and National Association of Theatre Owners (http://www.
natoonline.org/) for average US ticket price.

Note: Attendance equals total US gross revenues of the top three films, divided by average US ticket
price.

volatile than it had been in 1980. The same can be said for the attendance of the top five films.

7.6   When two become one

The aim of this chapter has been to understand how and to what extent Major Filmed Entertainment has increased its degree of confidence through the systemic reduction of risk (δ). Around 1980, Major Filmed Entertainment began to effectively determine the financial trajectory of its most valuable films. Since then, Hollywood has gotten better at predicting which films will best use the saturation-booking strategy to accumulate a greater share of all theatrical revenues. Moreover, the volatility of attendance has decreased for the top films, and this historical change is coeval with a shortening of the theatrical-release window, which in turn disadvantages platform releases. Overall, the institution of blockbuster cinema and the strategy of saturation booking signify a decrease in risk for Major Filmed Entertainment.

As we travel from 1980 to most recent years of Hollywood history, the two strategies of saturation booking and blockbuster cinema become entwined. The product is a "single" approach to risk reduction. Three consequences of this risk reduction, which are more systemic than microscopic, confirm that the business interest in differential accumulation is, to use Bichler and Nitzan's term, *creordering* our cinematic universe. If you love an endless stream of wide-released blockbusters, Major Filmed Entertainment's impact on the shape of our cinematic universe is praiseworthy. If you mourn what is crushed under the treads of Hollywood's risk-reducing machine, the future does not look as bright.

7.6.1   Major Filmed Entertainment versus theatre owners

In 2013 the *Los Angeles Times* reported a dispute between Disney and two major theatre owners, AMC Entertainment and Regal Entertainment. The dispute was over the release of *Iron Man 3* and how its theatrical revenues were going to be split between Disney and theatre owners. According to the *Los Angeles Times*, studios "typically collect 50% to 55% of ticket sales, depending on the movie". AMC and Regal were challenging Disney because, for *Iron Man 3*, "Disney was seeking an excessively large take of the box-office revenue — up to 65%" (Verrier, 2013).

How might we understand this dispute? Having recently acquired Marvel Studios and Lucasfilm, Disney is in a position to benefit from the future of blockbuster cinema, should its popularity continue. Disney's boldness about the distribution of *Iron Man 3* might also portend something more general: its degree of confidence about the future earnings of the Marvel cinematic universe and its other franchises. Because the order of cinema is currently structured to give the top tier of films the majority of theatrical revenues (McMahon, 2013; Weinstein, 2005), the threat to withhold anticipated blockbusters from the community at large is a big one.

The underlying power structure of this dispute can be seen if we take a historical view of the struggle between distribution and exhibition in contemporary Hollywood. Figure 7.7A shows the relationship of two time series. The x-axis measures the number of Major Filmed Entertainment releases from 1965 to

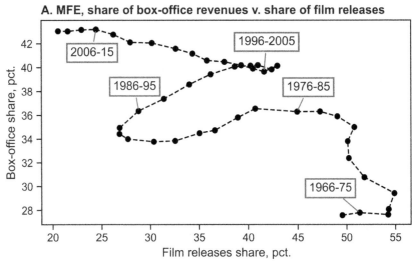

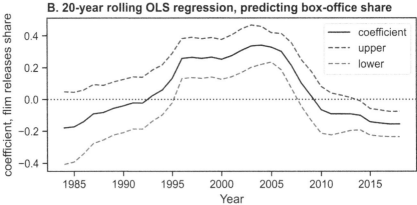

FIGURE 7.7 Major Filmed Entertainment's film releases and US theatrical revenues

Source: Time series of per cent shares of film releases and US theatrical revenues are created from three editions of Harold Vogel's *Entertainment Industry Economics* (2007, 2011, 2020).

2019. It is expressed as a percentage of the total number of films released in the United States per year, and the series is smoothed as a ten-year rolling average. The y-axis, from 1965 to 2019, measures Major Filmed Entertainment's share of all US box-office revenues per year, again as a ten-year moving average. This series is an indirect measure of the struggle between Major Filmed Entertainment and theatre owners – that is, there is a certain amount of theatrical revenues each year, and it is by means of contract negotiation that a certain share goes to the film distributors of Hollywood (Vogel, 2011, 2020).

The point in time when this dispute over *Iron Man 3* occurred is illuminating. Since the early 2000s, the rules of the game might be changing once again. AMC and Regal were challenging Disney in 2013, and in the period from the early 2000s to 2019, Major Filmed Entertainment's share of theatrical revenues increased as its share of all film releases is decreased. As we see in Figure 7.7B, Hollywood was operating with a positive relationship between film share and revenue share from the mid 1990s to the mid 2000s. The panel plots the coefficient and confidence intervals of predicting Major Filmed Entertainment's box-office share with its share of annual film releases.

We can look at Figure 7.7 in a way that is similar to how Crandall (1975) saw the Hollywood studios after the 1948 Supreme Court decision against the studio system. In the absence of bald-faced behaviour that is now infamous in the Hollywood studio system, Crandall correctly identified that a mechanism of control "at the distributors' disposal" was still there and that the power of film distribution was "quite straightforward – the control over the number of film releases per year". By "controlling the only non-substitutable input in theatrical exhibition – the film itself — the distributors continued to exercise market power" over theatrical exhibition (Crandall, 1975, p. 62). Since the 2000s, Major Filmed Entertainment's share of all films released in the United States has been declining to a level not seen since the late 1980s; however, the decline is not a signal of Hollywood losing control in its climb to ever-higher heights of theatrical revenue share. As Figure 7.8 shows with the R^2 values of Figure 7.7B, Major Filmed Entertainment has been on another wave of exercising control of theatrical releases since 2009 – this time with a *negative* relationship to its shares of theatrical revenues. The stable popularity of superhero franchises and other blockbusters appears to have created a situation whereby Major Filmed Entertainment can strategically sabotage without undermining revenues.

7.6.2   Have you seen this year's nominees?

One victim of Major Filmed Entertainment's risk reduction is a branch of *itself*. The attempt to redistribute attendance upwards, to the widest released films, is negatively affecting Hollywood's own branch of artistic cinema, which often competes with many foreign language films for awards and status.

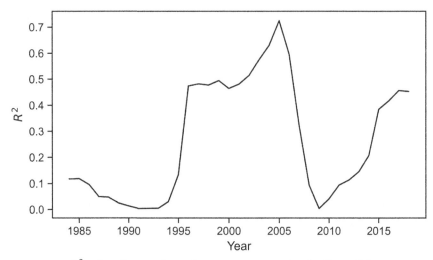

FIGURE 7.8 R^2 values from ordinary least squares regression in Figure 7.7

Sources: Time series of per cent shares of film releases and US theatrical revenues are created from three editions of Harold Vogel's *Entertainment Industry Economics* (2007, 2011, 2020).

In the wake of the independent-Hollywood wave of the 1990s – which started with films like *Pulp Fiction*, and was spearheaded *and sabotaged*[7] by Harvey Weinstein's Miramax studio – Major Filmed Entertainment has closed some of its independent, more artistically minded cinema divisions (Ortner, 2013). Furthermore, the budget range of $20 million to $85 million has become in Hollywood, according to director Steven Soderbergh, a "dead zone". It is possible for an art film to find financing below $20 million – although even that might be too generous – but a budget above $85 million is not even a conceivable possibility. "Above the 85 range you're into sort of the physically big movies that probably have movie stars in them or have some high concept behind them that they can sell" (Soderbergh, 2010, p. 62).

Figure 7.9 shows the effects of Hollywood's blockbuster strategy on the films that are considered for the Academy Award for Best Picture. The black time series is the theatrical attendance of every Best-Picture winner since *Patton* in 1970. The grey area plots the attendance for films that were nominated for Best Picture but did not win. The upper and lower boundaries of the area are the 5th and 95th percentile of theatrical attendance, respectively. For visual clarity, the area plot has been smoothed as a three-year moving average. Additionally, Figure 7.9 plots a vertical line in 2009, when the Academy increased the number of films to be nominated per year, from five to nine.

If Figure 7.5 shows the upward redistribution of box-office grosses (and attendance), Figure 7.9 presents the decline in theatrical attendance for what the

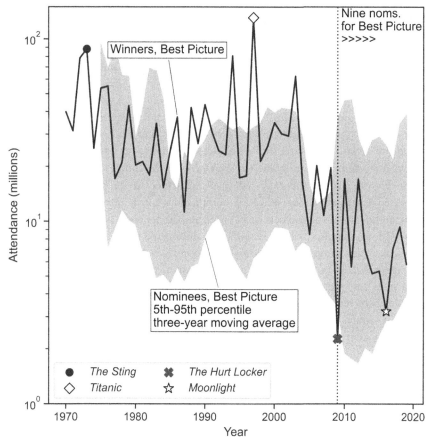

FIGURE 7.9   Academy Award for Best Picture: theatrical attendance of winners and nominees

Source: www.boxofficemojo.com for yearly gross revenues of individual films. National Association of Theatre Owners for average US ticket price.

Academy believes are the year's best films. Particularly since the win of *Titanic* in 1997, theatrical attendance has steadily declined for films that won an Oscar for best picture. In the years from 2009 to 2019, the wider spread of nominees acts as a counterbalance to the significant decline in attendance for the winners. For example, the attendances for such nominees as *Avatar, Up, Inception, Toy Story 3, American Sniper, Gravity* and *The Blind Side* are all at least five times larger than the attendances of such winners as *12 Years a Slave, The Artist, Spotlight, Birdman or (The Unexpected Virtue of Ignorance)*, and *Moonlight*.

There appears to be an easy retort to Figure 7.9: "While it is true fewer people are seeing Oscar-nominated films in theatres, moviegoers have plenty of opportunities to watch the Academy Awards ceremony in March and then see the films *post festum*, on video or through a streaming platform". Without video or streaming data, we cannot exclude the possibility that Oscar-nominated films use video and digital streaming to "compensate" for weak theatrical showings. However, performing a quick experiment will show the unlikelihood of there being enough cultural attention per year to allow Oscar-nominated films to catch up to the biggest films of the year.

The experiment takes, for each year, five thousand random samples from two sets of films: the top ten grossing films per year and films nominated for the Academy Award for Best Picture (including the eventual winner). Each sample draws three films randomly and the average of these samples (denoted as $\bar{T}$ and $\bar{O}$ in Figure 7.10) is the expected total attendance for each set of films. The expected total attendance of Oscar-nominated set ($\bar{O}$) is subtracted from the total attendance of the top-ten set ($\bar{T}$). The remainder is the additional attendance needed for a sample of three Best-Picture-nominated films to reach the level of attendance that three top-ten films achieved *in theatres*.

Figure 7.10 plots the results of our quick experiment. The solid line with grey area plots the average and standard deviation of the difference (in millions of people) between a random sample of three Best-Picture-nominated films and a random sample from the top ten. As some of Best-Picture-nominated films are in the top ten of their year, some random samples of Best-Picture-nominated

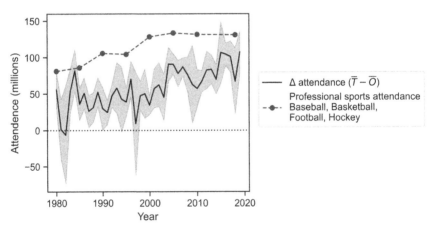

FIGURE 7.10   Additional attendance needed for Best-Picture-nominated films to reach the theatrical attendance of the top ten

Source: www.boxofficemojo.com for yearly gross revenues of individual films. National Association of Theatre Owners for average US ticket price. Three editions of Harold Vogel's *Entertainment Industry Economics* (2007, 2011, 2020) for total annual attendance for professional sports.

films do not need any "extra" attendance to be as popular as the biggest films of the year. However, as the time series travels from the 1980s to the 1990s, and then into the new Millennium, films nominated for Best Picture begin to need millions of post-theatrical viewings to achieve what the top ten simply accomplished in theatres. Not every Best-Picture nomination will need this much additional attendance to be profitable, or to be considered successful by Hollywood executives, but the size of the gap puts our imagination of post-theatrical popularity in context. For additional context, the dotted line plots the combined total attendance for the four major professional sports in the United States. With this additional context in mind, a random sample of three Best-Picture nominees will sometimes "require", in our thought experiment, digital viewings around the size of a full year of in-person attendances for the MLB, NBA, NFL and NHL combined.

7.6.3   Living among 120-minute-long action-adventures

This chapter has been building an empirical case against the argument that high risk in Hollywood is inherent to the film business. The argument we are challenging is problematic because it inoculates aspects of strategic sabotage in Hollywood – for example, stagnation, repetition, casting inequality, rejection of political projects. Under the narrative that "nobody knows anything" in Hollywood, the strategic sabotage of the American film industry is neither strategic nor intentional sabotage. Rather, any habit or obsession in the control over the industrial art of filmmaking is a so-called misguided fight against systemic risk: if risk is extremely high, any aggressive control of cinema's potential is just as fruitless for future success as any random walk from project to project.

Yet if strategic sabotage delivers results in risk reduction, the argument of inherently high risk loses yet another pillar in its foundation. For instance, we can investigate how the aesthetic dimension of cinema is being incorporated into the order of cinema – a concept introduced in Chapter 6.

Figure 7.11 presents evidence for this investigation. With IMDb data on the runtime of films theatrically released from 1983 to 2019, the figure plots the min-max range of runtime across a normalized opening-theatre rank – where 0 is lowest and 1 highest, per year. The minimum and maximum series are smoothed with locally weighted scatterplot smoothing. To exclude some extreme outliers – mostly film shorts, documentary screenings and retrospectives – the data are filtered to exclude films shorter than one hour and films longer than six hours. The full set totals 15,963 films; the 20 largest distributors (excluding Disney), sorted by total opening theatres, has 4,751 films; and Major Filmed Entertainment (excluding Disney) has 2,667 films.

Extra research is needed to explain how day-to-day activities in film financing and film production produce the outcome in Figure 7.11. Nevertheless, the figure

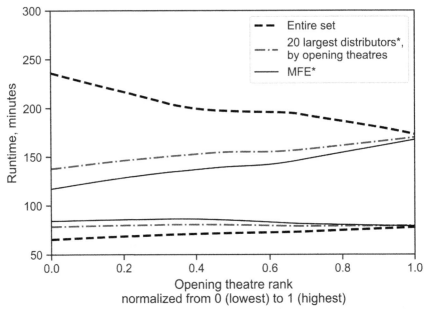

FIGURE 7.11 Minimum and maximum runtimes, by normalized opening theatre rank

Source: IMDb for film runtimes. www.boxofficemojo.com for opening theatre ranks, 1983–2019.

* Excluding Disney.

shows how Major Filmed Entertainment generally stays in a narrower range of film runtime. Additionally, lower-ranked films distributed by Major Filmed Entertainment do not have the freedom to be longer. This restraint is likely an effect of how business interests look at runtime differently than someone who is open to letting run time be dictated by the autonomous creation of form and content (Holman & McMahon, 2015). In terms of aesthetics, runtime is the time needed to tell a story in a certain way – no more, no less. Technologically speaking, especially with digital film cameras, you can make a ten-page script last 1,000 minutes. You can also create masterpieces like Chantal Akerman's *Jeanne Dielman, 23, quai du Commerce, 1080 Bruxelles*, a 201-minute film that uses long takes to allow for tension to slowly build beneath the surface as Jeanne performs domestic routines, such as preparing dinner.

For the entire set, higher-ranking films are, *on average*, longer in run time than films ranked lower in opening theatre rankings. In the era of comic book franchises and expensive adaptations of fantasy series like the Lord of the Rings and Harry Potter, the difference in runtime is pronounced. Figures 7.12 and 7.13 present two versions of locally weighted scatterplot smoothing; the two versions bin films by percentiles but in slightly different ways. The two figures illustrate

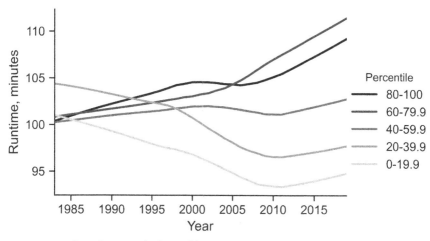

FIGURE 7.12   Runtime trends, binned by opening-theatre rank percentile, version 1
Source: IMDb for film runtimes. www.boxofficemojo.com for opening theatre ranks, 1983–2019.

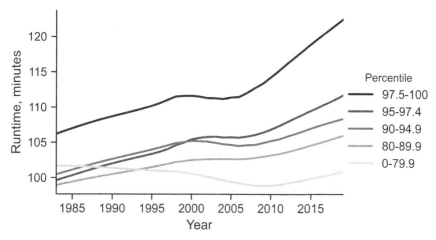

FIGURE 7.13   Runtime trends, binned by opening-theatre rank percentile, version 2
Source: IMDb for film runtimes. www.boxofficemojo.com for opening theatre ranks, 1983–2019.

the progressive increase in runtime for the top-tier films, ranked by opening theatres. In the same span of time, the middle and bottom percentiles either remained
in place or shortened.

On its own, run time is a variable without clear political economic implications –
the increase or decrease of run time is not obviously "good" for the Hollywood film
business, or even the average moviegoer. Combined with genre data – which was

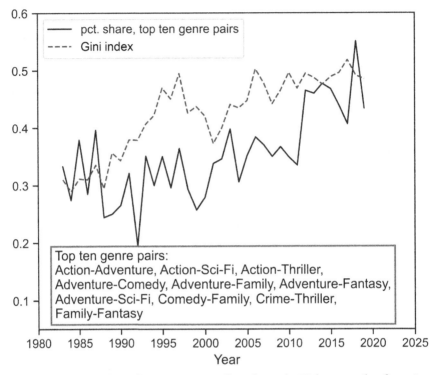

FIGURE 7.14 Inequality of genres per year, films above the 75th percentile of opening theatres, 1983–2019

Source: IMDb.

Note: Films with only one listed genre are excluded from the visualization.

used in Chapter 6 – the growing inequality in run time speaks to the impact of blockbusters on the order of cinema. Figure 7.14 plots two series with IMDb data on films above the 75th percentile in opening-theatre rank of its year. The solid line plots the per cent share of the ten most frequent genre pairs from 1983 to 2019. The dashed series measures inequality with an annual Gini index of the distribution of genre pairs – there are 168 pairs in total. Both series help us understand what is occurring in tandem with the lengthening of top-tier films. The top ten genre pairs are being used more frequently and the distribution of genre pairs has become more unequal.

7.6.4 The mirroring effect of US cultural imperialism

When a national competitor is *unable* to fight Hollywood for the top-grossing ranks of its own market, Hollywood is content to have its international strategies mirror its strategy in the United States. In other words, Hollywood's most straightforward strategy is to take what is successful at home and export it abroad (Fu & Govindaraju, 2010).

Figure 7.15 shows the successful overlap of Major Filmed Entertainment's international strategies and its dominance of the US market. The figure plots the results

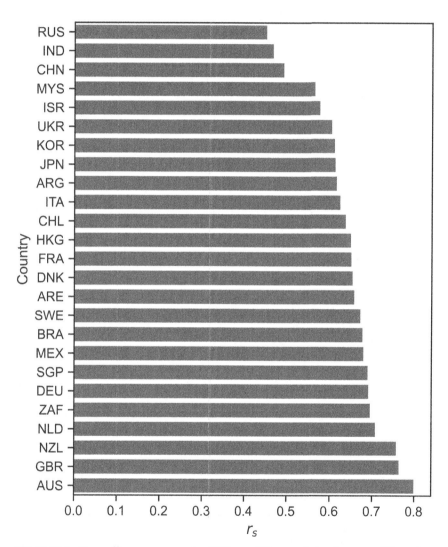

FIGURE 7.15   Box-office revenue rank of US top 100, correlation between US market versus foreign, 2007–2016

Source: www.boxofficemojo.com for gross revenue ranks of national theatrical markets.

Note: Data on France includes revenues from Algeria, Monaco, Morocco and Tunisia.

of Spearman correlations for films that have a US gross ranking and a non-US gross ranking. For each country, the rankings of films above 100 in US box-office rank are compared to their national box-office ranks, which can be any number. Data were retrieved for 25 countries and the biggest period of years is from 2000 to 2019. The number of values in each Spearman correlation is dependent on the number of films that are in the top 100 in the United States and released in a non-US market. The country with the fewest number of values is Russia, which has 100 films for comparison. Great Britain has the most films: 1,543.

Figure 7.15 demonstrates there is an international dimension of Major Filmed Entertainment's low risk after 2000. From 2000 to 2019 and across many countries around the world, top-ranking films in the United States tend to also be top-ranking in foreign markets. If that is the case, there is an added degree of confidence to giving certain films wide opening releases.

Few will be surprised about Hollywood's popularity abroad, and some readers will have seen arguments about Hollywood's deleterious effects on cultural diversity in global cinema before (Germann, 2005). However, there are considerable implications to seeing Hollywood's domination of global moviegoing through the lens of risk reduction. For example, a high predictability of US-foreign box-office rankings will likely have effects on American films that are deemed "unbankable" outside the United States. As Erigha (2019) shows, Hollywood's definition of "unbankable" is tied to race; there is a high probability that American films with a predominantly Black cast will *not* receive international distribution. Thus, the mirroring effect of top-ranking films in foreign markets strengthens the "logic" that Hollywood has constructed and continues to obey. In the name of "risk reduction", Major Filmed Entertainment can withhold substantial budgets from Black-cast films. This racial inequality is exacerbated with a double standard: many blockbusters – often with white leads – are given international distribution *regardless* of their failure in the US box office (Erigha, 2019, pp. 101–108).

Moreover, a strong positive Spearman correlation indicates that Hollywood can dominate global cinema with cold precision. Expressed as a degree of confidence in the capitalization of cinema, the international mirroring of the US box-office rank is an accounting tool for unexpected resistance to Hollywood's ubiquity. Indeed, it is always possible for future moviegoers to become tired of Hollywood's biggest films, especially if a country's national cinema has suffocated as a result. In the power-free worldview of neoclassical economics, this possibility is an imaginary demand-curve of consumer utility for imported Hollywood films, which endogenously shifts with changes to "cultural discounting".[8] In the capital-as-power worldview, Hollywood's top-tier domination of global cinema is gained or lost through power. And as consumer behaviour around the world begins to synchronize, Hollywood gains more confidence in obedience.

7.7   Conclusion

The aim of this chapter has been to understand how and to what extent Major Filmed Entertainment has increased its degree of confidence through the systemic reduction of risk (δ). Around 1980, Major Filmed Entertainment began to effectively determine the financial trajectory of its most valuable films. Since then, Hollywood has gotten better at predicting which films will best use the saturation-booking strategy to accumulate a greater share of all theatrical revenues. Moreover, the volatility of attendance has decreased for the top films, and this historical change is coeval with a shortening of the theatrical-release window, which in turn disadvantages platform releases. Overall, the institution of blockbuster cinema and the strategy of saturation booking signify a decrease in risk for Major Filmed Entertainment.

This decrease in risk has been a significant factor in Major Filmed Entertainment's drive to accumulate *differentially*. The reduction of risk was not only absolute; it was also differential, relative to Dominant Capital more broadly. Figure 7.16 plots the time series from Figure 7.1 beside a differential measure of risk. For both the numerator (Major Filmed Entertainment) and the denominator (Dominant Capital) in the differential measure, the time series measures a rolling 15-year standard deviation of the per cent change in operating income.

Figure 7.16 demonstrates that, overall, Major Filmed Entertainment reduced its risk faster than Dominant Capital after 1980. The spike of differential risk in 1980 is also a high watermark that signals when certain qualities of New Hollywood were no longer celebrated by business. If differential risk was rising, the *auteur*-ism and cinematic ambitions of a politically charged New Hollywood were parts to be amputated.

The next chapter will study the history of New Hollywood and analyse how its decline coincided with the rise of *high-concept* filmmaking, a cinematic style that pervades contemporary Hollywood. For now, we can reflect on the significance of understanding the role of risk reduction in Major Filmed Entertainment's quest to accumulate capital. Seeing quantitative evidence of risk reduction in Hollywood is analogous to possessing a device to measure air quality. Without this device, one can conjecture that the air quality of their environment has gotten worse, and perhaps symptoms such as headaches or coughing are reasonable clues. But possession of the device helps; it can be used to analyse the compounds of polluted air and it is the key to fighting doubts that anything is wrong.

This analogy, I believe, is helpful because lots of people complain about the quality of cinema produced and distributed by Major Filmed Entertainment, but they are not in possession of a device to measure the problem more accurately. These complaints are not simply coming from "everyday" consumers or journalists. In the March 2021 issue of *Harper's*, Martin Scorsese wrote an essay to pay tribute to Federico Fellini, the Italian director who directed such great films as

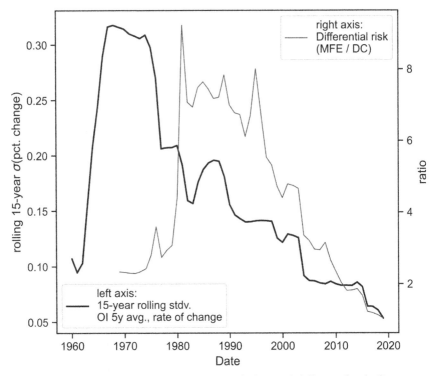

FIGURE 7.16 Major Filmed Entertainment's volatility and differential volatility

Source: Annual reports for operating income of Major Filmed Entertainment, 1943–1960. Compustat through WRDS for operating income of Major Filmed Entertainment, 1950–1992. Annual reports of Disney, News Corp, Viacom, Sony, Time Warner (Management's Discussion of Business Operations for information on their filmed entertainment interests) for operating income of Major Filmed Entertainment, 1993–2019. Compustat for operating income of Dominant Capital, 1950–2019.

La Strada, 8½, La Dolce Vita, Nights of Cabiria and *Satyricon*. News outlets reported the publishing of the essay and #scorcese trended on Twitter because Scorcese framed his tribute to Fellini – which was both personal and knowledgeable – with an argument about the decline of cinema as an art form. Here is a key example from the essay's conclusion:

> Everything has changed — the cinema and the importance it holds in our culture. Of course, it's hardly surprising that artists such as Godard, Bergman, Kubrick, and Fellini, who once reigned over our great art form like gods, would eventually recede into the shadows with the passing of time. But at this point, we can't take anything for granted. We can't depend on the movie business, such as it is, to take care of cinema. In the

movie business, which is now the mass visual entertainment business, the emphasis is always on the word "business", and value is always determined by the amount of money to be made from any given property — in that sense, everything from *Sunrise* to *La Strada* to *2001* is now pretty much wrung dry and ready for the "Art Film" swim lane on a streaming platform. (Scorcese, 2021)

Scorcese is telling a classic story: Hollywood is a business, and we keep learning the hard lesson that profit comes before art. Yet Scorcese can only imply the connection between the profit motive and the financial value of great film-makers. The capital-as-power approach focuses the lens on the "problem": to differentially accumulate, Major Filmed Entertainment has been pushing to reduce risk against its benchmark, which is composed of other giant firms that dominate their respective industries. Thus, a long period of risk reduction, from 1980 to 2019, will alter how Major Filmed Entertainment looks at the art of cinema. Major Filmed Entertainment needs social creativity to birth new films, but the (major) film business would only want another Fellini, Antonioni, Varda, Godard, Ackerman or Scorcese when these creative forms are instrumental to differential accumulation.

Notes

1 According to Ulin (2010), "the amount spent to open a film is disproportionately large because the theatrical launch of a film is the engine that drives all downstream revenues. Accordingly, the money spent up front marketing a film, creating awareness, develops an overnight brand that is then sustained and managed in most instances for more than a decade" (p. 499).

2 "Block booking" is perhaps the most notorious feature of the classical Hollywood studio system. Block booking occurred when studio films were sold to independent exhibitors in unalterable blocks, in a all-or-nothing deal. As Maltby (1983) notes, block booking was key to obstructing an independent film's route to a successful exhibition:

> Small independent exhibitors had little opportunity to cancel or choose films within the block and could not prevent distributors from including films of dubious commercial quality in the package. The main purpose of much of the majors' low-budget production…was to occupy exhibition time, foreclosing entry into the market by independent distributors and maintaining their own monopoly. (p. 45)

For more on the political economy of block booking, see Hanssen (2005), Hozic (2001), and Sedgwick and Pokorny (2005). For a defense of the studio system's "efficiency", which relied on anti-competitive practices like block booking, see Schatz (2010).

3 These two examples, *The Mummy Returns* and *O Brother, Where Art Thou?*, are taken from Maltby (2003, pp. 202–204).

4 As Rosenbaum (2000) speculates, this fear of giving wide releases to the wrong set of films – or rather not giving it to the right set – might explain the reactive co-optation of *The Blair Witch Project* by the mainstream media (pp. 45–46). The promotional coverage of *Blair Witch* by the big media conglomerates was aggressive, but, as Rosenbaum

notes, it was really a defensive manoeuvre to gloss over Major Filmed Entertainment's ignorance of and non-involvement with a film that rapidly accumulated $140 million at the US box-office. The media blitz began weeks after the independent film distributor, Artisan Entertainment, first released this low-budget film in 27 American theatres. *The Blair Witch Project* was far and away Artisan's most successful theatrical release. For all the films Artisan released from 1997 to 2003 – at which point Lionsgate acquired the firm – the theatrical revenues of *Blair Witch* were 17 times greater than the average Artisan release. For the same period, the film accounted for 36 per cent of Artisan's total theatrical revenues (my calculations from data retrieved from www.boxoffice-mojo.com).

5 While a tiered system was certainly in place, "first-run" theatres lost some of their advantages after 1948. For example, there was no longer a ticket-price difference between "first-run" theatres and lower tiered ones – most likely due to the post-1948 decline of double features (i.e., tickets that sell two back-to-back films). Also, the "clearance" tactic – where major studios would remove a film from all theatres for a block of time between its "first-run" exhibition and its "second-run" – was deemed illegal in the Supreme Court case against Paramount and the other major studios (Waterman, 2005, p. 57)

6   Spirit gains its truth only through finding itself within absolute rupture. Spirit is that power not as a positive which turns away from the negative, as when we say of something that it is nothing or false, and having thus finished with it we turn to something else; rather, spirit is that power only in so far as it looks the negative in the face and dwells in it. This dwelling is the magic force which converts the negative into being. (Hegel, 2005b, p. 129)

Yirmiyahu Yovel, in his running commentary on Hegel's (2005b) "Preface" to *The Phenomenology*, describes the self-reflective nature of Reason: "It is essential for knowledge to separate itself from the object and thus introduce falsity as a condition of the eventual reidentification" (p. 141).

7 As this book is being written, the contemporary conversations about Weinstein are, justifiably, related to the mountain of sexual abuse allegations that have been raised against him – and he is currently serving a sentence for one count of third-degree rape and one count of criminal sexual assault in the first degree. Alternative histories of Miramax and Weinstein's "support" of independent film have also been appearing in recent years, and they serve as critical contrasts to idyllic images of Miramax acting as a noble patron of independent filmmaking. For example, see McDonald (2009), Ortner (2013), and Rosenbaum (1997c).

8 The concept of "cultural discounting" first appeared in Hoskins and Mirus (1988). It refers to the amount of "discounting" a consumer makes when they are presented with media from a foreign culture – for example, you would be willing to pay $10 for a domestic film and $9.6 for a foreign film. The concept was designed to explain the clear asymmetry in media trade: American film and television are popular abroad, but the film and television of other countries are not popular in the United States. Hoskins and Mirus (1988) find key reasons for American cultural dominance. First, when the cultural discount is equal for all countries, the country with the largest domestic market wins: "If the costs of production are the same for all programme producers and the size of cultural discount is equal for all countries, then the cultural discount alone is sufficient to explain why the country with the largest domestic market, the US, dominates international trade". Second, cultural discounts are not equal across countries and the United States, argue Hoskins and Mirus, is discounted *less* than other cultures around the world. "The extremely competitive US broadcasting system", say Hoskins and Mirus (1988), "together with the Hollywood tradition has resulted in entertaining, common-denominator, tried-and-tested drama programming that is well received by viewers in

most foreign markets, markets long acclimatized to Hollywood products through cinema exposure. US viewers, on the other hand, appear unusually intolerant of foreign programming" (pp. 511–512).

Others have tested the effects of cultural discounting empirically (Shin & McKenzie, 2019). However, there is a critical problem that spans the theory and application of the concept. Under its current neoclassical economic form, the measure of cultural discounting is reliant on the assumption of revealed preferences, whereby sales data reveals the so-called effects of cultural discounting. Working backwards in this case, from prices to utility, is especially problematic because "discounting" the values of other cultures is hardly a "rational" comparison of alternatives. Instead, each cultural discount can contain any mixture of geopolitical power and region-centric ignorance, as it is entirely possible that a consumer could be heavily "discounting" foreign films and television programs with racism and xenophobia.

8
THE INSTITUTION OF HIGH-CONCEPT CINEMA

8.1 Introduction

This chapter, which is concerned with the history of American cinema and the political philosophy of art, complements the quantitative research of the previous chapter. The chapter provides a conceptual analysis of high-concept cinema, and it shows how, over the past three decades, the growing hegemony of high-concept cinema went hand in hand with the ability of Major Filmed Entertainment to significantly reduce its risk.

High-concept cinema in Hollywood involves the simplification of a film's message for marketing purposes. This strategy, which first emerged in the late 1970s, is the product of the rise and fall of American New Wave, which was briefly embraced during the period of "New Hollywood". By excising the complexity, ambiguity and, dare we say, politics from the aesthetic intentions of American New Wave, the application of high-concept cinema by Major Filmed Entertainment has been able to realign the aesthetics of Hollywood films with the contemporary strategies of saturation booking and blockbuster cinema.

The chapter explores how the aesthetic form of high-concept cinema complements Major Filmed Entertainment's need to strategically sabotage the industrial art of filmmaking. High-concept cinema is a product of "intensified continuity", which is a filmmaking technique that achieves clarity, simplicity and straightforward meaning through rapid cutting between shots. Intensified continuity need not be, in and of itself, a function of strategic sabotage. But it can easily become one when the rights of ownership allow Major Filmed Entertainment to transform the "raw" material created during film production into high-concept cinema. This discrepancy

DOI: 10.4324/9781003092629-10

between what is shot during actual production and what is finally presented to the audience is possible because American copyright law gives Major Filmed Entertainment the right to edit or re-arrange any film that is ostensibly completed by its filmmakers.

8.2   High-concept cinema

High concept is simultaneously an aesthetic and business term. It refers to a style of filmmaking that assumes that the essence of a film is broadly marketable when its main idea is as simple and straightforward as possible (Wyatt, 1994). According to the logic of high concept, the idea of a film should be communicated easily, as a modern audience is very likely to discover upcoming films through trailers and other advertisements. Thus, because of its aesthetic design, short descriptions adequately represent what high-concept films are about. (It may already appear that *low concept* is a more appropriate term; however, *high concept* is the term used by the film business.)

Who exactly invented high concept has yet to be settled. Wyatt notes that some people credit Barry Diller, while others point to Michael Eisner. Diller first used the high-concept standard when he was a programming executive for ABC television: "Since Diller needed stories which could be easily summarized for a thirty-second television spot, he approved those projects which could be sold in a single sentence" (Wyatt, 1994, p. 8). Eisner first practiced high concept when he was a creative executive for Paramount (he later moved to Disney). For Eisner, it was also about whether a film could be summarized briefly (Wyatt, 1994, p. 8).

This yearning for brevity is partly a consequence of Hollywood "pitch" meetings, which usually give writers or filmmakers only about 20 minutes to sell their idea or script to a producer or development executive (Elsbach & Kramer, 2003, p. 286). However, as Wyatt points out, the pitch to a studio executive or producer is also a hypothetical pitch to an audience that commonly learns about the plots of upcoming films through television commercials, movie posters or internet trailers. For example, Steven Spielberg, the most financially successful director in contemporary Hollywood and an executive producer of many films, uses the high-concept style to bridge pitched ideas and their hypothetical final products, the films themselves: "If a person can tell me the idea in 25 words or less, it's going to make a pretty good movie. I like ideas, especially movie ideas, that you can hold in your hand" (quoted in Wyatt, 1994, p. 13).

Twenty-five words or less is not very much, but as Wyatt points out, Hollywood has devised ways to achieve this reduction, whereby the gist of the film is expressed in a simple marketable idea. As we show in what follows, this reduction in cinematic complexity is coeval with the systematic reduction of risk for Major Filmed Entertainment.

8.2.1 The elements of high-concept cinema

In a high-concept film, one will find character types, a simple narrative or a take-away image or style — and sometimes all three elements.

High-concept films tend to rely on simple character types to make the motivation and goals of characters transparent. High-concept characters may have proper names, but they lack the richness and depth that often give individual desires, both real and imaginary, an ambivalent, obscure or even unconscious foundation. The main point of high-concept characterization is to highlight a single property in each character. For instance, in Steven Soderbergh's *Ocean's Eleven*, George Clooney plays a thief who steals for more than money, be it for love or revenge; Brad Pitt plays a thief who is always the cool counterweight to Clooney; and Matt Damon is the thief who is talented but always clueless about the master plan, to which Clooney and Pitt are always privy. Physical qualities can also stand in for personality and psychological motivation. In *Twins*, for instance, the narrative centres on "the physical difference between the twins," which, as Wyatt (1994) points out, "is reinforced by the casting of Danny DeVito and Arnold Schwarzenegger" (p. 55). This visual contrast between a stocky DeVito and brawny Schwarzenegger was also at the centre of the film's marketing campaign.

In Hollywood, complex stories are not always winnowed down to the point that they become high concept. Charlie Kaufman, for example, was forced to simplify his script for *Eternal Sunshine of the Spotless Mind*, yet the final product is complex enough to disqualify as high concept. As the analysis by Bordwell (2006) implies, *Eternal Sunshine* was still difficult to market because its simple narrative structure was buried too far beneath a visible façade of experimental exposition:

> As with the experiments of the 1940s and 1960s, most storytelling innovations since the 1990s have kept one foot in classical tradition. Because of the redundancy built into the Hollywood narrative system, unusual devices could piggyback on a large number of familiar cues. *Eternal Sunshine*, as Kaufman doubtless realizes, tells of boy meeting girl, boy losing girl, and boy getting girl. (p. 73)

By design, a high-concept film does not hide this simplicity. Instead, a high-concept film is the least likely candidate to veer from the established narrative standards of Hollywood cinema. With a straightforward premise and a cast of characters that lack psychological depth, high-concept films can cleanly and efficiently follow standard Hollywood procedure:

> Act 1 introduces the problems faced by the hero, ending with a crisis and the promise of major conflict. Act 2 consists of an extended struggle between the protagonist and his or her problem, and it ends at a point of even more severe testing for the hero. Act 3 shows the protagonist solving the

problem. Taking a two-hour film as the norm and assuming that one script page equals a minute of screen time, [it is recommended] that act 1 run about thirty pages, act 2 about sixty pages, and act 3 another thirty pages. (Bordwell, 2006, p. 28)

This ratio of page count to screen time suggests that Adorno was not exaggerating when he stated that the total duration of a Hollywood film "is regulated as if by a stopwatch" (Adorno, 2004d, p. 75).

The third element, the high-concept image, can be described as "excessive". In order to explain what that means, though, we need to briefly examine the role of images in art films. As described later in this chapter, art films, like high-concept ones, will often delay narrative progression, sometimes by holding a shot and creating memorable images. However, there is a qualitative difference between high-concept imagery and, for example, the images of perpendicular female faces in *Persona* and *Mulholland Drive*. The latter two films use the same type of shot to add complexity, mystery and ambiguity to stories that are already discontinuous. As Bordwell (2003) notes, an art film generally alternates between imagery and narration to announce that "life is more complex than art can ever be, and . . . the only way to respect this complexity is to leave causes dangling and questions unanswered" (p. 43).

By contrast, the narrative-imagery relationship of high-concept film aims to have the opposite effect. The first job of high concept is to keep the film's marketable qualities on the surface (Wyatt, 1994, p. 63). Thus, a pause in narrative is "excessive" because the style of high-concept imagery is never an alternative road to substantial meaning. Thus, having Tom Hanks play the foot-operated piano at FAO Schwarz in *Big*, or John Cryer's lip-synch and dance to "Try A Little Tenderness" in *Pretty in Pink*, does not make the films richer, and after the pause in narrative, their stories resume as if nothing had ever happened (Wyatt, 1994, p. 44). Moments of "excessive" style can also be used to showcase a much beloved quality of an actor. Wyatt (1994) comments on the role of Eddie Murphy in the story of *Beverly Hills Cop*:

> Murphy's performance in *Beverly Hills Cop* breaks the development of the story at several occasions due to Murphy's extraordinary "transformations". In order to gain access to information, Murphy playing Detective Axel Foley, assumes strikingly different identities: from an irate *Rolling Stone* reporter to a dedicated floral delivery-man to an effeminate gay lover. Each of these transformations is accomplished solely through Murphy's acting: through his speech patterns, gestures, and manner of presentation, rather than through physical disguises. The abruptness with which Murphy assumes each new character, along with the apparently arbitrary choice of persona, serves to break the world of the film. (p. 33)

This same method of "storytelling" was used in many Jim Carrey films in the 1990s, particularly *Ace Ventura: Pet Detective*, *The Mask* and *The Cable Guy*. In each of these films, the story is thin because the true purpose is to have Carrey-the-actor showcase his abilities in physical comedy and impersonations.

The excessiveness of high-concept imagery actually increases the need for the story of a high-concept film to be straightforward and easy to follow. If the imagery does not add any complexity to a film, the time left over for narrative development might not be enough to produce the experience of following the progression of a good story. As Mamet (2007) notes, great films of various genres *slowly* build anticipation and excitement because dramatic experience is "essentially the enjoyment of the postponement of enjoyment" (p. 130). But for this deferred form of enjoyment, the screenwriter needs a lot of pages and the director needs every scene. When films are, instead, built around scenes or images that do little to deepen meaning, what is generally left over for story are simply pretexts for action, or a "loose assemblage" of visual effects or scenes.

8.3 Capitalizing (low) artistic expectations

As Wyatt observes, the elements of high-concept cinema come together such that they weaken our identification with character and narrative. Instead of building a complicated relationship between subject and object,

> the viewer [of a high-concept film] becomes sewn into the "surface" of the film, contemplating the style of the narrative and the production. The excess created through such channels as the production design, stars, music, and promotional apparati, all of which are so important to high concept, enhances the appreciation of the films' surface qualities. (Wyatt, 1994, p. 60)

But how does high-concept filmmaking reduce risk? On the surface, the answer seems apparent: high-concept films are less risky because their stories are simpler and more straightforward, and the superficial style – be it through the marketing of a star, the music or even the look of the film – is a quick and easy "argument" about why you, the typical moviegoer, should see a film. While this may be partly true, it is merely the first step. In order to understand the apparent box-office appeal of simplicity, we need to consider and historicize the social relationship between filmmaking and film consumption.

High-concept filmmaking helps Major Filmed Entertainment by deepening social familiarity with the Hollywood style of cinema. Not every Hollywood film is high concept, nor is every film of this type wildly popular. Rather, the general persistence of high-concept films shapes and reinforces social expectations about what cinema should and should not be. If the belief that films should be simple and straightforward is strongly held by managers, producers, directors, screenwriters, actors, artists and the consumers of their films, Major Filmed Entertainment can, with a greater ability, quantify its expectations about the repeatability and regularity of high-concept cinema. Thus, the social institution of high-concept cinema relies on the social-historical foundation of aesthetic experience (Adorno, 1997, p. 269). Low, pessimistic expectations about the aesthetic potential of cinema can reinforce the institution of a narrow aesthetic horizon. Prevailing cinematic habits and expectations can also disadvantage filmmakers and audiences that would otherwise wish that films discovered the artistic alternatives within cinema. With respect to the pursuit of alternative narrative styles, for example, Iranian filmmaker Abbas Kiarostami highlights Hollywood's problematic effects on the way we watch films: "we want to follow everything or we think the film has failed" (Baumbach, 2014).

The wide social acceptance of high-concept cinema is assisted by other characteristics of the Hollywood film business. For instance, the Hollywood star system is commonly used to develop a film project that can be sold in one or two sentences. The use of well-known stars, whose fame has come from repeatedly playing certain character types, gives a film a "certain pre-sold identity" (Wyatt, 1994, p. 24). By virtue of Tom Cruise or Meryl Streep being cast in a film, we already imagine what this film is about or, at the very least, what it is likely *not* about. From the perspective of Major Filmed Entertainment, our mental associations between movie stars and their typical movie roles can be sold back to us. Moreover, Major Filmed Entertainment can sabotage the art of filmmaking to guarantee that the advertisements of films follow through on their promises. If an advertisement suggests that I keep holding on to my idea of what a typical Julia Roberts film is, it is also promising that this particular Julia Roberts film, the one being advertised, will deliver the goods; it will be what I already expect it to be.

On this count, high-concept cinema is a variation of what Hollywood has been doing for many decades. In the past, the form and content of a typical Hollywood film also served to reinforce and solidify the social relations that Hollywood needed to extend itself as the most dominant cinematic tradition. For instance, in the 1930s, MGM attempted to develop an MGM style that the audience would identify as any film with high production values and a lot of movie stars. Through repetition of this "style", MGM created a feedback loop in which more and more "MGM-type" films were made because moviegoers had come to associate aesthetic quality with high production values and lots of movie stars (Christensen, 2012). Other studios also learned how a business-led institution of aesthetic standards was simultaneously an ideological and financial strategy. Once, in the words of Maltby (1983), the "fabled extravagances of film production" had become "central to the myth of Hollywood the Dream Factory", the ideological predominance of the Hollywood style of cinema had "the practical effect of restricting the number of companies which could afford to mount A-feature productions" (p. 48). Only the major studios could afford to produce A-feature productions, and if moviegoers developed a habituated taste for nothing but A-feature productions, films with smaller budgets, or even an alternative cinematic style, were technically not in competition for the same streams of revenues.

What sort of empirical evidence can we offer in support of our arguments about risk and high-concept filmmaking? Wyatt (1994) has his own statistical evidence, and his conclusion that "high concept lowers the risk and uncertainty within the movie marketplace" reinforces the argument of this section (p. 172). Yet Wyatt acknowledges that his method carries a statistical bias for high-concept films. Wyatt looks at the revenue impacts of a film's "elements", as if every film in the data set could be broken down as a production function of inputs. Such elements as "stars, bankable director, merchandising tie-ins, and genre", however, already favour high-concept cinema's method of income generation:

> The modular, packaged high concept films, with marketing hooks inherent in the projects, lend themselves to this analytical breakdown. Consequently, it is not surprising perhaps that the statistical model illustrates that high concept is actually more predictable than other forms of production. The model works most successfully with genre-bound, linear narrative and pre-packaged films — all categories which overlap with high concept. (Wyatt, 1994, p. 172)

Instead of retaining the assumptions that underlie Wyatt's quantitative analysis of high-concept "elements", we can offer an alternative method that treats high concept as a world within a larger cinematic universe. As was established in Figure 5.7, US theatrical attendance per capita has remained at roughly the same level for over 50 years. If we treat this average moviegoing habit as an outer limit of the social world of American cinema, we can then ask how much of the average movie consumption (~4–5 films per year) goes to high-concept films. We can also ask whether the general fixation on high-concept films has strengthened over the years. If US theatrical attendance per capita of high-concept films has increased as a share of attendance, we can conclude that these films have a greater degree of social longevity. Concomitantly, we can infer that capitalist confidence in high-concept filmmaking has increased – though, by exactly how much, our method cannot determine.

Changes in the share of high concept cinema offer a rough approximation of changes in risk perception. Yet US theatrical attendance per capita has been more or less stable for some time, so an increase in attendance for high-concept cinema means that this type of film is being substituted for other types of films. And if, over the long term, high-concept films are watched with greater frequency, that increase suggests that moviegoing habits are locked into a narrowing

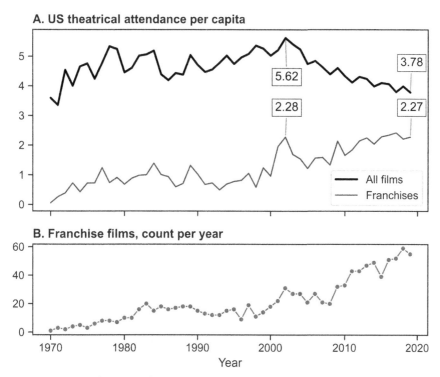

FIGURE 8.1   Franchise attendance per capita, United States

Source: Franchise data (via Python) taken from https://www.boxofficemojo.com/franchise/. Bordwell (2006), "Appendix: A Hollywood Timeline, 1960–2004", for total attendance 1970–2004; www. natoonline.org/data/admissions/ for attendance 2005–2019. IHS Global Insight for total United States population.

range of film types. Stronger dedication to high-concept filmmaking, even if only in relative terms, speaks to the durability of Hollywood's social-historical foundations, which could always change in light of new creation.

Figure 8.1 presents data on US franchise films, a term denoting a film that has the copyright to exploit images, characters, environments and stories of intellectual property (e.g., James Bond, the Ghostbusters, Indiana Jones, Jurassic Park, Marvel superheroes, Harry Potter). The intellectual property of a film franchise can originate from other media, such as literature, television shows and comic books. The production of sequels or "spin-offs" can also create or extend a film franchise. Not every high-concept film is a franchise, but all film franchises are high concept. A typical franchise film is reducible to its marketable element, which is often one or many of its characters. This marketable element is the franchise film's essence because the franchise is primarily designed to carry its theatrical success to or from other channels: television, novels, fast-food chains, toys and video games

(Drake, 2008, p. 77). Additionally, if a franchise was created in media other than film, the very first film release of the franchise is its own shorthand advertisement, as the essential idea is already familiar to its audience.

Figure 8.1 shows three series. In Panel A, the figure shows the US attendance per capita of all theatrical releases and the per-capita attendance of franchise films. Franchise films are tallied from the list of franchises compiled by boxofficemojo. Examples from the list include films from "Marvel Cinematic Universe", "Star Wars", "Disney Live Action Reimaginings" and "J.K. Rowling's Wizarding World". Some of the franchise sets overlap – for example, films in the "Avengers" category are also in the "Marvel Cinematic Universe". To prevent double counting, a Python script is used to tally each theatrical release once, which means a film can only appear again if it is formally given a re-release. Panel B counts the annual number of films in the franchise set from 1970 to 2019.

The figure demonstrates that the average American moviegoer is giving proportionally more attention to franchise films than non-franchise films. In particular, franchise cinema has made significant gains during the decline of *total* theatrical attendance per capita in the twenty-first century. In 2002, for example, the average American moviegoer was already giving 40 per cent of their theatrical attendance to franchise films. By 2019, this share of attendance has increased to 60 per cent. Increased consumer dedication to this small world corroborates the film criticism of Rosenbaum (1997b, 2000). As Rosenbaum often argues, our collective comfort in the mainstream of Hollywood cinema perpetuates our ignorance of the larger universe of cinema, which is much more expansive than we habitually imagine.

An audience usually knows what it wants to get out of franchise films, and Hollywood, for its part, is committed to delivering it. Only so much originality, or even abnormality, is tolerated in a franchise film because there is always a more pressing task: the film must touch upon many or all of the established themes and images of the franchise in question. Christopher Nolan, for example, injected his love of monochromatic visuals and film noir into *Batman Begins*, *The Dark Knight* and *The Dark Knight Rises*, which creates a stylistic continuity between these three franchise films and his non-franchise projects, such as *The Following* or *Memento*. However, the key elements of the Batman universe are nevertheless given primacy in Nolan's Batman trilogy. A Batman film without the Batmobile, the Batcave and the Bat-Signal is taboo. It is also never a cliché to reuse the villains of previous Batman films: the Joker, Bane and Two-Face.

To get a better sense of how American cinematic habits are narrowing, we need to answer the following question: what is the average American not watching? Figure 8.2 examines annual total theatrical attendance per capita for the 1,000 largest foreign-language films released in the United States from 1979 to 2019. The difference between the sizes of franchise films and foreign-language films is stark. US theatrical attendance per capita for franchise films is currently above 2.

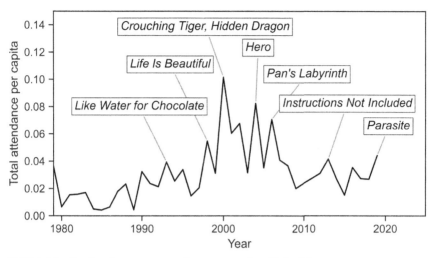

FIGURE 8.2 Foreign-language attendance per capita, United States

Source: Foreign-language data (via Python) taken from https://www.boxofficemojo.com/genre/sg4208980225/. IHS Global Insight for total US population.

Note: Data points are annual totals of all foreign-language films. Annotations are indications of when popular foreign-language films were released.

By comparison, foreign-language films are a small fraction of American attendance. If attendance-per-capita was cumulative, whereby someone could watch one foreign-language film in annual shifts, the average American would need over thirty years to watch a single foreign-language film in theatres.

Some readers might already know how unpopular foreign-language films are in America. However, when examined more closely, low American attendance for foreign-language films says something important on the degree of confidence of Major Filmed Entertainment. First, there is a small wave of increased American attendance for foreign-language films from 1998 to 2006. Interestingly, this period does not signal a threat to Major Filmed Entertainment. This wave was primarily the result of four hits that were distributed by Major Filmed Entertainment's subsidiaries. The films, distributors and the corporate parents of the distributors are *Life is Beautiful* (1998, Miramax, at the time owned by Disney); *Crouching Tiger, Hidden Dragon* (2000, Sony Pictures Classics, Sony); *Hero* (2004, Miramax) and *Pan's Labyrinth* (2006, Picturehouse, Time Warner). All four films are part of Hollywood's aggressive-but-common strategy of investing and over-inflating the artistic merits of only a few foreign-language films per year. *Life is Beautiful; Crouching Tiger, Hidden Dragon;* and *Pan's Labyrinth* won awards at the Golden Globes and the Oscars, and distributors like Miramax and Sony Pictures Classics have been known for stubbornly focusing on the foreign-language films they believe can be easily tailored for the tastes of North American audiences (McDonald, 2009). The two biggest films involved in the most recent spikes – the years of *Instructions Not Included* and *Parasite* – are technically "outside" the ownership of Major Filmed Entertainment. *Instructions Not Included*, a Spanish-language Mexican film, was distributed through a joint-venture of Grupo Televisa S.A.B. and Lionsgate. *Parasite*, the Korean-language film that won Best Picture at the 2019 Academy Awards, was theatrically distributed by Neon. After the Oscars wins for *Parasite*, the *Los Angeles Times* described Neon as a "scrappy" David in a David-and-Goliath battle (Faughnder, 2020). Yet this characterization might be misleading if the distributor, although excluded from Major Filmed Entertainment, is supported by the The Friedkin Group, which owns, among other things, the Italian football club A.S. Roma.

Second, the trend of the foreign-language series in Figure 8.2, however short, suggests that Major Filmed Entertainment can be quite confident about what its potential consumers are unlikely to watch. Decades-long *disinterest* in foreign-language films, be they German, French or Hindi, is stable overall; there is little threat for foreign-language films to suddenly steal consumer attention away from Hollywood's franchise films. Thus, the existence of foreign-language films is not a barrier to the continued, and possibly intensified, strategy of making more and more franchise films. Weak threats to the popularity of franchise films are also ripe for reification. Here, Adorno's (1997) argument about the repetitive cycle of a type of music listening can be applied to franchise cinema:

> Aesthetic norms that are said to correspond to the perceiving subject's invariant forms of reaction are empirically invalid; thus the academic psychology is false that, in opposing new music, propounds that the ear is unable to perceive highly complex tonal phenomena that deviate too far from the natural overtone relations: There is no disputing that there are individuals who have this capacity and there is no reason why everyone should not be able to have it; the limitations are not transcendental but social, those of second nature. If an empirically oriented aesthetics uses quantitative averages as norms, it unconsciously sides with social conformity. What such an aesthetics classifies as pleasing or painful is never a sensual given of nature but something performed by society as a whole, by what it sanctions and censors, and this has always been challenged by artistic production. (p. 267)

8.4 Before high concept

Figures 8.1 and 8.2 corroborate the argument that high concept helps increase Major Filmed Entertainment's degree of confidence because it has become a socially acceptable style. However, it is still possible to continue pondering why high-concept cinema, of all possible cinematic styles, is related to the risk-reduction strategies of Major Filmed Entertainment. Why is this style of cinema an effective component in risk reduction?

It would be an exaggeration to state that high concept was, logically, the only aesthetic style capable of helping Major Filmed Entertainment reduce risk from 1980 onwards. Yet we can pinpoint the importance of high-concept aesthetics another way. The institution of high-concept filmmaking is, as a particular risk-reduction strategy, the product of a two-stage process that began in the late 1960s. By briefly looking at Hollywood cinema during the American New Wave years, from roughly 1968 to 1977, we can see that the Hollywood film business purposefully instituted high-concept filmmaking in order to negate ambiguity and indeterminacy as filmmaking techniques. In comparison to the style of cinema it superseded, high-concept filmmaking was a much more suitable aesthetic style for saturation booking and contemporary marketing efforts. Overall, Major Filmed Entertainment used high-concept filmmaking to go back to what Hollywood does best: sustain a social world of cinema through repetition and sameness. In comparison to American New Wave, high-concept films affirm, with much greater intensity, what Adorno and Horkheimer would describe as the schema of mass culture.

8.4.1 The aesthetics dimension and the auteurism of American New Wave

American New Wave is associated with the period of institutional rebirth, when out of the ashes of the crumbled studio system came the phoenix of New Hollywood. A partial list of New Hollywood filmmakers includes Hal Ashby, Robert Altman, Peter Bogdonovich, John Cassavetes, Francis Ford Coppola, Sidney Lumet, Alan Pakula, Arthur Penn and Bob Rafelson.[1] These filmmakers, and others like them, share two influences. American New Wave was predominantly European in form and American in content. With respect to form, the aesthetic of New Hollywood was imported from European cinema of the 1950s and 1960s – for example, lengthy shots, location shooting, handheld cameras, the use of natural light and a grainy colour palette achieved through the exposure of film negatives. Its stories were also character driven and the plot, often non-linear, was typically used to explore a political issue conceptually. European art cinema has had a small but stable place in American consumerism since the 1920s (Guzman, 2005). In the business environment of New Hollywood, the influence of European cinema was pronounced and much more direct.

New-Hollywood filmmakers consciously mixed many of the artistic techniques of European New Wave with "raw" American content – not the idealized imaginations of "America the beautiful" but contemporary issues about American society in the mid-twentieth century. An American New Wave film does not always make explicit references to the Vietnam War, President Nixon, civil rights or the women's liberation movement and the sexual revolution, but the Hollywood film business hired many young and previously inexperienced directors because they had the eyes and ears for an America that was in the midst of social and political upheaval. In fact, to the extent that youth in America were developing a "new sensibility" in the 1960s and 1970s (Marcuse, 1969), some American filmmakers had chances to practice a freer form of *auteur* filmmaking in the Hollywood system. As D. Cook (1996) notes, "the studios' transitional managers briefly turned the reigns of creative power to a rising generation of independents and first-time directors" because their "values seemed to resonate with the newly emerging 'youth culture' market" (p. 156).

However monumental the rise of American New Wave was, its aesthetic and commercial successes were eventually overshadowed by the rapidity of its death. Around 1980, it had become clear that Major Filmed Entertainment's embrace of New Wave cinema would only ever be an exception to Hollywood's usual aesthetic style. What had changed? Why was this aesthetic movement, which appeared to be temporarily loved by investors and critics alike, suddenly buried as a brief experiment in the long history of Hollywood cinema?

The quantitative research of Part II provides some answers. As Figure 5.5 shows, the differential profits of Major Filmed Entertainment were highest in the 1970s (at least for the roughly 60 years for which data are available). Yet the relatively high volatilities of earnings (Figure 7.1) and of attendance for the same period (Figure 7.6) are indicators that risk was a serious issue for Major Filmed Entertainment. That these volatilities of profits and attendance were sharply reduced in the 1980s is no coincidence. In the twilight of American New Wave, the delicate balance between *auteur* filmmaking and studio management had, after almost a decade of functioning well, suddenly tipped over and smashed to pieces, having been replaced by the far less risky high-concept style.

A brief summary of Marcuse's theory of the aesthetic dimension will enable us to frame this process. His theory orients us to the form-content question in aesthetics, which in turn allows us to highlight the aspect of American New Wave that was such a problem from the late 1970s onwards. American New Wave was risky for business not simply because its artists addressed or were inspired by political issues of the 1960s, from America's controversial war in Vietnam to the social movements that were organizing themselves in cities like Washington, New York and Chicago. Rather, it was risky because young filmmakers were using the spirit of the times to reimagine the industrial practices of filmmaking and to take the form-content relationship of aesthetics *very seriously* – and that shift in industry threatened to undermine the control of business. In fact, when Major Filmed Entertainment was ready to steer the film industry towards high-concept filmmaking, the aesthetic spirit of New Wave cinema had become a nuisance that needed to return to the outskirts of American filmmaking.

As Marcuse argues, the form–content problem in art is the responsibility of the artist. It is the unity of the form and content that gives an artwork the "power to break the monopoly of established reality (i.e., of those who established it) to define what is real". There is certainly a multitude of artistic styles to choose from, but great artworks of various styles demonstrate the same point: "aesthetic form, autonomy and truth are related" (Marcuse, 1978, p. 9). For Marcuse, this common denominator lies beneath different styles of artistic representation because, in each case, the artist is deciding how to represent the essence of reality "through estrangement". Thus, tackling the form-content problem is a crucial step in the production of "critical mimesis", which works with the content of established reality but has the power to make the invisible visible and the familiar unfamiliar. For example, "mimesis in literature occurs in the medium of language; it is tightened or loosened, forced to yield insights otherwise obscured. Prose is subjected to its own rhythm. What is normally not spoken is said; what is normally spoken too much remains unsaid if it conceals that which is essential" (Marcuse, 1978, p. 45). Therefore, form is what gives historical content "aesthetic meaning and function" and once formed, the content of an artwork is "re-presented" as something in need of conscious reexamination.

This artistic ideal is fundamentally social: "in its very elements (word, color, tone) art depends on the transmitted cultural material; art shares it with the existing society" (Marcuse, 1978, p. 41). American New Wave tried to let the light of this social-artistic ideal shine with great intensity. It was trying to establish a form of filmmaking that, as art, was able to represent the estrangement of the ideal from the real. A New-Hollywood film like *The Friends of Eddie Coyle*, for example, extols happiness and fulfillment as human needs, but this message only comes across in the negative, as a repressed ideal: the amelioration of life is not possible in the present, in social conditions in which friends are not really friends at all (Kirshner, 2012).

Looking at the form–content relationship reveals the qualitative change brought on by American New Wave. The content of a New Hollywood film, while often pushing the envelope regarding how much sex and violence could be shown in a mainstream film, is only half the story. In fact, the freedom for an American filmmaker to show more adult-oriented content on the silver screen was gained in the 1950s, when both the US Supreme Court granted First Amendment rights to films distributed in the United States and the Hays Production Code effectively died.[2] The other half of the story was the form of American New Wave. It was aesthetically powerful because it was trying to reveal the ambiguity and indeterminacy of the content: an American society that was in turmoil since its established values were losing legitimacy.

At least for the filmmakers themselves, New Hollywood was an opportunity to make cinema political without shamelessly appropriating the news of the day or "hot-topic" subjects like gender, race, class and the rights of the individual.

Rather, the point was to develop a style of cinema that could focus on, rather than gloss over, the moral ambiguity, complexity and difficulty of being a citizen in an unequal society that only paid lip service to the universal ideals of life, liberty and the pursuit of happiness.[3] New Hollywood cinema was fundamentally about the political: it found ways to look at the different processes, decisions and rationalizations that go into the institution of a social order. This artistic study of the political is what leads Kirshner to state that New Hollywood was truly an "adult" cinema. It was in this brief period that we found, in mainstream American filmmaking, "characters with morally complex choices, not necessarily between right and wrong, but made by imperfect people trying to find the best alternative from the menu of compromised choices that circumstances have made available to them" (Kirshner, 2012, p. 21).

As a type of "adult" film, New Hollywood cinema showed, for example, more explicit sexuality than had hitherto been shown in mainstream American cinema. Yet, argues Kirshner, greater amounts of "frank sexuality (admittedly at times vulnerable to the charge of pandering and titillation) were embraced as an important vehicle for exploring characters' challenges and complexity, and acknowledging that sex and gender are inescapable elements of adult relationships" (Kirshner, 2012, p. 21). Moreover, many American *auteurs* of the 1960s and 1970s were consciously trying to counterbalance the affirmative character of cinema. Since the cinematic image has a technological capacity to, with good-looking people, the right lighting and excellent picture quality, make almost anything look beautiful, New Wave filmmakers avoided any style that would give the facts of a bad reality a smooth gloss and sparkle.

Consequently, American filmmakers such as Scorcese, De Palma and Altman used cinematic form to deepen the moral and ideological incongruities of a complex narrative (Wyatt, 1994, p. 34). As Berliner (2011) notes about *Nashville*, Altman's film is not complex just because it has a lot of main characters – 24, to be exact. The style of *Nashville* gives the interwoven narratives a political quality. By making a multitude of characters move in and out of the same scene, or by using parallel editing techniques to have different lifestyles and attitudes collide into one another, Altman reveals that many of the characters are inconsistent in their motivations and actions. In fact, Altman's lengthy presentation of these inconsistencies does not let the moviegoer use cinema to escape from real social antagonisms that lie outside of the movie theatre (or, in the twenty-first century, the living room; Berliner, 2011).

Speaking about the form–content relationship in protest films such as *Medium Cool*, Peter Lloyd states: "No engagement with the subject-matter can be possible if the 'style' is directed towards . . . superficial ends, without any sense of structure or the organic relation of every frame to the total conception of the movie itself" (quoted in Wyatt, 1994, p. 34). As was the case for Haskell Wexler, the director of *Medium Cool*, the artistic sincerity of American New Wave was often the result of "*auteur* filmmaking", which is an idea that was first instituted by French New Wave. Originally articulated by Francois Truffaut in 1954, the fundamental idea of *auteur* filmmaking was that the director was the principal author of a film (Kirshner, 2012, p. 28). "Principal author", not sole author – there are many branches of filmmaking (costume, lighting, design, makeup, sound, film scoring), and copyright law and trade union regulations require the contributions of these branches are credited on professional film productions (MacCabe, 2003, p. 36). The philosophy of *auteur* cinema gives the film director principal authorship because directors have the exceptional task of having to express, on film, their attitudes about the visual amalgamation of all the content being used. Thus, as Andrew Sarris (2003) describes, the job of the director is to take in everything that goes into a cinematic image – "cutting, camera movement, pacing, the direction of players and their placement in the décor, the angle and distance of the camera, and even the content of the shot" (p. 27).

Auteur cinema does not praise film direction as such but directors who take responsibility for their creative role in a medium that is primarily visual.[4] This aesthetic principle was antithetical to the corporate structure of film production in the first half of the twentieth century, when directors traditionally were attached to film projects late in the creative process. It was often the case that in the studio system the director joined a film project that had already been "imagined" by others – for example, the project had already been written by a screenwriter who had been hired to shape the preliminary visions of a producer or a studio executive (Balio, 1993; Bordwell et al., 1985). Consequently, the idea of creative control was being turned on its head when, for instance, Robert Newman and David Benton, the screenwriters of *Bonnie and Clyde*, publicly extolled the role of the director: "if there is one thing we learned beyond any question in the movie business it is this: once there is a director, he [*sic*] is the boss" (Christensen, 2012, p. 257).

8.4.2   *The party is over*

Capitalist interests were certainly never wholly absent from the production of American New Wave films – in fact, the logic of capitalist investment always, at some level, needed to instrumentalize what was being filmed for profit, the ultimate end of any capitalist endeavour. Yet by the end of the 1970s, the industrial practices of American New Wave had become a severe irritant to Major Filmed Entertainment. The instrumentalization of American New Wave filmmakers had grown to be difficult, especially in comparison to less "resistant" filmmaking techniques.

In the golden years of American New Wave – from about 1968 to 1977 – the balance between business and industry could be considered mutually beneficial. Many filmmakers were able to, for example, acquire autonomous creative control – from project approval to final cut – but only as long as they kept within the budgets that were decided on by the respective studios. Woody Allen, an *auteur* in his own right but not necessarily associated with New Hollywood cinema, was able to negotiate this freedom to do whatever he wanted with United Artists as long as he stayed on budget (Bach, 1985, p. 51). Similarly, the six-picture deal between Columbia and BBS productions, the production house that made *Easy Rider*, stipulated that Columbia would only keep its hands off development and production if all budgets stayed under $1 million (D. A. Cook, 2000, p. 109).

Outside of the strong examples of business–industry harmony, certain films revealed that New Hollywood was not necessarily open to any form of American New Wave. For instance, the $600,000 deal between Francis Ford Coppola's film development project, American Zoetrope, and Warner Bros. was abruptly canceled after the latter was thoroughly displeased with the rough cut of the first Zoetrope project, George Lucas's *THX-1138* (D. A. Cook, 2000, p. 135). The treatment of Elaine May portended the willingness of Major Filmed Entertainment to protect, to the very end, the right of business to control industry. When the editing of *A New Leaf* began to go over budget, Paramount took away her rights to produce a near-final cut. The studio then shortened the film and drastically changed the ending. After May sued the studio in 1971, a judge ruled in favor of Paramount's version. May and Paramount joined again for *Mikey and Nicky*, which was written and directed by May. When the relationship broke down during the editing process, in part because May was not producing a comedy but a film that emphasized the melodramatic acting of John Cassavetes and Peter Falk, the studio sued May. A judge ordered May to hand the film canisters over to the studio. According to Barry Diller, who replaced Frank Yablans as Paramount's studio head when *Mikey and Nicky* was still in production, May initially held two film canisters hostage only to deliver them after additional legal threats were made (Smukler, 2019, pp. 78–93).

American New Wave's twilight occurred when blockbuster cinema proved to be the next major strategy of Hollywood. *Auteur*-inspired films such as *Barry Lyndon*; *New York, New York*; *Sorcerer* and *Apocalypse Now* had budgets the size of some contemporaneous blockbusters, but the style and substance of these particular films were far more esoteric. These films fell well below their financial expectations, and the blame for budget overruns fell on the philosophy of *auteurism*. Kubrick, for instance, was once praised by Warner Bros. management for keeping the production of his films on budget and schedule, but the huge cost of *Barry Lyndon* was the effect of shooting the film on location in Ireland and Kubrick's obsession with achieving an extremely detailed visual representation of English aristocratic life in the eighteenth century. Similarly for Terrence Malick, the production of *Days of Heaven* ran well over schedule because many of its beautiful long shots could only be achieved in the light of each day's "magic hour", the brief period when, during a sunrise or sunset, the top of the sun is just above the horizon (D. A. Cook, 2000).

Perhaps the greatest impetus for instituting stricter controls over the pace and direction of Hollywood filmmaking was the production and distribution of *Heaven's Gate*, one of Hollywood's infamous financial disasters. Inspired by the Johnson County War of 1892, Michael Cimino's film was an ambitious portrayal of the conflict between the big and small players of the American frontier. With much of the film shot on location in Montana, Cimino was obsessive about every detail that went into the story of cattle barons, the Wyoming Stock Growers Association, conspiring to kill settlers who, because of poverty, rustled cattle. Cimino's repeated demands to reconstruct sets, shoot multiple takes for virtually every shot and delay the daily shooting schedule in wait for potentially more beautiful shots ballooned the production budget to $30 million, up from the planned $11 million. At the end of shooting, there were over 1 million feet of footage, which is over 200 hours of running time.

Having lost Woody Allen to the newly formed Orion Pictures, United Artists hired Cimino on the hopes that *Heaven's Gate* would match the success of *The Deer Hunter*, a winner of five Academy Awards and Cimino's first film. By the time *Heaven's Gate* was actually released in 1980 – Cimino cut and recut the film himself in post-production – United Artists had the task of advertising and distributing a film that was 3 hours 39 minutes long and which ultimately cost $44 million to produce and distribute. The domestic sales for its theatrical release were roughly $3.5 million. On top of being unsuccessful financially, *Heaven's Gate* won little to no critical acclaim during its initial theatrical run. All it ever became in the initial years of its release was the ultimate reason for Transamerica to sell United Artists to MGM in 1981. In addition, Cimino himself became the public face of massive egotism and uncontrollable creativity in a Hollywood system that could no longer tame its own directors – Francis Ford Coppola being one of the other well-publicized examples (Corrigan, 2003, pp. 102–108).

The sector-wide impact of *Heaven's Gate* is addressed in Steven Bach's memoir. As one of the United Artists vice-presidents involved with the financing and theatrical distribution of *Heaven's Gate*, Bach (1985) attempts to draw conclusions that are relevant to the business of Hollywood as a whole:

> Movies matter. Because they do, and because they are created and manufactured in both artistic and industrial contexts, their costs matter, too. Signs that costs are once again escalating wildly and could one day make movies simply a prohibitively expensive "luxury" should be deeply sobering to those who care about them and most sobering of all to those who make them, the auteurs and artists whose assiduous pursuit of final cut or this or that other contractual advantage is a meaningless, even destructive luxury unless accompanied by the salutary force of discipline which no union, management, or conglomerate can impose. Like art, it comes from within.
> (p. 416)

Having worked with Cimino directly, Bach's memoir remains partly sympathetic to the aesthetic goals of *Heaven's Gate*. He is also clear that before production began, Bach and the rest of United Artists management wanted Cimino to ambitiously make an artistic masterpiece like his other film, *The Deer Hunter*. Yet Bach's conclusion on the *Heaven's Gate* fiasco also speaks to the changing attitude of management and investors, who were suddenly in no mood to deal with the "next Cimino", whomever that may be.

High concept contributed to the death of American New Wave because it, through its general application, built the platform for business concerns to identify and articulate why films like *Heaven's Gate* were such bad investments. Once high concept because the strategy *du jour*, any film without a "simple" essence became, by definition, "low concept". Take, for instance, the words of Dawn Steel, former president of Columbia Pictures,

> [the movie business in 1978] was all about capturing the spirit of the times with high-concept pictures geared to the youth audience – movies whose themes could be explained in a sentence or two. These were movies like *Saturday Night Fever* that were, as they were called at the time, critic-proof, so that they could bypass all the old ways of thinking. Following this premise, those films which are high concept could be matched by marketing campaigns that accurately represent their content, while marketing for low concept films would be more problematic, since the marketing, which inevitably operates through a reduction of the film's narrative, misrepresents the film as a whole. (quoted in Wyatt, 1994, p. 9)

As Steel and other executives began to yearn for films that could be marketed in a straightforward manner, the ambiguity and complexity of many New Hollywood films began to be judged according to their perceived inability to fit the mould of high-concept cinema. Steel is right to imply that some films, by virtue of their style and content, cannot be reduced to one or two sentences; but this was now, in 1978, a problem in serious need of a "solution".

The rise and fall of Robert Altman's career in Hollywood reflects the changing attitude toward American New Wave. In the first half of the 1970s his films were acclaimed for being imaginative, self-reflexive approaches to film genre and other staples of Hollywood storytelling. *McCabe and Mrs. Miller* is an anti-Western western. Played by Warren Beatty, John McCabe is stubborn, but his stubbornness in the face of an encroaching mining company, a much larger foe, is not presented as a courageous virtue. Rather, McCabe is a bumbling character, unsure as to why, in the first generation of American trusts and cartels, he holds so strongly to the myth of the small entrepreneur (M. J. Shapiro, 2008, p. 58). Altman himself said that that the point of *McCabe and Mrs. Miller* was to turn "a number of Western conventions on their sides", such as "male dominance and the heroic standoff; gunplay is a solution only after reputation, wit, and nonviolent coercion fail; and law and order do not always prevail" (quoted in M. J. Shapiro, 2008, p. 5).

Altman's *The Long Goodbye*, a film adaptation of a Philip Marlowe detective story, is a neo-noir version fit for the American social consciousness of the 1970s. As Kirshner (2012) argues, Altman fought for and kept the revisionist ending of his film version, where, unlike in Raymond Chandler's novel, Marlowe (played by Elliott Gould) kills his friend, Lennox. Altman's intention was to indict the "times he was living in. In the 1970s, not only was the world corrupt, but also there was no sanctuary to be found through the shared understanding of [a moral] code" (p. 173).

The dissonance between the aesthetic and commercial value of Altman's *Nashville* symbolizes the changing perceptions of "low-concept" films best. For its cultural and political value to the community at large, *Nashville* is excellent because it is so ambitious. With its ensemble cast of 24 characters, the film follows multiple storylines yet impressively reserves over one hour for musical performances. As Molly Haskell (2013) argues, *Nashville* has, with respect to cinematic ambition,

> no successors except Altman's own films – it was simply too complicated, too ambitious, too original in its improvisatory style, its huge cast, in other words, too inimitable. Think of it: twenty-four main characters – singers, musicians, wannabes, hangers-on – orbiting around the Grand Ole Opry and its satellite clubs, wandering into one another's lives and limelight; twenty-four actors, free to work up their own material but staying in character through long crowd scenes, never knowing whether the camera was on them or not, never knowing whether what they sang or said would end up in the final cut. (Haskell, 2013)

However, under the gaze of a film business that was, in 1975, beginning to prefer simpler, more straightforward films, *Nashville* malfunctioned financially. It became the typical "low-concept" film. Marketing-wise, the film had too many characters and no single narrative to advertise. The original poster featured photos of the entire main cast of 24 characters. The advertising copy ignored the narrative and the complex social and political themes and instead suggested that the consumer would feel an array of emotions because the film was "wild, wonderful, sinful, laughing [*sic*], explosive" (Wyatt, 1994, p. 117). In contrast, this type of marketing problem did not affect *Jaws*, which was released in the same year as *Nashville*. The style, imagery and story of *Jaws* could be reduced "to a single marketing image without severe distortion, or oversimplification" (Wyatt, 1994, p. 117). The iconic poster of *Jaws*, one of the first high-concept films in Hollywood, is not just clever marketing. The single image of an enormous shark approaching a woman swimming in the ocean is an adequate representation of what *Jaws* is all about (Wyatt, 1994, p. 117).

8.5   The hegemony of high concept

For the period when Major Filmed Entertainment was willing to give anti-Establishment youth of America what they wanted, business interests could tolerate the artistic principles of *auteur* filmmaking. For instance, Jack Warner and the rest of the Warner Bros. management originally hated almost everything about *Bonnie and Clyde*, but the corporate mood in Hollywood turned 180 degrees when the film became the first of many commercial successes for American New Wave (Christensen, 2012). And like the American New Wave films that followed on its heels, the writers and directors of *Bonnie and Clyde* were useful to business enterprise because they had access to social pipelines that were virtually invisible to out-of-touch studio heads: European New Wave cinema, the American New Left, the Hippie movement, civil rights, women's liberation and a generational desire among young Americans to opt out of the social structures they were supposed to inherit from their parents and grandparents.

Because American New Wave's main source of inspiration was the cultural and political transformations of the late 1960s and early 1970s, it is certainly possible that this cinematic movement would have faded anyways, as the norms and values of America became more conservative by the beginning of the 1980s. And as Berliner (2011) notes, it is common for academic literature to focus on the content of American New Wave, which is then connected to the "ideological conflicts and social upheavals of [its] era" (p. 16). While certainly important, this focus on the ideological content of American New Wave is still too narrow. By neglecting the *form* of American New Wave filmmaking, especially the form–content relationship, a one-sided view misses the part of the story that explains how Hollywood's shift from counterculture to high concept was also an effect of strategic sabotage. Beneath the visible shift from a critical American New Wave to an affirmative high-concept cinema was a structural, more subterranean shift in the ways in which Major Filmed Entertainment sabotaged filmmaking. This shift took place in the institutional "asthenosphere" of film production, which is beneath the "lithosphere" of Hollywood aesthetics.

By looking at some of the institutional conditions surrounding the rise of high concept, we can make some connections between Hollywood's style of cinema and the pecuniary interests of Major Filmed Entertainment. In fact, the "what-might-have-been?" question – namely, "what if the political and aesthetic principles of New Wave filmmaking had remained mainstream for many more decades?" – should flare in our minds because social problems did not suddenly disappear. The social and political issues of modern civilization are also reified just a bit more when the critical potential of cinema, and other mediums of mass culture, is being deflated by the pressures of business.[5]

If Major Filmed Entertainment had no institutional means to sabotage the art of filmmaking, the synchronization of creative output in film production with

Hollywood's distribution and exhibition strategies would be beyond the control of capitalists. But with the institutional means to sabotage the art of filmmaking, as we will elaborate further, Major Filmed Entertainment has been able to incorporate high-concept cinema in its greater project of reducing risk through blockbuster cinema and saturation booking. The power of the Hollywood film business over the social creativity of filmmaking mitigates the threat that, over time, the social relations of high-concept cinema will be undermined by a cultural-political project of autonomy.

The *telos* of a typical high-concept film is to produce the elements mentioned earlier – character types, simple narrative and superficial imagery – and institutional power is the efficient cause of making high concept become a cinematic movement. To appropriate Marcuse's (2005a) insights into the dialectical quality of persistence in historical time, the identity of high-concept cinema is "only the continuous negation" of any cinematic style that opposes its essence (p. 446). In other words, American New Wave is in the oppositional camp; it is "other than" high concept.

Two institutional characteristics of Hollywood have, on the one hand, enabled high concept to persist for so many years after the fall of American New Wave, and, on the other, foreclosed the possibility that another radical *auteur*ism will sprout up in an era in which Hollywood has lost its tolerance for an autonomous film industry. The first characteristic is the intensification of the continuity style, which, for the Hollywood film business, is closely entangled with the second characteristic, the rights of ownership in American copyright law.

8.5.1   Intensified continuity

What Bordwell (2006) calls "intensified continuity" is the contemporary version of what classical Hollywood cinema often used to make the temporal and spatial construction of each film coherent. Classical continuity techniques involved "opening a scene with master shots, handling it through matched shot/reverse-shot coverage, going in [with close-ups] to underscore a point" (Bordwell, 2006, p. 161). Intensified continuity adopts these techniques and the "classical precepts of Hollywood spatial construction: break the dramatic interaction into segments according to the dramatic curve, keep eyelines and posture coherent so that we always understand who is looking at whom" (Bordwell, 2006, p. 161). But as its name suggests, the technique of intensified continuity also heightens the classical Hollywood style by using "rapid editing, bipolar extremes of lens lengths, reliance on close shots, and wide-ranging camera movements" (Bordwell, 2006, p. 121).

To empirically investigate the intensity of continuity, we can use measurements of average shot length (ASL). ASL data have been compiled with Cinemetrics software, which enables a user to time shots of what is being watched. As simply a measure of time, ASL is never a direct measure of the continuity style; there can always be an experimental film that uses its low ASL to disorient the audience. However, a low ASL suggests the presence of intensified continuity in a mainstream Hollywood film. We can infer intensified continuity, in this instance, because a low-ASL Hollywood film cannot abandon the requirements for character and plot to remain accessible to a mainstream audience. For example, when "every shot is short," writes Bordwell (2006), "when establishing shots are brief or postponed or nonexistent, the eyelines and angles in a dialogue need to be even more unambiguous, and the axis of action is likely to be respected quite strictly" (p. 124).

Figure 8.3 uses the ASL data provided by Barry Salt, whose data set of 10,137 films has its own section on the Cinemetrics website; the data set is separated from ASL timings submitted by registered users. Salt's data are not exhaustive, but there is presently no standard methodology to support the amalgamation of multiple

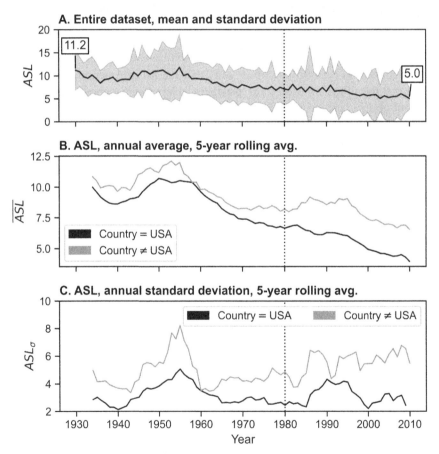

FIGURE 8.3 Average shot length (ASL), 1930–2010

Source: Barry Salt's Cinemetrics data: http://www.cinemetrics.lv/satltdb.php.

user-created data sets into one large Cinemetrics database. Salt also offers the largest data set made by one person, and he has also published his methods of ana-lysing ASL data (Salt, 1974). For the sake of visualization, I have filtered the data to films within six standard deviations of the mean ASL (the outlier that skews the data the most is Hitchcock's *Rope*). Remaining are 9,758 films.

Figure 8.3 demonstrates how, in the history of cinema from 1930 to 2010 and with almost ten thousand measurements, the era of high concept (1980–present) has pushed ASL to its lowest point: an annual average of 5.03 seconds. Figure 8.3 also visualizes the difference in editing timings between American and non-American films. After 1980, American films continued its trend to make quicker cuts. By 2010, an average American film has an ASL of 3.93 seconds, which is 2.81 seconds faster than an average American film in 1980. Non-American films, by contrast, were actually slower paced in the late 1990s than in the 1980s. Like their American competitors, non-American films were at their lowest ASL by 2010; however, the decline from 1980 was not as severe. The average non-American film in 1980 was 7.97 seconds. In 2010 it was 6.53, which gives a difference of 1.44 seconds.

For the moviegoer, the value of intensified continuity is aesthetic. From the perspective of the Hollywood film business, the aesthetic consequences of inten-sified continuity are entangled with financial fears of inflated budgets and uninter-ested audiences. Thus, as "double-digit ASLs, still found during the 1970s, virtually vanished from mass-entertainment cinema" (Bordwell, 2006, p. 122), Hollywood film production, Bordwell argues, relied on a set pattern of shooting and editing techniques, all of which are designed to achieve a tighter degree of coherence and continuity. As an extreme form of cutting between multiple quick shots, intensified continuity exploits, for the vested interests of Hollywood, what Bazin (2005) thought was deficient about montage techniques:

> Through the contents of the image and the resources of montage, the cinema has at its disposal a whole arsenal of means whereby to impose its interpretation of an event on the spectator. (p. 26)

> In analyzing reality, montage presupposes of its very nature the unity of meaning of the dramatic event. . . . In short, montage by its very nature rules out ambiguity of expression. (p. 36)

When films are not comprised of constant cutting between quick shots, cinema is capable of producing ambiguity and non-identity in the subject–object relationship of moviegoer and film. For Bazin (2005), the works of Orson Welles and Italian neo-realism are examples of how the absence of montage can "give back to the cinema a sense of the ambiguity of the reality" (p. 37). Deep focus and single shots of greater duration also imply "a more active mental attitude on the part of the spectator" (Bazin, 2005, p. 35). Interestingly, Bazin's perspective is similar to Adorno's. The "static character" of Antonioni's *La Notte* is, according to Adorno, a good example of how lengthy takes can resuscitate a "subjective mode of experience" that is not simply a "technique of consumer exploitation". Much like the experience of the person who, "after a year in the city, spends a few weeks in the mountains abstaining from all work", the slowness of *La Notte* gives the subject an opportunity to explore unfamiliar and discontinuous images (Adorno, 2004e, p. 180).

Apart from its aesthetic functions, intensified continuity is a means for high concept to become the intended product of strategic sabotage. Achieved through quick shots and a lot of editing in post-production, intensified continuity marginalizes other filmmaking techniques, such as the ones liked by Bazin and Adorno: "fixed-camera long takes, sustained two-shots, frequent long shots and mid-range framings" (Bordwell, 2006, p. 138). Furthermore, as these alternative methods have shrunk before the established standard of intensified continuity, the predominance of the latter has transformed the actual structure of film production in Hollywood. It has given capitalists a form of insurance over principal photography, the stage of shooting when directors and other creative personnel can significantly shape the form and content of a film project.

As the principal photography of *Heaven's Gate* demonstrated, the day–to-day process of film production can become a source of financial disaster. Costs can balloon when directors are not satisfied with the takes they already have or when a shooting schedule is delayed or cancelled in hopes of achieving just the "right" look for a shot. Moreover, location shooting has been a common practice since the end of the classical studio system (Hozic, 2001), which means that upper management might not always be on location to closely supervise filmmakers. Regardless of whether fast cutting between a lot of close shots has an aesthetic function in specific instances, the repeated use of intensified continuity is good for business because coherence is mainly achieved in *post*-production, where producers and distributors have, as a result of contract agreements and the structure of the contemporary Hollywood system, the upper hand.[6] Their right over final cut gives them the ability to use post-production editing to alter, cut or altogether second-guess the footage that was shot in principal photography, even if it was shot far away on location. Therefore, the threat of aesthetic overproduction from *auteur*-ism is greatly reduced; when desired, Major Filmed Entertainment can take the "raw material" of film projects out of the hands of its creators and give it to people who may care much more about reducing financial risk.

Once again, the work of Bordwell can help us perceive strategic sabotage in the filmmaking techniques of intensified continuity. As a result of what can happen to a film in post-production, contemporary Hollywood now demands *complete coverage* from film production. Complete coverage means "shooting every scene from half a dozen angles to defer choices until the months of editing" (Bordwell, 2006, p. 118). It also means that the director is not automatically in control of the form–content relationship. There were certainly limitations to what a director could or could not do with cinematic form in previous decades, but intensified continuity is a much more formless process:

> If you were a director [during the studio era], your choices were constrained by tacit but strongly felt boundaries, matters of taste and judgement as much as anything else. You could move the camera, but you couldn't cut in the middle of a movement. You could shoot extreme close-ups, but rarely. Every piece of action demanded one right spot for the camera, which it was your task to find. You didn't (for reasons of economy as much as professional pride) set up four cameras to grab action haphazardly. From this perspective, the casual setups and abrupt cuts that emerged in the 1960s could only look amateurish. (Bordwell, 2006, p. 118)

In the opinion of Sven Nykvist (1981), the Swedish cinematographer who is noted for working on many Ingmar Bergman films, Hollywood's

> requirement for so many cover shots . . . comes from the fact that the producers really have the final cut and they want to have all the material they can get in order to speed up the pace of the film or make other changes that may be necessary. (Nykvist, 1981, p. 377)

And as Steven Soderbergh, Billy Bob Thornton, Jodie Foster and likely countless other filmmakers have learned while working in contemporary Hollywood, single long takes are antithetical to a business that demands that contemporary filmmakers will cover all the angles during principal photography (Bordwell, 2006). It is difficult to cut a carefully constructed lengthy shot into smaller pieces, and anything shot in one take leaves post-production with less material to work with.

If the reader is holding on to the idea that the shift of creative control from production to post-production is not much of a problem because directors often participate in the editing of a film, this idea can be put to rest. In fact, the symbiotic relationship between complete coverage and intensified continuity is only exacerbating the mechanization of cinema. Here is it useful to quote Bordwell (2006) at length:

> With demands for complete coverage and a belief that the movie could be made in the cutting room, directors were overshooting wildly. A 100-minute movie runs nine thousand feet, but to arrive at that the editor might hack through as much as six hundred thousand feet of material. Directors and producers began to subdivide editing labor. Rather than handle all the footage, the principal editor might supervise a team of

several cutters, often making each responsible for one reel of the final cut. (This was called, with typical Hollywood delicacy, "gang banging" the film.) The introduction of computerized editing systems allowed producers to demand even faster output. Now databases could track all the takes, the physical act of splicing was not needed until the very last moment. Producers began to expect to see a rough cut in as little as a week. Editors complained that they were overworked and didn't have enough time to fine-tune the film. Under these conditions, they evidently felt obliged to fall back on the default settings of the dominant style. "I'm concerned", remarked one director at the beginning of the trend, that "management will assume electronic equipment means editors should work faster. And faster means formula. Go to the master, two shot, closeup, close-up and get out". Likewise, assigning each editor a reel of a big project favoured a neutral, standardized way of handling footage so that the completed film looked uniform throughout. (p. 156)

This quotation enables us to add another level of interpretation to Figure 8.3. The intensification of ASL likely tightens the relationship between coverage and formulaic editing. The pressure for film production to contribute to the goal of intensified continuity is that much greater when the average shot in an American film is now less than four seconds.

8.5.2 The rights of ownership

In its attempt to reduce risk, the Hollywood film business discovered a method of transforming the social-aesthetic principle of continuity into a business tool of strategic sabotage. The institution of intensified continuity is complementary to the means and ends of high-concept cinema, which is in turn part of the saturation-booking and blockbuster strategy. With this backdrop in mind, the question naturally arises: can the indeterminacy and ambiguity of American New Wave resurface in another form of Hollywood cinema? What are the chances that Major Filmed Entertainment will allow aesthetic experimentation and alternative methods of cinematic expression in the foreseeable future?

The scope of these two questions is wider than our present discussion of high-concept cinema. Nevertheless, we can use them to add one more level to our analysis of high concept. Major Filmed Entertainment's pushing of the art of filmmaking towards high-concept cinema has been made possible by Hollywood owning the legal business right to sabotage the art of cinema. Indeed, Hollywood needed an institutional mechanism to have blockbuster cinema dominate for over 30 years.

A key institutional mechanism for Major Filmed Entertainment to control Hollywood cinema is American copyright law (Decherney, 2012; Kamina, 2002;

Salokannel, 2003). In American law, as in other Anglo-American legal systems, the rights associated with the ownership of film copyright are always established through contract negotiation and guild rules. Moreover, American filmmakers are not perceived to naturally possess "moral rights", which give original creators (filmmakers) an inalienable claim over the manner in which their films are exhibited to the public (Salokannel, 2003). By contrast, European copyright law recognizes that "those who provide the original creative effort in the generation of the work should, *prima facie*, be considered the authors of the work" (Kamina, 2002, p. 285). This type of assumption about the authorship of original creator(s) grants the following moral rights:

1   "the right of paternity, i.e. the right to be identified as the author of the work";
2   "the right of integrity, i.e. the right to object to derogatory treatments of the work";
3   "the right of divulgation or of dissemination, i.e. the right to decide when and how a work should be made public (including the right not to make it public)";
4   "the right to revoke a grant of right or to withdraw a work from commerce, on the condition that the author indemnifies the transferee for any loss (sometimes called the 'right of reconsideration')" (Kamina, 2002, p. 285)

Moral rights have sometimes been implicitly recognized in American law (Decherney, 2012). But without the backing of Supreme Court decisions or strong legislation from Congress, a filmmaker in the United States has generally been left to contractually negotiate the rights to control the aesthetic dimension of filmmaking from production to distribution and exhibition. In Europe, by contrast, there are examples of moral rights and the aesthetic principles behind them trumping the demands of a film's distributor. As Salokannel (2003) notes, an Italian appellate court "held that breaking [the television presentation of *Serafino*] up with commercials infringed the moral rights of its director [Pietro Germi]" (Salokannel, 2003, p. 165). Even more remarkably, the estates of John Huston and Ben Maddow were able to convince a French court to stop Turner Entertainment from broadcasting on French television a colourized version of *The Asphalt Jungle*, Huston's black-and-white American film (Decherney, 2012, p. 244).

These examples are certainly small drops in the massive pool of films ever to have been distributed in Europe. And the point is not to exaggerate the effectiveness of moral rights, especially with respect to the insertion of commercials into the television broadcasts of films. Rather, the point is to demonstrate that there are important differences between Europe and the United States with regard to copyright law. In Europe, the ideals of *auteur*-ism have a legal counterpart in the Berne Convention, which states that

Independently of the author's economic rights, and even after the transfer of the said rights, the author shall have the right to claim authorship of the work and to object to any distortion, mutilation or other modification of, or other derogatory action in relation to, the said work, which would be prejudicial to his [*sic*] honour or reputation. (Kamina, 2002, p. 286)

In the American system, in contrast, the principles of *auteur*-ism can only win the day by battling through a system of contract negotiation, which involves filmmakers, writing and directing guilds, agents, producers and studios.

Ever since the inclusion of cinematic art in American copyright law, which recognizes film as its own artistic medium rather than an appendage of either photography or theatre, the rights of cinematic expression have almost always gone to the film producer, the distributor or both. In other words, they went not to the film creators, but to its owners. And while the United States did implement the Berne Convention in 1988, Congress also made it explicit that it would take a "minimalist" approach to the issue of moral rights. Thus, unless a filmmaker lives on the margins of independent film for the express reason of trading financing opportunities for more creative control (Sayles, 1987), it is rare for any of the key creators (director or screenwriter) to retain authorial rights in mainstream American cinema. Consequently, there is no authorial right based in natural law that stands in the way of American film distribution and its strategies of doing business. In other words, Major Filmed Entertainment has the power to use its dominance over distribution to significantly leverage its rights of ownership against the industrial art of filmmaking, and the creators and artists have little legal recourse to object to what the former does with its property.

A 1990 United States Congressional Hearing before the Subcommittee on Courts, Intellectual Property and the Administration of Justice illustrates how frustrated filmmakers have become with this state of affairs. According to Joe Dante (1990), film director and the Directors Guild of America representative before the subcommittee,

State statutes systematically exclude motion pictures from protective status, the Lanham Act leads on to consumer's rights through labeling, and contracts in the motion picture business more and more routinely include boilerplate denying moral rights to creative participants for all time. Moral rights provide the legal tools for creators to protect their work from alterations that undermine their honor or reputation. There are no moral rights for filmmakers in the United States, and no arcane legal theories can alter that simple fact. (p. 184)

Phil Alden Robinson, screenwriter, director and the representative for the Writers Guild of America, shared the same feelings before the subcommittee. At one point in the hearing, Robinson (1990) argued that moral rights can only exist if the objections of principal artists (directors and screenwriters) are *actually* effective:

> Mr. Robinson. Well, in fact, what we are asking for, we are saying, "You can do whatever you want to but we retain the right to object to it, if you change it in a way that"—.
>
> Mr. Berman. [Congressman for California's 26th district]. Here is my problem, this word objection.
>
> Mr. Robinson. Yes, sir.
>
> Mr. Berman. Consultation, I understand. And I understand your version of consultation which is, "Come on in; tell us what you think. If we like what you say, we may do it, but we are going to decide and all the cards are in our hand". That is what consultation is. It is better to have it than not.... But now registering your right to object, what does that mean? Is that, you can block [a film] from being shown in an [edited] form?
>
> Mr. Robinson. To me the right to object is the right to objectively object. It is not to have freedom of speech, to say, "Wait I object." And they say, "Thank you, goodbye". . . . And my limited understanding of the Berne Convention is that moral rights includes the right to object. It seems to me that we need some way to redress our grievances. Right now, we do not have one other than the individual clout of the director or the writer. When they cut up my film or when they change it in a way that I feel damages me, where can I go? Who do I talk to under the present system? (p. 209)

Major Filmed Entertainment has an institutional mechanism to enforce its will. Artists can be kept at arm's length once a film is finished and ready to be distributed through the different windows of exhibition (theatres, pay-per-view cable, DVDs and Blu-ay, the internet and television). This seemingly innocuous fact is actually, according to Robinson's testimony, a licence to strategic sabotage. Film production can create a product, a film, but the technological capacity to alter, edit, rearrange or add to any film that is ostensibly completed, at least in the eyes of the director, screenwriter, actors and other members of the film crew, can be abused by business interests when there is a proprietary distinction between authorship and ownership:

> [M]aybe all over America, all over the world, people will sit in dark rooms and watch something that once existed only in your imagination. And they will be moved or entertained or enlightened or somehow touched by it. And this movie that you imagined that is the product of so many people working so hard for so long, this movie that against all odds, somehow turned out pretty good, this movie that bears your name, will outlive you. . . . Mr. Chairman, to accomplish that is an extraordinarily moving thing. To have even a chance of accomplishing that is the prime reason

we create. But to go through all that and then to have somebody who did not put any of his sweat and tears and passion, much less a big chunk of his life into it, turn around and say, "Hey, pal, I own this and I think it would be better if we painted it green or cut off the ending or put in some rock music, or slapped in some nudity or lopped off the beginning", for someone to do that is the ultimate degradation, discouragement, insult, crime. It is a moral crime, not just against the creators, but against the people for whom that work was intended because they will not get to see it the way it was meant to be seen. So, instead of being moved by an artist who put part of his life into this, they will be ripped off by a merchant who gave it maybe 5 minutes of thought. (P. A. Robinson, 1990, p. 197)

8.6 Conclusion

The arguments in this chapter followed in the footsteps of Chapter 7. The series of figures in Chapter 7 collectively suggest that Major Filmed Entertainment has been able to increase its degree of confidence about its blockbuster and saturation booking strategies. Furthermore, the 1980s appear to have been a key turning point in Hollywood's risk perceptions – this was the decade in which the systematic reduction of risk in the contemporary period gained momentum.

Building on these results, this chapter analysed some of the underlying transformations that enabled and boosted Major Filmed Entertainment's risk reduction strategies. If the 1980s was the decade when blockbuster cinema and saturation booking increased in effectiveness, the 1970s was the decade when the institution of high concept cinema helped redefine Hollywood's business-industry relationship according to these strategies. High-concept cinema narrows the horizon of aesthetic potential; filmmakers might still have a personal desire for ambiguity and discontinuity, as these qualities can become ingredients for political cinema, but the Hollywood system generally wants ideas, stories and characters that can be marketed in a simple and straightforward manner. Intensified continuity and the US legal framework of film copyright also protect business interests from a film industry that can become "uncontrollably" obsessed with the truths of the aesthetic dimension, whereby filmmakers inflate costs with artistic improvisations or deliver films whose cinematic meanings are too obscure for wide theatrical releases. Overall, the historical evolution of Hollywood's aesthetics are related to changes in the business–industry relationship in Hollywood, which is an effect of Major Filmed Entertainment seeking to accumulate differentially by reducing its risk and differential risk.

Notes

1 We should not ignore the fact that New Hollywood was just as male-dominated as other periods of Hollywood cinema. Some women filmmakers were employed by major

Hollywood studios during the period of American New Wave, but employment discrimination kept many women from accessing creative or managerial roles in film production. For the handful of women directors working in New Hollywood, gender discrimination continued. As Sheehan (2020) demonstrates, executives, crew members and film critics instituted a severe gender gap by treating directors like Elaine May differently than her male counterparts. Even if Hollywood studios would eventually grow to dislike the majority of American New Wave directors irrespective of gender, executives and male crew members heavily scrutinized the experience, knowledge and skills of women *auteurs*. When her film was eventually released – sometimes with final cut being rejected by the studio, as in the case of May's *A New Leaf* – a woman director's box-office failure was neither forgiven nor forgotten. Sheehan (2020) notes, "Their failures were read as proof of their gendered inability to direct movies. Seen as representative of all women, they were under enormous performance pressure and close scrutiny" (p. 16).

2 The collapse of the Hays Code was the result of more and more films, like those of Otto Preminger and Alfred Hitchcock, being released without a PCA seal of approval. A Supreme Court decision was also handed down in *Burstyn v. Wilson* in 1952, which dealt with the attempt to ban *The Miracle* (the first part of Rossellini's *L'Amore*) in New York for being "sacrilegious". For more details about the granting of First Amendment rights to motion pictures and the abandonment of the PCA seal of approval, see (Kunz, 2007; Lewis, 2002).

3 Of all these terms, *ambiguity* may be the key one. For instance, David Newman and Robert Benton, the writers of *Bonnie and Clyde*, declared that filmmakers in the late 1960s had good reasons to let ambiguous meaning roam free:

> It is safe to assume . . . cinema lends itself to such a variety of interpretations because visual images tend to be more ambiguous than words in a book. The director can make his [*sic*] setup and call his shot, but you might get a fix on a table lamp in the corner of the frame and decide that's the real meaning of the image. . . . This quest for ambiguity has, to a great extent, been encouraged by filmmakers in the last few years. Odd juxtapositions of subject matter or of images themselves have been so freely used that audiences have become educated to expect the shattering of "continuity". (quoted in Christensen, 2012, p. 250)

4 Who exactly these directors are is a matter of debate, subject to time and place. But some names kept coming up when *auteur* cinema was first articulated: Chabrol, Ford, Godard, Hawks, Hitchcock, Mizoguchi, Ray, Renoir, Resnais, Rivette and Rossellini.

5 For example, income inequality and crime and punishment in the United States more or less rose in tandem from 1980 to 2000 (Bichler & Nitzan, 2014). And aside from *RoboCop* (1987), there are no mainstream Hollywood films that, without resorting to allegory, present the systemic causes and effects of crime in the contemporary era. Beyond the mainstream, I can think of only two American films in which it is argued that crime in United States is structural: *Repo Man* and *Homicide*.

6 As Powdermaker (1950) revealed in her anthropological study of Hollywood in 1950, the current power of producers and management in post-production has an ancestor in the classical studio system.

9

CONCLUSION

This book has operated at two levels of analysis. At the level of theory, the presentation of the capital-as-power approach followed from a critique of Marxist political economy. While Marxist theory has advanced a great number of arguments about mass culture and its function in capitalism, the capital-as-power approach enables us to break new ground on this subject. It helps us demonstrate why the politics–economics separation in Marxism makes it difficult – if not impossible – to jointly theorize mass culture and accumulation in advanced capitalism. The capital-as-power approach also helps us theorize how Major Filmed Entertainment capitalizes an order of cinema that is predominantly formed, shaped and transformed through capitalist power. Hollywood is an expression of capitalist power because its dominant firms, in their pursuit of differential accumulation, are compelled to delimit the possibilities of cinema through strategic sabotage. Strategic sabotage is used to predetermine, as much as possible, the place of new social creation in an instituted field of social significations.

At the empirical level, the book has applied the capital-as-power approach to the historical trends and details of the Hollywood film business and the aesthetics of its cinema, with a particular focus on the theory and practice of risk reduction. The research on risk connects to two related questions: How is Hollywood cinema sabotaged? and How is sabotage in Hollywood cinema capitalized? The research on risk has sought to explain why aesthetic overproduction matters to the business of film and how the reduction of risk, both absolute and differential, bore on the differential accumulation of Major Filmed Entertainment.

While risk is only one of many aspects of the political economy of Hollywood, this type of research demonstrates the usefulness of transcending the politics-economics duality that is commonly assumed by political economic theories. The

DOI: 10.4324/9781003092629-11

creative labour of the Hollywood film industry is still a part of our story about risk reduction, but this story also includes the institutional creation of ideology through the repression of meaning and the control of social behaviour. This institutional activity is political because it is about the power of Major Filmed Entertainment to do the following: to effectively block unwanted creativity from finding the mainstream, to create a habituated social system of creation and consumption through the establishment of its own aesthetic principles and to narrow our collective expectations about the aesthetic potentials of cinema. These aspects of institutional power are mostly understood qualitatively, as they are rooted in the social relations of Hollywood cinema. Yet by challenging the politics–economics separation in Part I, we opened the door to research how, in our case, the logic of capitalization includes the control of ideology, meaning and other social characteristics of cinema. From this perspective, these qualitative aspects have a direct bearing on Hollywood's accumulation strategies.

More specifically, Part II argued that the Hollywood film business's ability to strategically sabotage the aesthetic, political and social qualities of cinema have a bearing on Major Filmed Entertainment's degree of confidence. Expected future earnings can be predicted with a greater degree of confidence when the qualities of cinema begin to function according to a level of predictability. Thus, the capitalization of cinema assumes that culture and art should behave like other determinate systems; elements "must be connected together by relations of causal determination, linear or cyclical (reciprocal), categorical or probabilist – relations which themselves are amenable to univocal definition" (Castoriadis, 1998, p. 177).

To passionate filmmakers and avid consumers of films alike, the capitalization of cinema does not capture the experience of creating and engaging with good films, especially novel ones. Yet this logic shapes the worldview of those who seek to profit from mass culture. Capitalization pushes capitalists to define where human creativity becomes aesthetic overproduction, which itself relates to the order of cinema. Furthermore, the chance to reduce risk compels capitalists to sabotage the industrial art of filmmaking, whose improvisations, experimentations and desires for new aesthetic forms can translate into greater business uncertainty and, therefore, lower capitalization.

9.1   Paths of future research

The empirical and theoretical levels of this book can each be developed further, in future research on the political economy of Hollywood. For the sake of clarity, let us temporarily split empirical research and theory.

9.1.1   Empirical paths

New opportunities for empirical research keep appearing. The foundation of this book was built on my doctoral dissertation, which was completed in 2015. Data and research were updated from the spring of 2020 to the winter of 2021. All of my updates made 2019 the end-point of my historical research. Deciding to make 2019 my historical endpoint ended up making me nervous, as I would be completing a book that had its historical research stop on the eve of a global pandemic, which forced Hollywood to postpone theatrical releases everywhere and left moviegoers with one option for cinema: Video-on-Demand (VOD).

As I prepared my final draft of the manuscript in 2020 and 2021, friends and family asked me about my thoughts on the future of Hollywood. Will Hollywood recover from the crash of theatrical revenues caused by the COVID-19 pandemic? Will consumers return to theatres in a post-COVID world? Answers to these questions are connected to the political economy of VOD, which is the dominant alternative to theatrical moviegoing. Yet like the invention and direct sale of video technology to consumers in the 1980s (Wasser, 2002), the precise impact of VOD has not been disaggregated in Major Filmed Entertainment's business operations data. Thus, this book can only contribute to an answer that, to be comprehensive, will require a dedicated search for financial data on VOD revenues and profits. So far we know that the risk of Major Filmed Entertainment continued to decrease after the inventions of Betamax and VHS tape, and it still decreased in the age of the internet. We still remain unsure about the precise impacts of these technologies on the volatility of income or the predictability of theatrical releases.

Before the pandemic, future research on Netflix was going to be important. As the pandemic continues in 2021 – with events that are infinitely more tragic than people not being able to see a movie on a big screen – future research on Netflix has grown in importance. A key step in future research would be to study Major Filmed Entertainment's relationship to the rise and dominance of Netflix, a portion of which came in 2020. Two figures can help us understand the importance of 2020 for the world's biggest VOD service. Figure 9.1 visualizes the impact of the pandemic on US theatrical revenues. When lockdowns, social distancing measures and quarantine rules were first implemented across Canada and the United States, the seasonal pattern of monthly theatrical revenues collapsed. Similar to the public health risks of theatres during the Spanish Flu pandemic of 1918 (Strassfeld, 2018), present-day theatres were not designed for social distancing indoors – notwithstanding the variables of adequate ventilation and sanitation. The Olympian "bounce-back" of theatrical moviegoing in April 2021 is misleading, in part because the per cent increases will be huge when the starting number is extraordinarily low. The *total* gross revenues of April 2020 were $52,015.

Figure 9.2 compares to differential operating income of Netflix to firms within Major Filmed Entertainment. Netflix's differential earnings have risen significantly and 2020 was its best year. For the sake of presentation, firms within Major Filmed Entertainment have been put into two groups. Group A contains studios that are heavily invested in franchise cinema (Disney owns Marvel Studios, Lucasfilm and,

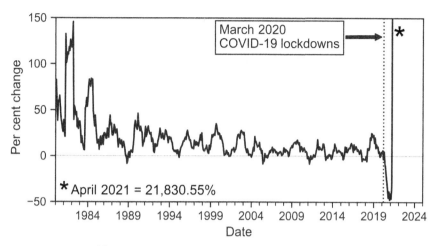

FIGURE 9.1   Monthly gross revenues, per cent change from year before, 12-month moving average

Source: https://www.boxofficemojo.com/month/ for monthly gross revenues of US domestic box office.

Note: The vertical line representing COVID-19 lockdowns is general placeholder for national, regional and local government measures that took place in North America.

most recently, Twentieth Century-Fox; Warner Bros. owns DC Comics and produced the Harry Potter film adaptations). Group B, in comparison to A, has stagnated in terms of its differential earnings.

Media analysts and economists were curious about Netflix's threat to Hollywood film distribution before the COVID-19 pandemic. M. D. Smith and Telang (2016), for example, argued a few years ago that VOD service has the potential to be a disruptive force much greater than its technological predecessors, the VCR and pay-per-view cable. After the first wave of the global pandemic, VOD appears to have won consumer attention by default. Consumers have nowhere to go and the freshly unemployed have endless hours to binge-watch films and television shows. Some argue this exceptional consumer lifestyle is quickening the pace of our exodus from "traditional" media consumption. "Hollywood television and film industries", writes Johnson Jr. (2021), "will capitalize upon this current public health crisis by moving towards streaming platforms as the new preferred distribution mechanism, and that their decision to do so would be [a] permanent one" (p. 7). The trend of Figure 9.2 suggests this future is a possibility, but one datum in the figure also gives us an important perspective on the power of VOD. Netflix joined the Motion Picture Association in 2019. VOD might be the future of Hollywood cinema, and theatrical peformance might not have a primary role in future risk reduction – but Netflix is no longer "disrupting"

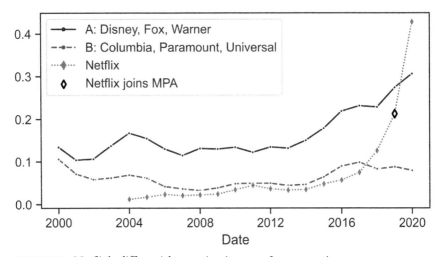

FIGURE 9.2 Netflix's differential operating income, 3-year moving average

Source: Compustat through WRDS for firm data of Dominant Capital and for operating income of Netflix. Annual reports for operating income of Major Filmed Entertainment.

Hollywood from the outside. As Major Filmed Entertainment expands its own VOD services (Disney+, Hulu, HBO Max), they can also use the trade-association partnership with Netflix to collectively control the erosion of theatrical movie-going. And as Veblen made clear in his distinction between business and industry, there is also no business impediment to Netflix going "backwards" in terms of industry, by investing in film distribution for theatrical release. In fact, Netflix showed its first signs of acquiring claims on theatrical earnings with small, international theatrical releases of *Roma*, *The Irishman* and *Marriage Story*.

The Netflix-pandemic research question is, I believe, connected to questions about conglomerated ownership in film and television media. When companies like Disney, Apple and Amazon joined Netflix in VOD services, they followed a decades-long trend of media firms seeking to own both "software" (film, TV, music) and "hardware" (servers, portable devices, satellite systems, cable networks and other digital technology). This question is important to understanding how the complexity of media intellectual property is constituted by its networks of distribution. For instance, the transaction costs, sales and profits of AT&T (owner of Time Warner after 2018) stay "in house" when its intellectual property is produced at Warner Bros. studio facilities and then traverses cable subscription (e.g., HBO, TNT, CNN, Cartoon Network), newsprint (e.g., *Entertainment Weekly*, *Time* magazine, *People*) and the internet (e.g., HBO Max, CNN.com). Conglomeration in Hollywood is also affecting labour relations in the film industry. Conglomeration in the age of the internet has given Hollywood a big opportunity to produce or re-release content as digital media. When business interests initially created new revenue streams from digital media, there was no update to creative labour compensation – primarily through residuals for usage. The Writers Guild strike of 2007 was a consequence of this dissonance between business and industry (Handel, 2011).

Another research question concerns the apparent inverse relationship between the volatility and level of Major Filmed Entertainment's earnings. As Major Filmed Entertainment's differential risk declined, its differential earnings have stagnated. Can the risk of mainstream Hollywood be reduced further, or has it reached its limits? As of this writing, Hollywood remains committed to the distribution of blockbuster, high-concept cinema, but can this commitment cause further increases in theatrical attendance per capita, profits per firm and differential profits per firm? If Hollywood's contemporary strategies are effective at reducing risk but ineffective at increasing earnings, its largest firms might need to reconsider how it will sabotage industry in the future. One way or the other, though, a new business–industry relationship that accommodates autonomous creativity might not be welcomed by Hollywood's vested interests. American New Wave gave Major Filmed Entertainment its longest differential increase in profits, but its wave of creativity also engendered Hollywood's most unstable relationship among business, industry and consumerism.

9.1.2 Theoretical paths

Theoretically, the next step would be to extend our analysis of the political costs of achieving risk reduction through the control of social creativity. Much of this book spoke of cinema's political value in the inverse, by showing that Hollywood, in its quest to accumulate differentially, must sabotage the potentials of human creativity.

Outside of an institution that, because of its financial goals, tightly controls its artistic labour, cinema can blossom in different ways and for alternative social ends. The capacity for humans to create new, unexpected cultural forms can support a democratic mode of being, which does not have a vested interest to negate the potential of social creativity. With Christopher Holman, my interest in this democratic potential has mainly worked with the political theory of Castoriadis, who helped us outline and justify the value of a democratic relationship between a film-maker and her audience (Holman & McMahon, 2015). To study this mediated relationship between filmmaker and audience in further detail, future research can theorize how audiences can give authority to the autonomous creative practices of filmmakers by valuing films as objects for a deliberative civil society. The audience in this relationship seeks art that can fuel an open struggle over political issues, but it is the task of filmmakers to decide how certain cinematic techniques can, in a specific situation, interrogate an aspect of modern society. Filmmakers, for their part, would not produce an aimless cinema; there are material and aesthetic reasons for putting limits on the style and methods of a film production (Bordwell, 2003). Yet democratic cinema flourishes as an autonomous cultural-political activity. It depends on the degree to which filmmakers have opportunities to self-limit themselves and decide how a film's form and content will effectively engage with established norms and values.

We can also study the history of cinema and find films that have been effective at opening the audience to political questions that are not already answered by the films themselves. For example, I would argue that such films as *The Night of the Hunter, Hiroshima, Mon Amour, Ivan's Childhood, Medium Cool, Sans Soleil* and *A Brighter Summer Day* use discontinuous narratives and ambiguous meanings to have film and audience question a political issue together. Audiences are participating alongside these films because, in a vein similar to theories of democratic activity, the filmmakers have provided no fixed resolutions to stories filled with irreconcilable duties, moral ambiguities and inconsistent social behaviour.

9.1.3   What makes Hollywood run?

We can certainly choose to ignore the capitalist character of Hollywood cinema, but doing so severely limits our ability to understand how filmmakers, actors, writers, designers and other related artists will or will not conflict with business interests. As Lowenthal (1961) suspected, when "we talk about art" we tend to "reflect upon a specific product, its inner structure, its norms, and the relationship of such structure and norms to those of other individual products" (p. xix). What is missing from this perspective, however, are all the decisions and institutional dimensions that could very well impact the creation of art, including its claims to truth:

> [W]ho makes decisions about the kinds of entertainment and art offered in a given society? To indicate the scope of the problem briefly, one need only ask: who decides about the form and content of productions which may become, or are intended from the beginning to be, products of popular culture? If one can determine the conditions under which the decisions are made, one has moved at least a step toward answering the question of whether the gap between art and popular culture is unbridgeable. Decisions which are taken by joint conferences of financial groups, advertising agency and media corporation executives, engineers, directors and script writers have become so far removed from the realm of responsibility of the individual artist that no ready answers suggest themselves. (Lowenthal, 1961, p. xx)

Analysing the political economic dimensions of Hollywood force us to situate the cultural and political value of filmmaking against the goals of the film business.

Moreover, the political economic dimensions of Hollywood give us the means to judge whether the business control of industry is legitimate. While the creation and distribution of culture, particularly in a highly complex technological setting, will never be entirely separate from acts of administration (Adorno, 2004a), the degree of power that the Hollywood film business imposes over the social creativity of filmmaking is not an inevitable fact. There are degrees of institutional control, just as the scope and effect of political power change with the type of political organization that is predominant in society. As the work of Castoriadis emphasizes, decisions on the limitations imposed on society and its institutions need not be heteronomous; they can also be made autonomously, through democratic activity.

The logic of repressing social creativity for the purpose of accumulating differentially is very different from the logic of artists constraining their work according to ideas about the form and content of art. These logics are certainly mixed in capitalist society, but it is the difference between them that makes the political economy of Hollywood so interesting. Just like Al Manheim's Hollywood experience in Schulberg's novel *What Makes Sammy Run?* we see the ways Major Filmed Entertainment's drive to profit *undermines but never exhausts* the potentials of cinema as art.

REFERENCES

Adorno, T. (1973). *Negative Dialectics* (E. B. Ashton, Trans.). New York: Continuum.

Adorno, T. (1997). Paralipomena (R. Hullot-Kentor, Trans.). In G. Adorno & R. Tiedemann (Eds.), *Aesthetic Theory* (pp. 262–324). Minneapolis: University of Minnesota Press.

Adorno, T. (2004a). Culture and Administration. In J. M. Bernstein (Ed.), *The Culture Industry: Selected Essays on Mass Culture* (pp. 107–131). New York: Routledge.

Adorno, T. (2004b). Culture Industry Reconsidered. In J. M. Bernstein (Ed.), *The Culture Industry: Selected Essays on Mass Culture* (pp. 98–106). New York: Routledge.

Adorno, T. (2004c). Free Time. In J. M. Bernstein (Ed.), *The Culture Industry: Selected Essays on Mass Culture* (pp. 187–197). New York: Routledge.

Adorno, T. (2004d). The Schema of Mass Culture. In J. M. Bernstein (Ed.), *The Culture Industry: Selected Essays on Mass Culture* (pp. 61–97). New York: Routledge.

Adorno, T. (2004e). Transparencies on Film. In J. M. Bernstein (Ed.), *The Culture Industry: Selected Essays on Mass Culture* (pp. 178–186). New York: Routledge.

Adorno, T. (2005a). *Minima Moralia: Reflections on a Damaged Life* (E. Jephcott, Trans.). New York: Verso.

Adorno, T. (2005b). On the Fetish Character in Music and the Regression of Listening. In A. Arato & E. Gebhardt (Eds.), *The Essential Frankfurt School Reader* (pp. 270–299). New York: The Continuum International Publishing Group.

Agee, J. (2005). Comedy's Greatest Era. In *James Agee: Film Writing and Selected Journalism* (pp. 9–33). New York: The Library of America.

Althusser, L. (2001). Ideology and Ideological State Apparatuses: Notes Towards an Investigation. In B. Brewster (Trans.), *Lenin and Philosophy and Other Essays* (pp. 85–126). New York: Monthly Review Press.

Anonymous. (2003, January). The Entertainment Industry: Lights! Camera! No Profits! *The Economist*, 4.

Anonymous. (2014, December). *Christian Bale and Ridley Scott defend Exodus Casting at Film's New York Premiere*. Retrieved 2015-01-13, from http://www.cbc.ca/1.2864090

Aristotle. (1999). *Nicomachean Ethics* (2nd ed.; T. Irwin, Trans.). Indianapolis, IN: Hackett.

Arvidsson, A. (2005a). Brands: A Critical Perspective. *Journal of Consumer Culture, 5*(2), 235–258.

Arvidsson, A. (2005b). *Brands: Meaning and Value in Media Culture.* Florence, KY: Routledge.

Asimakopulos, A. (1978). *An Introduction to Economic Theory: Microeconomics.* Oxford: Oxford University Press.

Babe, R. E. (2009). *Cultural Studies and Political Economy: Toward a New Integration.* Lanham: Lexington Books.

Bach, S. (1985). *Final Cut: Dreams and Disaster in the Making of Heaven's Gate.* New York: William Morrow and Company, Inc.

Bagdikian, B. H. (2004). *The New Media Monopoly.* Boston: Beacon Press.

Bakker, G. (2004, March). Selling French Films on Foreign Markets: The International Strategy of a Medium-Sized Film Company. *Enterprise & Society, 5*(1), 45–76.

Bakker, G. (2005). America's Master: The European Film Industry in the United States, 1907–1920. In J. Sedgwick & M. Pokorny (Eds.), *An Economic History of Film* (pp. 24–47). New York: Routledge.

Balio, T. (1993). *Grand Design: Hollywood as a Modern Business Enterprise, 1930–1939* (No. 5). New York: C. Scribner.

Baran, P. A. (1954, May). *Paul A. Baran to Herbert Marcuse.* Retrieved from http://monthly review.org/commentary/baran-marcuse-correspondence/

Baran, P. A., & Sweezy, P. M. (1966). *Monopoly Capital: An Essay on the American Economic and Social Order.* New York: Monthly Review Press.

Barnes, B. (2013, May). Solving Equation of a Hit Film Script, With Data. *The New York Times.* Retrieved 2013-08-22, from http://www.nytimes.com/2013/05/06/business/media/solving-equation-of-a-hit-film-script-with-data.html

Bataille, G. (1991). *The Accursed Share: An Essay on General Economy* (Vol. 1; R. Hurley, Trans.). New York: Zone Books.

Baumbach, N. (2014). *Like Someone in Love: On Likeness.* Retrieved 2014-07-21, from http://www.criterion.com/current/posts/3170-like-someone-in-love-on-likeness

Bazin, A. (2005). The Evolution of the Language of Cinema. In H. Gray (Ed. & Trans.), *What is Cinema? Volume I* (pp. 23–40). Berkeley, CA: University of California Press.

Benjamin, W. (1968a). *Illuminations: Essays and Reflections* (H. Arendt, Ed.). New York: Schocken Books.

Benjamin, W. (1968b). The Work of Art in the Age of Mechanical Reproduction. In H. Arendt (Ed.), *Illuminations* (pp. 217–252). New York: Schocken Books.

Benjamin, W. (1978). *Reflections: Essays, Aphorisms, Autobiographical Writings* (P. Demetz, Ed.). New York: Schocken Books.

Berliner, T. (2011). *Hollywood Incoherent: Narration in Seventies Cinema.* Austin, TX: University of Texas Press.

Bernardoni, J. (1991). *The New Hollywood: What the Movies Did with the New Freedoms of the Seventies.* Jefferson, NC: McFarland.

Best, J., & Paterson, M. (Eds.). (2009). *Cultural Political Economy.* Florence, KY: Routledge.

Bichler, S., & Nitzan, J. (2012, June). The Asymptotes of Power. *Real-World Economics Review, 60*, 18–53.

Bichler, S., & Nitzan, J. (2013). Francis' Buy-to-Build Estimates for Britain and the United States: A Comment. *Review of Capital as Power, 1*(1), 73–78.

Bichler, S., & Nitzan, J. (2014). No Way Out: Crime, Punishment and the Capitalization of Power. *Crime, Law and Social Change*, *61*(3), 251–271.

Bichler, S., & Nitzan, J. (2016, December). A CasP Model of the Stock Market. *Real-World Economics Review*, *77*, 118–154.

Biltereyst, D., & Winkel, R. V. (Eds.). (2013). *Silencing Cinema: Film Censorship Around the World*. New York: Palgrave Macmillan.

Bloch, E. (1988). Ideas as Transformed Material in Human Minds, or Problems of an Ideological Superstructure (Cultural Heritage). In J. Zipes & F. Mecklenburg (Trans.), *The Utopian Function of Art and Literature: Selected Essays* (pp. 18–70). Cambridge, MA: The MIT Press.

Bohm, S., & Land, C. (2009). No Measure for Culture? Value in the New Economy. *Capital & Class*, *33*(1), 75–98.

Bohm, S., & Land, C. (2012). The New "Hidden Abode": Reflections on Value and Labour in the New Economy. *The Sociological Review*, *60*(2), 217–240.

Bordwell, D. (2003). Authorship and Narration in Art Cinema. In V. W. Wexman (Ed.), *Film and Authorship* (pp. 42–49). New Brunswick, NJ: Rutgers University Press.

Bordwell, D. (2006). *The Way Hollywood Tells It: Story and Style in Modern Movies*. Berkeley, CA: University of California Press.

Bordwell, D., Thompson, K., & Staiger, J. (1985). *The Classical Hollywood Cinema: Film Style & Mode of Production to 1960*. New York: Columbia University Press.

Braverman, H. (1998). *Labor and Monopoly Capital: The Degradation of Work in the Twentieth Century* (25th Anniversary Edition ed.). New York: Monthly Review Press.

Buchsbaum, J. (2017). *Exception Taken: How France Has Defied Hollywood's New World Order*. New York: Columbia University Press.

Buzgalin, A. V., & Kolganov, A. I. (2013, October). The Anatomy of Twenty-First Century Exploitation: From Traditional Extraction of Surplus Value to Exploitation of Creative Activity. *Science & Society*, *77*(4), 486–511.

Caporaso, J. A., & Levine, D. P. (1992). *Theories of Political Economy*. New York: Cambridge University Press.

Castoriadis, C. (1984a). Technique. In K. Soper & M. H. Ryle (Trans.), *Crossroads in the Labyrinth* (pp. 229–259). Cambridge, MA: The MIT Press.

Castoriadis, C. (1984b). Value, Equality, Justice, Politics: From Marx to Aristotle and From Aristotle to Ourselves. In K. Soper & M. H. Ryle (Trans.), *Crossroads in the Labyrinth* (pp. 260–339). Cambridge, MA: The MIT Press.

Castoriadis, C. (1991). Power, Politics, Autonomy. In D. A. Curtis (Ed.), *Philosophy, Politics, Autonomy* (pp. 143–174). New York: Oxford University Press.

Castoriadis, C. (1995). The Dilapidation of the West. *Thesis Eleven*, *41*(1).

Castoriadis, C. (1998). *The Imaginary Institution of Society* (K. Blamey, Trans.). Cambridge, MA: The MIT Press.

Child, B. (2014, December). *Christian Bale Defends Ridley Scott over Exodus 'Whitewashing'*. Retrieved 2015-01-13, from http://www.theguardian.com/film/2014/dec/09/ christian-bale-defends-ridley-scott-exodus-whitewashing

Christensen, J. (2012). *America's Corporate Art: The Studio Authorship of Hollywood Motion Pictures*. Stanford, CA: Stanford University Press.

Christopherson, S. (2013). Hollywood in Decline? US Film and Television Producers beyond the Era of Fiscal Crisis. *Cambridge Journal of Regions, Economy and Society*, *6*, 141–157.

Compaine, B. M., & Gomery, D. (2000). *Who Owns the Media? Competition and Concentration in the Mass Media* (3rd ed.). Mahwah, NJ: Lawrence Erlbaum Associates.

Cook, D. (1996). *The Culture Industry Revisited: Theodor W. Adorno on Mass Culture.* Lanham, MD: Rowman & Littlefield Publishers.

Cook, D. (2015, December). "Is Power Always Secondary to the Economy?": Foucault and Adorno on Power and Exchange. *Foucault Studies, 20,* 180–198.

Cook, D. A. (2000). *Lost Illusions: American Cinema in the Shadow of Watergate, 1970–1979* (C. Harpole, Ed.) (No. 9). New York: C. Scribner.

Coombe, R. J. (1998). *The Cultural Life of Intellectual Properties: Authorship, Appropriation, and the Law.* Durham and London: Duke University Press.

Corrigan, T. (2003). The Commerce of Auteurism. In V. W. Wexman (Ed.), *Film and Authorship* (pp. 96–111). New Brunswick, NJ: Rutgers University Press.

Crandall, R. W. (1975). The Postwar Performance of the Motion-Picture Industry. *The Antitrust Bulletin, 20*(49), 49–88.

Crane, D. (2014). Cultural Globalization and the Dominance of the American Film Industry: Cultural Policies, National Film Industries, and Transnational Film. *International Journal of Cultural Policy, 20*(4), 365–382.

Cucco, M. (2009). The Promise is Great: The Blockbuster and the Hollywood Economy. *Media, Culture & Society, 31*(2), 215–230.

Curtin, M. (2016). What Makes them Willing Collaborators? The Global Context of Chinese Motion Picture Co-productions. *Media International Australia, 159*(1), 63–72.

Dante, J. (1990, January). *Moral Rights and the Motion Picture Industry.* Los Angeles, CA: U.S. Government Printing Office.

De Vany, A. S. (2004). *Hollywood Economics: How Extreme Uncertainty Shapes the Film Industry.* New York: Routledge.

De Vany, A. S., & Walls, W. D. (2002). Does Hollywood Make Too Many R-Rated Movies? Risk, Stochastic Dominance, and the Illusion of Expectation. *The Journal of Business, 75*(3), 425–451.

Decherney, P. (2012). *Hollywood's Copyright Wars: From Edison to the Internet.* New York: Columbia University Press.

Denisoff, R. S., & Plasketes, G. (1990). Synergy in 1980s Film and Music: Formula for Success or Industry Mythology? *Film History, 4*(3), 257–276.

Doyle, G. (2010). Why Culture Attracts and Resists Economic Analysis. *Journal of Cultural Economics, 34*(4), 245–259.

Drake, P. (2008). Distribution and Marketing in Contemporary Hollywood. In P. McDonald & J. Wasko (Eds.), *The Contemporary Hollywood Film Industry* (pp. 63–82). Malden, MA: Blackwell Publishing.

Dreamworks Animation SKG, I. (2010). *Form 10-K for the Year Ended December 31, 2010* (Annual Report).

Dunne, J. G. (1998). *The Studio.* New York: Vintage Books.

Dyer-Witheford, N. (1999). *Cyber-Marx: Cycles and Circuits of Struggle in High-technology Capitalism.* Champaign: University of Illinois Press.

Eagleton, T. (2011). *Why Marx Was Right.* New Haven: Yale University Press.

Earl, P. E., & Potts, J. (2013, May). The Creative Instability Hypothesis. *Journal of Cultural Economics, 37*(2), 153–173.

Elberse, A. (2007). The Power of Stars: Do Star Actors Drive the Success of Movies? *Journal of Marketing, 71*(4), 102–120.

Elberse, A. (2013). *Blockbusters: Hit-Making, Risk-Taking, and the Big Business of Entertainment.* New York: Henry Holt and Company.

Elsbach, K. D., & Kramer, R. M. (2003, June). Assessing Creativity in Hollywood Pitch Meetings: Evidence for a Dual-Process Model of Creativity Judgments. *The Academy of Management Journal*, *46*(3), 283–301.

Erigha, M. (2019). *The Hollywood Jim Crow: The Racial Politics of the Movie Industry*. New York: NYU Press.

Faughnder, R. (2020, February). "Parasite" Oscars are a Huge Win for Neon. Why the Scrappy Indie Bet on Bong Joon Ho. *Los Angeles Times*. Retrieved 2021-04-21, from https://www.latimes.com/entertainment-arts/business/story/2020-02-10/parasiteoscars-are-a-huge-win-for-neon-why-the-scrappy-indie-bet-on-bong-joon-ho

Fine, B., & Saad-Filho, A. (2004). *Marx's Capital* (4th ed.). London: Pluto Press.

Finler, J. W. (2003). *The Hollywood Story*. New York: Wallflower Press.

Fix, B. (2019). Energy, Hierarchy and the Origin of Inequality. *PLoS ONE*, *14*(4), e0215692. Retrieved from https://doi.org/10.1371/journal.pone.0215692

Foley, D. K. (2012). The Political Economy of Postcrisis Global Capitalism. *South Atlantic Quarterly*, *111*(2), 251–263.

Francis, J. A. (2013). The Buy-to-Build Indicator: New Estimated for Britain and the United States. *Review of Capital as Power*, *1*(1), 63–72.

Frater, P. (2018, January). Will the Force Be With 'The Last Jedi' in China? *Variety*, Online. Retrieved from https://variety.com/2018/film/asia/will-force-be-with-the-last-jedi-china-1202653042/

Fu, W. W., & Govindaraju, A. (2010). Explaining Global Box-Office Tastes in Hollywood Films: Homogenization of National Audiences' Movie Selections. *Communication Research*, *37*(2), 215–238.

Galbraith, J. K. (1997). *The Affluent Society*. New York: Mariner Books.

Garnham, N. (1995). Political Economy and Cultural Studies: Reconciliation or Divorce? *Critical Studies in Mass Communication*, *12*(1), 62–71.

Garvin, D. A. (1981, June). Blockbusters: The Economics of Mass Entertainment. *Journal of Cultural Economics*, *5*(1), 1–20.

Germann, C. (2005). Content Industries and Cultural Diversity: The Case of Motion Pictures. In B. Hamm & R. Smandych (Eds.), *Cultural Imperialism: Essays on the Political Economy of Cultural Domination* (pp. 93–113). Broadview Press.

Giedion, S. (1948). *Mechanization Takes Command: A Contribution to Anonymous History*. New York: W. W. Norton & Company.

Gill, R., & Pratt, A. (2008). In the Social Factory? Immaterial Labour, Precariousness and Cultural Work. *Theory, Culture & Society*, *25*(7–8), 1–30.

Gladwell, M. (2006, October). The Formula: What If You Built a Machine to Predict Hit Movies? *The New Yorker*, 138–149.

Google. (2013, June). *Quantifying Movie Magic with Google Search* (Google Whitepaper). Google Whitepaper: Industry Perspectives + User Insights.

Grantham, B. (2012). Motion Picture Finance and Risk in the United States. In M. Hjort (Ed.), *Film and Risk* (pp. 197–208). Detroit: Wayne State University Press.

Greenberg, J. (2016, August). How Star Wars Is Trying to Rule China's Tough Box Office. *Wired*, Online. Retrieved from https://www.wired.com/2016/01/star-wars-force-awakens-china/

Guzman, T. (2005). The Little Theatre Movement: The Institutionalization of the European Art Film in America. *Film History: An International Journal*, *17*(2/3), 261–284.

Habermas, J. (1991). *The Structural Transformation of the Public Sphere: An Inquiry into a Category of Bourgeois Society* (T. Burger, Trans.). Cambridge, MA: MIT Press.

Hacking, I. (1965). *Logic of Statistical Inference*. Cambridge: Cambridge University Press.

Hadida, A. L. (2010). Commercial Success and Artistic Recognition of Motion Picture Projects. *Journal of Cultural Economics*, *34*(1), 45–80.

Haiven, M. (2012). Can Pikachu Save Fannie Mae? *Cultural Studies*, *26*(4), 516–541.

Handel, J. (2011). *Hollywood on Strike! An Industry at War in the Internet Age*. Los Angeles, CA: Hollywood Analytics.

Hanssen, F. A. (2005). Revenue Sharing and the Coming of Sound. In J. Sedgwick & M. Pokorny (Eds.), *An Economic History of Film* (pp. 86–120). New York: Routledge.

Harris, D. J. (1972). On Marx's Scheme of Reproduction and Accumulation. *Journal of Political Economy*, *80*(3), 505–522.

Harris, M. (2009). *Pictures at a Revolution: Five Movies and the Birth of the New Hollywood*. New York: Penguin Books.

Harvey, D. (2006). *The Limits to Capital*. New York: Verso.

Harvey, P. (1985). The Value-Creating Capacity of Skilled Labour in Marxian Economics. *Review of Radical Political Economics*, *17*(1/2), 83–102.

Haskell, M. (2013). *Nashville: America Singing*. Retrieved 2013-12-09, from http://www.criterion.com/current/posts/2978-nashville-america-singing

Hegel, G. W. F. (1977). *Phenomenology of Spirit* (A. V. Miller, Trans.). New York: Oxford University Press.

Hegel, G. W. F. (2005a). *Elements of the Philosophy of Right* (A. W. Wood, Ed. & H. B. Nisbet, Trans.). New York: Cambridge University Press.

Hegel, G. W. F. (2005b). *Hegel's Preface to the Phenomenology of Spirit* (Y. Yovel, Trans.). Princeton, NJ: Princeton University Press.

Heilbroner, R. (1992). *Twenty-First Century Capitalism*. Toronto: Anansi.

Hilferding, R. (1966). Bohm-Bawerk's Criticism of Marx. In P. M. Sweezy (Ed.), *Karl Marx and the Close of His System/by Eugen von Bohm-Bawerk; & Bohm-Bawerk's Criticism of Marx, by Rudolf Hilferding; together with an appendix consisting of an article by Ladislaus von Bortkiewicz on the transformation of values into prices of production in the Marxian system*. New York: A.M. Kelley.

Hobbes, T. (1985). *Leviathan*. London, UK: Penguin Books.

Holman, C. (2013). *Politics as Radical Creation: Hebert Marcuse and Hannah Arendt on Political Performativity*. Toronto: University of Toronto Press.

Holman, C., & McMahon, J. (2015). From Power Over Creation to the Power of Creation: Castoriadis on Democratic Cultural Creation and the Case of Hollywood. *TOPIA: Canadian Journal of Cultural Studies*, *33*, 157–182.

Horkheimer, M. (2002a). Materialism and Metaphysics. In M. J. O'Connell (Trans.), *Critical Theory: Selected Essays* (pp. 10–46). New York: The Continuum Publishing Company.

Horkheimer, M. (2002b). Traditional and Critical Theory. In M. J. O'Connell (Trans.), *Critical Theory: Selected Essays* (pp. 188–243). New York: The Continuum Publishing Company.

Horkheimer, M. (2005a). The Authoritarian State. In A. Arato & E. Gebhardt (Eds.), *The Essential Frankfurt School Reader* (pp. 95–117). New York: The Continuum International Publishing Group.

Horkheimer, M. (2005b). On the Problem of Truth. In A. Arato & E. Gebhardt (Eds.), *The Essential Frankfurt School Reader* (pp. 407–443). New York: The Continuum International Publishing Group.

Horkheimer, M., & Adorno, T. (2002). *Dialectic of Enlightenment: Philosophical Fragments* (G. S. Noerr, Ed. & E. Jephcott, Trans.). Stanford, CA: Stanford University Press.

Horowitz, G. (1977). *Repression: Basic and Surplus Repression in Psychoanalytic Theory: Freud, Reich, and Marcuse*. Toronto: University of Toronto Press.

Horowitz, G. (1987). The Foucaultian Impasse: No Sex, No Self, No Revolution. *Political Theory*, *15*(1), 61–80.

Hoskins, C., & Mirus, R. (1988). Reasons for the US Dominance of the International Trade in Television Programmes. *Media, Culture & Society*, *10*, 499–515.

Hozic, A. A. (2001). *Hollyworld: Space, Power, and Fantasy in the American Economy*. Ithaca, NY: Cornell University Press.

Hudson, M. (2000). How Interest Rates Were Set, 2500 BC-1000 AD: Máš, Tokos and Foenus as Metaphors for Interest Accruals. *Journal of the Economic and Social History of the Orient*, *43*(2), 132–161.

Jameson, F. (2007). *Late Marxism: Adorno, Or the Persistence of the Dialectic*. New York: Verso.

Jay, M. (1984). *Marxism and Totality: Adventures of a Concept from Lukacs to Habermas*. Berkeley, CA: University of California Press.

Jay, M. (1996). *The Dialectical Imagination: A History of the Frankfurt School and the Institute of Social Research 1923–1950*. Berkeley, CA: University of California Press.

Jin, D. Y. (2011). A Critical Analysis of US Cultural Policy in the Global Film Market: Nationstates and FTAs. *International Communication Gazette*, *73*(8), 651–669.

Johns, A. (2009). *Piracy: The Intellectual Property Wars From Gutenberg to Gates*. Chicago, IL: University of Chicago Press.

Johnson Jr., M. (2021). Hollywood Survival Strategies in the Post-COVID 19 Era. *Humanities and Social Sciences Communications*, *8*(100), 1–8.

Kalecki, M. (1971). Costs and Prices. In *Selected Essays on the Dynamics of the Capitalist Economy, 1933–1970* (pp. 43–61). Cambridge: Cambridge University Press.

Kamina, P. (2002). *Film Copyright in the European Union*. Port Chester, NY: Cambridge University Press.

Keen, S. (2001). *Debunking Economics: The Naked Emperor of the Social Sciences*. New York: Zed Books.

Kellner, D. (1989). *Critical Theory, Marxism, and Modernity*. Baltimore: Johns Hopkins University Press.

Kempers, B. (1994). *Painting, Power and Patronage: The Rise of the Professional Artist in Renaissance Italy* (B. Jackson, Trans.). London: Penguin Books.

Kirshner, J. (2012). *Hollywood's Last Golden Age: Politics, Society, and the Seventies Film in America*. Ithaca, NY: Cornell University Press.

Kliman, A. (2012). *The Failure of Capitalist Production: Underlying Causes of the Great Recession*. London: Pluto Press.

Knight, F. H. (1921). *Risk, Uncertainty and Profit*. Boston, MA: Houghton Mifflin Company.

Koestler, A. (2014). *The Sleepwalkers: A History of Man's Changing Vision of the Universe*. New York: Penguin Books.

Kokas, A. (2017). *Hollywood Made in China*. Oakland, CA: University of California Press.

Krasznahorkai, L. (2012). *Sátántangó* (G. Szirtes, Trans.). Cambridge, MA: New Directions.

Kunz, W. M. (2007). *Culture Conglomerates: Consolidation in the Motion Picture and Television Industries*. Lanham, MD: Rowman & Littlefield Publishers.

Langfitt, F. (2015, May). *How China's Censors Influence Hollywood*. Retrieved 2017-03-28, from http://www.npr.org/sections/parallels/2015/05/18/407619652/how-chinas-censors-influence-hollywood

Langford, B. (2010). *Post-classical Hollywood: Film Industry, Style and Ideology Since 1945.* Edinburgh: Edinburgh University Press.

Lazzarato, M. (1996). Immaterial Labor (P. Colilli & E. Emory, Trans.). In P. Virno & M. Hardt (Eds.), *Radical Thought in Italy: A Potential Politics* (pp. 133–147). Minneapolis: University of Minnesota Press.

Leaver, A. (2010, August). A Different Take: Hollywood's Unresolved Business Model. *Review of International Political Economy, 17*(3), 454–480.

Levin, S. (2019, September 14). Netflix Co-founder: "Blockbuster Laughed at Us... Now There's One Left". *The Guardian.* Retrieved from https://www.theguardian.com/media/2019/sep/14/netflix-marc-randolph-founder-blockbuster

Lewis, J. (2002). *Hollywood v. Hard Core: How the Struggle over Censorship Saved the Modern Film Industry.* New York University Press.

Lewis, J. (2013). "American Morality is Not to be Trifled With": Content Regulation in Hollywood after 1968. In D. Biltereyst & R. V. Winkel (Eds.), *Silencing Cinema: Film Censorship Around the World.* New York: Pal-grave Macmillan.

Litman, B. R. (1983). Predicting Success of Theatrical Movies: An Empirical Study. *Journal of Popular Culture, 16*(4), 159–175.

Litman, B. R. (1998). *The Motion Picture Mega-Industry.* Boston, MA: Allyn and Bacon.

Lowenthal, L. (1961). Popular Culture in Perspective. In *Literature, Popular Culture, and Society* (pp. 1–13). Englewood Cliffs, NJ: Prentice-Hall, Inc.

Lukacs, G. (1968). *History and Class Consciousness: Studies in Marxist Dialectics* (R. Livingstone, Trans.). Cambridge, MA: MIT Press.

MacCabe, C. (2003). The Revenge of the Author. In V. W. Wexman (Ed.), *Film and Authorship* (pp. 30–41). New Brunswick, NJ: Rutgers University Press.

Machiavelli, N. (1999). *The Prince* (G. Bull, Trans.). London: Penguin Books.

Maltby, R. (2003). *Hollywood Cinema* (2nd ed.). Malden, MA: Blackwell Publishing.

Maltby, R. (1983). *Harmless Entertainment: Hollywood and the Ideology of Consensus.* Lanham, MD: Scarecrow Press.

Maltby, R. (1993). The Production Code and the Hays Office. In *Grand Design: Hollywood as a Modern Business Enterprise, 1930–1939* (pp. 37–72). New York: C. Scribner.

Mamet, D. (2007). *Bambi vs. Godzilla: On the Nature, Purpose, and Practice of the Movie Business.* New York: Pantheon Books.

Mandel, E. (1976). *Late Capitalism* (J. De Bres, Trans.). London: NLB.

Marcuse, H. (1991). *One-Dimensional Man: Studies in the Ideology of Advanced Industrial Society.* Boston, MA: Beacon Press.

Marcuse, H. (1965). Remarks on a Redefinition of Culture. *Daedalus, 94*(1), 190–207.

Marcuse, H. (1966). *Eros and Civilization: A Philosophical Inquiry into Freud.* Boston, MA: Beacon Press.

Marcuse, H. (1968a). The Affirmative Character of Culture. In J. J. Shapiro (Trans.), *Negations: Essays in Critical Theory* (pp. 88–133). Boston, MA: Beacon Press.

Marcuse, H. (1968b). The Concept of Essence. In J. J. Shapiro (Trans.), *Negations: Essays in Critical Theory.* Boston, MA: Beacon Press.

Marcuse, H. (1968c). Industrialization and Capitalism in the Work of Max Weber. In J. J. Shapiro (Trans.), *Negations: Essays in Critical Theory* (pp. 201–226). Boston, MA: Beacon Press.

Marcuse, H. (1968d). On Hedonism. In J. J. Shapiro (Trans.), *Negations: Essays in Critical Theory* (pp. 159–200). Boston, MA: Beacon Press.

Marcuse, H. (1968e). Philosophy and Critical Theory. In J. J. Shapiro (Trans.), *Negations: Essays in Critical Theory* (pp. 134–158). Boston, MA: Beacon Press.

Marcuse, H. (1969). *An Essay on Liberation*. Boston, MA: Beacon Press.

Marcuse, H. (1972). *Counterrevolution and Revolt*. Boston, MA: Beacon Press.

Marcuse, H. (1978). *The Aesthetic Dimension: Toward A Critique of Marxist Aesthetics*. Boston, MA: Beacon Press.

Marcuse, H. (2005a). A Note on the Dialectic. In A. Arato & E. Gebhardt (Eds.), *The Essential Frankfurt School Reader* (pp. 444–451). New York: The Continuum International Publishing Group.

Marcuse, H. (2005b). Postscript: My Disillusionment with Heidegger. In R. Wolin & J. Abromeit (Eds.), *Heideggerian Marxism* (p. 176). Lincoln: University of Nebraska Press.

Marcuse, H. (2005c). Some Social Implications of Modern Technology. In A. Arato & E. Gebhardt (Eds.), *The Essential Frankfurt School Reader* (pp. 138–162). New York: The Continuum International Publishing Group.

Marramao, G. (1975, June). Political Economy and Critical Theory. *Telos, 24*, 56–80.

Marx, K. (1988). Economic and Philosophic Manuscripts of 1844. In M. Milligan (Trans.), *Economic and Philosophic Manuscripts of 1844 and The Communist Manifesto* (pp. 13–170). Amherst, NY: Prometheus Books.

Marx, K. (1990). *Capital: A Critique of Political Economy* (Vol. 1; B. Fowkes, Trans.). New York: Penguin Books.

Marx, K. (1993). *Grundrisse: Foundations of the Critique of Political Economy (Rough Draft)* (M. Nicolaus, Trans.). New York: Penguin Books.

Marx, K. (1994). *Economic Works of Karl Marx 1861–1864: The Process of Production of Capital, Draft Chapter 6 of Capital: Results of the Direct Production Process*. Retrieved from http://www.marxists.org/archive/marx/works/1864/economic/ch02b.htm

Marx, K. (1999). *A Contribution to the Critique of Political Economy*. New York: International Publishers.

McDonald, P. (2009, December). Miramax, Life is Beautiful, and the Indiewoodization of the Foreign-film Market in the USA. *New Review of Film and Television Studies, 7*(4), 353–375.

McMahon, J. (2011). The Role of Technology in Marcuse's Eros and Civilization. *Annual Review of Critical Psychology* (9), 38–47.

McMahon, J. (2013). The Rise of a Confident Hollywood: Risk and the Capitalization of Cinema. *Review of Capital as Power, 1*(1), 23–40.

McMahon, J. (2015). Risk and Capitalist Power: Conceptual Tools to Study the Political Economy of Hollywood. *The Political Economy of Communication, 3*(2), 28–54.

McMahon, J. (2019). Is Hollywood a Risky Business? A Political Economic Analysis of Risk and Creativity. *New Political Economy, 24*(4), 487–509.

McMahon, J. (2020). Selling Hollywood to China. *Forum for Social Economics*, 1–18. doi: 10.1080/07360932.2020.1800500

McNally, D. (2001). *Bodies of Meaning: Studies on Language, Labor, and Liberation*. Albany, NY: State University of New York Press.

Miller, T., Govil, N., McMurria, J., Maxwell, R., & Wang, T. (2005). *Global Hollywood 2*. London: Palgrave Macmillan.

Mohun, S. (1996). Productive and Unproductive Labor in the Labor Theory of Value. *Review of Radical Political Economics, 28*(4), 30–54.

Moor, L., & Lury, C. (2011, November). Making and Measuring Value: Comparison, Singularity and Agency in Brand-Valuation Practice. *Journal of Cultural Economy, 4*(4), 439–454.

Moore, B. (1993). *Social Origins of Dictatorship and Democracy: Lord and Peasant in the Making of the Modern World*. Boston, MA: Beacon Press.

Mumford, L. (1970). *The Myth of the Machine: The Pentagon of Power*. New York: Harcourt Brace Jovanovich.

Mumford, L. (2010). *Technics and Civilization*. Chicago, IL: University of Chicago Press.

Neale, S. (2000). *Genre and Hollywood*. New York: Routledge.

Nelson, R. A., & Glotfelty, R. (2012, May). Movie Stars and Box Office Revenues: An Empirical Analysis. *Journal of Cultural Economics, 36*(2), 141–166.

Neumann, F. (1942). *Behemoth: The Structure and Practice of National Socialism*. London: Victor Gollancz Ltd.

Nitzan, J. (2001). Regimes of Differential Accumulation: Mergers, Stagflation and the Logic of Globalization. *Review of International Political Economy, 8*(2), 226–274.

Nitzan, J., & Bichler, S. (2000). Capital Accumulation: Breaking the Dualism of 'Economics' and 'Politics'. In R. Palan (Ed.), *Global Political Economy: Contemporary Theories* (pp. 67–88). New York: Routledge.

Nitzan, J., & Bichler, S. (2009). *Capital as Power: A Study of Order and Creorder*. New York: Routledge.

Noerr, G. S. (2002). Editor's Afterword. In *Dialectic of Enlightenment: Philosophical Fragments*. Stanford, CA: Stanford University Press.

Nykvist, S. (1981, April). Photographing "Cannery Row". *American Cinematographer, 62*(4).

O'Connor, S., & Armstrong, N. (2015, October). *Directed by Hollywood, Edited by China: How China's Censorship and Influence Affect Films Worldwide* (Staff Research Report). U.S.-China Economic and Security Review Commission.

Ollman, B. (1976). *Alienation: Marx's Conception of Man in Capitalist Society*. New York: Cambridge University Press.

Ollman, B. (2003). *Dance of the Dialectic: Steps in Marx's Method*. Urbana, IL: University of Illinois Press.

Olson, M. (1982). *The Rise and Decline of Nations: Economic Growth, Stagflation, and Social Rigidities*. New Haven: Yale University Press.

Ortner, S. B. (2013). *Not Hollywood: Independent Film at the Twilight of the American Dream*. Durham and London: Duke University Press.

Palmer, B. (2014, December). How White Were Ancient Egyptians? Not as white as Christian Bale. *Slate*. Retrieved 2015-01-13, from http://www.slate.com/articles/health_and_science/explainer/2014/12/ridley_scott_s_exodus_were_ancient_egyptians_white_black_or_brown.html

Pendakur, M. (2008). Hollywood and the State: The American Film Industry Cartel in the Age of Globalization. In P. McDonald & J. Wasko (Eds.), *The Contemporary Hollywood Film Industry* (pp. 167–181). Malden, MA: Blackwell Publishing.

Pokorny, M. (2005). Hollywood and the Risk Environment of Movie Production in the 1990s. In J. Sedgwick & M. Pokorny (Eds.), *An Economic History of Film* (pp. 277–311). New York: Routledge.

Pokorny, M., & Sedgwick, J. (2012). The Financial and Economic Risks of Film Production. In M. Hjort (Ed.), *Film and Risk* (pp. 181–196). Detroit, MI: Wayne State University Press.

Polanyi, K. (2001). *The Great Transformation: The Political and Economic Origins of Our Time.* Boston, MA: Beacon Press.

Pollock, F. (2005). State Capitalism: Its Possibilities and Limitations. In A. Arato & E. Gebhardt (Eds.), *The Essential Frankfurt School Reader* (pp. 71–94). New York: The Continuum International Publishing Group.

Postone, M. (1996). *Time, Labor, and Social Domination: A Reinterpretation of Marx's Critical Theory.* New York: Cambridge University Press.

Postone, M., & Brennan, T. (2009). Labor and the Logic of Abstraction: An Interview. *South Atlantic Quarterly, 108*(2), 305–330.

Powdermaker, H. (1950). *Hollywood the Dream Factory: An Anthropologist Looks at the MovieMakers.* Boston, MA: Little, Brown and Company.

PricewaterhouseCoopers. (2009, December). *Filmed Entertainment: Cost Capitalization, Amortization, and Impairment* (Tech. Rep.). Author.

Prince, S. (2000). *A New Pot of Gold: Hollywood Under the Electronic Rainbow, 1980–1989* (No. 10). New York: C. Scribner.

Ravid, S. A. (1999). Information, Blockbusters, and Stars: A Study of the Film Industry. *The Journal of Business, 72*(4), 463–492.

Reijen, W. V., & Bransen, J. (2002). The Disappearance of Class History in "Dialectic of Enlightenment": A Commentary on the Textual Variants (1994 and 1947). In *Dialectic of Enlightenment: Philosophical Fragments.* Stanford, CA: Stanford University Press.

Robinson, J. (1964). *Economic Philosophy.* Middlesex, England: Penguin Books.

Robinson, J. (1976). *An Essay on Marxian Economics.* London: The Macmillan Press.

Robinson, P. A. (1990, January). *Moral Rights and the Motion Picture Industry.* Los Angeles, CA: U.S. Government Printing Office.

Rosenbaum, J. (1997a). Entertainment as Oppression. In *Movies as Politics* (pp. 81–90). Berkeley, CA: University of California Press.

Rosenbaum, J. (1997b). *Movies as Politics.* Berkeley, CA: University of California Press.

Rosenbaum, J. (1997c). The World According to Harvey and Bob. In *Movies as Politics* (pp. 159–165). Berkeley, CA: University of California Press.

Rosenbaum, J. (2000). *Movie Wars: How Hollywood and the Media Conspire to Limit What Films We Can See.* Chicago, IL: A Cappella Books.

Rosenbaum, J. (2004). The Importance of Being Sarcastic: Sátántangó. In *Essential Cinema: On the Necessity of Film Canons.* Baltimore: Johns Hopkins University Press.

Ross, L. (2002). *Picture.* Cambridge, MA: De Capo Press.

Ryan, B. (1992). *Making Capital From Culture: The Corporate Form of Capitalist Cultural Production.* New York: Walter de Gruyter.

Salokannel, M. (2003). Cinema in Search of Its Authors: On the Notion of Film Authorship in Legal Discourse. In V. W. Wexman (Ed.), *Film and Authorship* (pp. 152–178). New Brunswick, NJ: Rutgers University Press.

Salt, B. (1974). Statistical Style Analysis of Motion Pictures. *Film Quarterly, 28*(1), 13–22.

Sanbonmatsu, J. (2010). *The Postmodern Prince: Critical Theory, Left Strategy, and the Making of a New Political Subject.* New York: Monthly Review Press.

Sarris, A. (2003). The Auteur Theory Revisited. In V. W. Wexman (Ed.), *Film and Authorship* (pp. 21–29). New Brunswick, NJ: Rutgers University Press.

Sayles, J. (1987). *Thinking in Pictures: The Making of the Movie Matewan.* Boston, MA: Houghton Mifflin Company.

Schatz, T. (2008). The Studio System and Conglomerate Hollywood. In P. Mc-Donald & J. Wasko (Eds.), *The Contemporary Hollywood Film Industry* (pp. 13–42). Malden, MA: Blackwell Publishing.

Schatz, T. (2010). *The Genius of the System: Hollywood Filmmaking in the Studio Era.* Minneapolis: University of Minnesota Press.

Schmidt, A. (1981). *History and Structure: An Essay on Hegelian-Marxist and Structuralist Theories of History* (J. Herf, Trans.). Cambridge, MA: MIT Press.

Schumpeter, J. (2008). *Capitalism, Socialism and Democracy.* New York: Harper Perennial.

Scorcese, M. (2021, March). *Il Maestro: Federico Fellini and the Lost Magic of Cinema.* Retrieved from https://harpers.org/archive/2021/03/il-maestro-federico-fellini-martin-scorsese/

Sedgwick, J., & Pokorny, M. (2005). The Characteristics of Film as a Commodity. In J. Sedgwick & M. Pokorny (Eds.), *An Economic History of Film* (pp. 6–23). New York: Routledge.

Sedgwick, J. (2005). Product Differentiation at the Movies: Hollywood 1946 to 1965. In J. Sedgwick & M. Pokorny (Eds.), *An Economic History of Film* (pp. 186–218). New York: Routledge.

Shapiro, M. J. (2008). Robert Altman: The West as Countermemory. In J. Phillips (Ed.), *Cinematic Thinking: Philosophical Approaches to the New Cinema* (pp. 52–67). Stanford, CA: Stanford University Press.

Shapiro, S. (2009). Intellectual Labor Power, Cultural Capital, and the Value of Prestige. *South Atlantic Quarterly, 108*(2), 249–264.

Sheehan, R. J. (2020). "One Woman's Failure Affects Every Woman's Chances": Stereotyping Impossible Women Directors in 1970s Hollywood. *Women's History Review*, 1–23.

Shin, S. Y., & McKenzie, J. (2019). Asymmetric Cultural Discounting and Pattern of Trade in Cultural Products: Empirical Evidence in Motion Pictures. *The World Economy, 42*, 3350–3367.

Simon, S. J. (2019). Hollywood Power Brokers: Gender and Racial Inequality in Talent Agencies. *Gender, Work & Organization, 26*(9), 1340–1356. https://doi.org/10.1111/gwao.12365

Smith, A. (1991). *The Wealth of Nations.* New York: Alfred A. Knopf.

Smith, M. D., & Telang, R. (2016). *Streaming, Sharing, Stealing: Big Data and the Future of Entertainment.* Cambridge, MA: MIT Press.

Smukler, M. M. (2019). *Liberating Hollywood: Women Directors and the Feminist Reform of 1970s American Cinema.* New Brunswick, NJ: Rutgers University Press.

Soderbergh, S. (2010). Toward a Universal Cinema: A Talk with Steven Soderbergh. *World Policy Journal, 27*(3), 57–65.

Song, X. (2018). Hollywood Movies and China: Analysis of Hollywood Globalization and Relationship Management in China's Cinema Market. *Global Media and China, 3*(3), 117–194.

Spinoza, B. D. (2007). *Theological-Political Treatise* (M. Silverthorne & J. Israel, Trans.). New York: Cambridge University Press.

Starosta, G. (2012, July). Cognitive Commodities and the Value-Form. *Science & Society, 76* (3), 365–392.

Stiglitz, J. E., Sen, A., & Fitoussi, J.-P. (2009). *Report by the Commission on the Measurement of Economic Performance and Social Progress* (Tech. Rep.). France: CMEPSP.

Strassfeld, B. (2018). Infectious Media: Debating the Role of Movie Theaters in Detroit during the Spanish Influenza of 1918. *Historical Journal of Film, Radio and Television, 38*(2), 227–245.

Su, W. (2011, April). Resisting Cultural Imperialism, or Welcoming Cultural Globalization? China's Extensive Debate on Hollywood Cinema from 1994 to 2007. *Asian Journal of Communication, 21*(2), 186–201.

Suhail, M., & Phillips, A. (2012). Tainted Love: Art's Ethos and Capitalization. In *Contemporary Art and Its Commercial Markets: A Report on Current Conditions and Future Scenarios*. Berlin: Sternberg Press.

Swank Motion Pictures, Inc. (2016). *Film & Video Copyright Infringement: What Your College or University Needs to Know about the Public Performance of Movies*. Online. Retrieved from https://www.swank.com/media/263573/180920college-copyright-brochure.pdf

Thomas, P., & Nain, Z. (Eds.). (2004). *Who Owns the Media? Global Trends and Local Resistances*. London: Zed Books.

Thompson, K. (1985). *Exporting Entertainment: America in the World Film Market, 1907–34*. London: British Film Institute.

Trumpbour, J. (2002). *Selling Hollywood to the World: U.S. and European Struggles for Mastery of the Global Film Industry, 1920–1950*. Cambridge: Cambridge University Press.

Ulin, J. (2010). *The Business of Media Distribution: Monetizing Film, TV, and Video Content*. Waltham, MA: Focal Press.

UNESCO Institute for Statistics. (2013, May). *Feature Film Diversity* (UIS Fact Sheet No. 24). UNESCO.

Veblen, T. (2004). *Absentee Ownership: Business Enterprise in Recent Times: The Case of America*. New Brunswick, NJ: Transaction Publishers.

Veblen, T. (2006a). On the Nature of Capital: II. Investment, Intangible Assets, and the Pecuniary Magnate. In *The Place of Science in Modern Civilization: and Other Essays* (pp. 352–386). New Brunswick, NJ: Transaction Publishers.

Veblen, T. (2006b). On the Nature of Capital: I. The Productivity of Capital Goods. In *The Place of Science in Modern Civilization: and Other Essays* (pp. 324–351). New Brunswick, NJ: Transaction Publishers.

Veblen, T. (2006c). *The Theory of Business Enterprise*. New Brunswick, NJ: Transaction Publishers.

Verrier, R. (2013, April). Regal Pulls Marketing Materials for 'Iron Man 3'. *Los Angeles Times*. Retrieved 2014-01-31, from http://articles.latimes.com/2013/apr/24/entertain-ment/la-et-ct-regal-iron-man-fight-20130423

Vogel, H. L. (2007). *Entertainment Industry Economics: A Guide for Financial Analysis* (7th ed.). New York: Cambridge University Press.

Vogel, H. L. (2011). *Entertainment Industry Economics: A Guide for Financial Analysis* (8th ed.). New York: Cambridge University Press.

Vogel, H. L. (2020). *Entertainment Industry Economics: A Guide for Financial Analysis* (10th ed.). New York: Cambridge University Press.

Wang, T. (2007). Hollywood's Pre-WTO Crusade in China. *Jump Cut: A Review of Contemporary Media*, (49), 1–22.

Warner, T. (2011). *Form 10-K for the Year Ended December 31, 2011* (Annual Report).

Wasko, J. (1982). *Movies and Money: Financing the American Film Industry*. Norwood, NJ: ABLEX Pub Corp.

Wasko, J. (1994). *Hollywood in the Information Age: Beyond the Silver Screen*. Austin, TX: University of Texas Press.

Wasko, J. (2003). *How Hollywood Works*. London: SAGE.

Wasko, J. (2008). Financing and Production: Creating the Hollywood Film Commodity. In P. McDonald & J. Wasko (Eds.), *The Contemporary Hollywood Film Industry* (pp. 43–62). Malden, MA: Blackwell Publishing.

Wasser, F. (2002). *Veni, Vidi, Video: The Hollywood Empire and the VCR*. Austin, TX: University of Texas Press.

Waterman, D. (2005). *Hollywood's Road to Riches*. Cambridge, MA: Harvard University Press.

Weber, M. (2002). *The Protestant Ethic and the Spirit of Capitalism*. New York: Routledge.

Weinstein, M. (2005). Movie Contracts: Is "Net" "Gross"? In J. Sedgwick & M. Pokorny (Eds.), *An Economic History of Film* (pp. 240–276). New York: Routledge.

Wiese, M. (1991). *Film & Video Financing*. Studio City, CA: Focal Press.

Williams, R. (2005). Base and Superstructure in Marxist Cultural Theory. In *Culture and Materialism: Selected Essays* (pp. 31–49). New York: Verso.

Willmott, H. (2010). Creating 'Value' beyond the Point of Production: Branding, Financialization and Market Capitalization. *Organization, 17*(5), 517–542.

Wolff, R. P. (1981). A Critique and Reinterpretation of Marx's Labor Theory of Value. *Philosophy & Public Affairs, 10*(2), 89–120.

Wu, T. (2010). *The Master Switch: The Rise and Fall of Information Empires*. New York: Alfred A. Knopf.

Wyatt, J. (1994). *High Concept: Movies and Marketing in Hollywood*. Austin, TX: University of Texas Press.

Yeh, E. Y., & Davis, D. W. (2008). Re-nationalizing China's film Industry: Case Study on the China Film Group and Film Marketization. *Journal of Chinese Cinemas, 2*(1), 37–51.

Yuen, N. W. (2016). *Reel Inequality: Hollywood Actors and Racism*. New Brunswick, NJ: Rutgers University Press. Retrieved from https://doi.org/10.36019/9780813586328

INDEX

INDEX OF FILMS

Printed in the United States
by Baker & Taylor Publisher Services